Alexy's Theory of Law

Edited by Júlio Aguiar de Oliveira / Stanley L. Paulson / Alexandre Travessoni Gomes Trivisonno

ARCHIV FÜR RECHTS- UND SOZIALPHILOSOPHIE

ARCHIVES FOR PHILOSOPHY OF LAW AND SOCIAL PHILOSOPHY

ARCHIVES DE PHILOSOPHIE DU DROIT ET DE PHILOSOPHIE SOCIALE

ARCHIVO DE FILOSOFÍA JURÍDICA Y SOCIAL

Herausgegeben von der Internationalen Vereinigung

für Rechts- und Sozialphilosophie (IVR)

Redaktion: Dr. Annette Brockmöller, LL. M.

Beiheft 144

Alexy's Theory of Law

Proceedings of the Special Workshop "Alexy's Theory of Law" held at the 26th World Congress of the International Association for Philosophy of Law and Social Philosophy in Belo Horizonte, 2013

Edited by Júlio Aguiar de Oliveira / Stanley L. Paulson / Alexandre Travessoni Gomes Trivisonno

Franz Steiner Verlag

Nomos

Bibliografische Information der Deutschen Nationalbibliothek:
Die Deutsche Nationalbibliothek verzeichnet diese Publikation in der Deutschen Nationalbibliografie; detaillierte bibliografische Daten sind im Internet über <http://dnb.d-nb.de> abrufbar.

Satz: DTP + TEXT Eva Burri
Druck: Druckhaus Nomos, Sinzheim
Gedruckt auf säurefreiem, alterungsbeständigem Papier.
Printed in Germany.
Franz Steiner Verlag: ISBN 978-3-515-11043-3 (Print)
Franz Steiner Verlag: ISBN 978-3-515-11093-8 (E-Book)
Nomos Verlag: ISBN 978-3-8487-2332-4

Contents

Part IV – Law and Rights

Introduction

If this short introduction bore a title, we might well be tempted to write: "Robert Alexy, the Agreeably Unyielding Legal Philosopher". Whereas other analytical jurists embrace legal positivism, Alexy goes his own way, developing a non-positivist position. Whereas other jurists are fond of using "formalism" as a negative label – a practice with a long tradition, most notoriously in the Weimar period, where participants in the politico-constitutional confrontations dismissed Hans Kelsen as a "formalist" – Alexy is quite happy to be called a formalist, reading formalism as shorthand for a conceptual approach to jurisprudential issues. We are thinking, here, of Jeremy Bentham's and, much later, Georg Henrik von Wright's contributions to deontic logic, of Georg Jellinek's development of the Theory of Legal Status (elegantly reconstructed by Alexy in *A Theory of Constitutional Rights*), of Kelsen's effort to work out a principle of normativism that underlies, indeed makes possible, legal science, and we are thinking, too, of Alexy's own weight formula in its ramified form. In short, if legal science is a serious enterprise, then conceptual work – formalism – has an important role to play. This, after all, is what Georg Friedrich Puchta and Rudolf von Jhering had in mind with their *Verwissenschaftlichung des Rechts*, their effort "to render the law scientific".

Martin Borowski, a contributor to the present volume, writes in a review article in *Jurisprudence*, 2 (2011), 575–595, that three treatises of Alexy's represent the core of his work – *A Theory of Legal Argumentation*, *A Theory of Constitutional Rights*, and *The Argument from Injustice – A Reply to Legal Positivism*. "They lay the foundation for the three main strands in his œuvre: discourse theory, principles theory, and a non-positivist concept of law."

Happily, the present volume reflects work in all three areas – and in a fourth area, too, Alexy's work on human rights. Specifically, the first part of the volume, devoted to discourse theory and related topics, contains contributions from Carsten Bäcker, Gonzalo Villa Rosas, and Alexandre Travessoni Gomes Trivisonno. The second part of the volume, on Alexy's conception of human rights, consists of a contribution from Jean-Christophe Merle. The third part, devoted to principles theory, contains contributions from Martin Borowski, João Andrade Neto, Ralf Poscher, and Jan Sieckmann. The last part of the volume, which takes up issues related to the concept of law, contains contributions from Júlio Aguiar de Oliveira and Stanley L. Paulson.

The authors of the essays published here were participants in the workshop "Alexy's Theory of Law" at the 26th World Congress of the International Association for Philosophy of Law and Social Philosophy (IVR), held in Belo Horizonte, Brazil, on 21–26 July 2013. While the authors represented here recognize the uncommon significance of Alexy's work, they have not settled for a mere restatement of his views. Rather, they engage in criticism and the exploration of new approaches. The editors of the present volume wish to express their gratitude to these authors.

Kiel and Belo Horizonte, November 2014

Júlio Aguiar de Oliveira
Stanley L. Paulson
Alexandre Travessoni Gomes Trivisonno

Part I – Legal Discourse

Carsten Bäcker

Rationality without Ideality

Outlines of a Relativistic Discourse Theory of Law*

Introduction

By contrast to the most significant discourse theory in philosophy, that of Jürgen Habermas, Robert Alexy's discourse theory[1] can lay claim to be of the greatest significance in legal philosophy.[2] A central reason for this significance might well be that Alexy's theory has been conceptualized from the beginning as the basis of a special discourse theory of law, whereas Habermas commenced his work in this field with the development of a general theory of communicative action. To be sure, Alexy developed his discourse theory under the influence of Habermas,[3] whose theory served as a point of departure for Alexy's own.[4] With an eye to this genesis, the relativization of general discourse theory to be presented here begins with Alexy's conceptualization, for the aim is to reconstruct the discourse theory of law.

Part One: The Two-Dimensional Model of Discourse in Alexy's Theory

According to the familiar discourse-theoretic point of view, as reflected in Alexy's theory, the distinction between two kinds of discourse is significant: ideal discourse on one hand and real discourse on the other.[5] Ideal discourse is understood as a perfect discourse, whereas real discourse is limited. Ideal discourse serves as something approximating a standard for real discourse. In this way, a two-dimensional

* First published in German in *Junge Rechtsphilosophie*, C. Bäcker and S. Ziemann (eds.), ARSP-Beiheft 135, Stuttgart 2012, 9–22. Unless otherwise declared, translations in the text and notes stem from the author.

1 Alexy's variant of discourse theory is independent from Habermas's theory, see Peter Gril, *Die Möglichkeit praktischer Erkenntnis aus Sicht* der *Diskurstheorie. Eine Untersuchung zu Jürgen Habermas und Robert Alexy*, Berlin 1998, 14, a "self-contained variant of discourse-theory". However, Alexy's theory has been profoundly influenced by Habermas's work; see below, n. 3.

2 This is emphasized in Bernd Rüthers, *Rechtstheorie*, 4th ed. München 2008, 373 n. 586; who remarks here that discourse theory "has been introduced into legal methodology through, above all, the work of R. Alexy".

3 This coinage of the Alexyian theory by Habermas is underscored by Ulfrid Neumann, *Juristische Argumentationslehre*, Darmstadt 1986, 95, n. 6: "Alexy's outline ties [...], above all, to Habermas's theory of practical discourse with its broad scope". Robert Alexy, *A Theory of Legal Argumentation. The Theory of Rational Discourse as Theory of Legal Justification*, transl. by R. Adler and N. MacCormick, Oxford 1989, 101, holds "Habermas's consensus theory of truth and the theory of practical deliberation of the Erlangen School" to be of the greatest significance for his enquiry, as far as theories "conducted in German" are concerned. For a portrayal of some similarities and differences between Alexy's and Habermas's theories see Gril (n. 1), 129–135.

4 The subtitle reads *The Theory of Rational Discourse as Theory of Legal Justification*, Alexy (n. 3).

5 See Robert Alexy, "Hauptelemente einer Theorie der Doppelnatur des Rechts", in *Archiv für Rechts- und Sozialphilosophie* 95 (2009), 151–166, 157.

model of discourse emerges – the ideal discourse serves as the ideal dimension, the real discourse as the real dimension.

A. Alexy's Concept of Ideal Discourse qua Ideal Dimension

Alexy defines the ideal practical discourse as follows:[6]

> [The ideal discourse] is defined by searching for an answer to a practical question under the conditions of unlimited time, unlimited participation, and complete freedom of constraints by way of achieving complete linguistic-conceptual clearness, complete empirical information, complete ability and willingness to change roles and complete freedom from prejudice.[7]

Ideal discourse performs two essential tasks in the two-dimensional model. First, it serves as the criterion of correctness. Since, however, ideal discourse, as Alexy puts it, "cannot be carried out by definition"[8], it will serve as "a criterion for correctness" only if one asks "whether a norm N *could* be the result of an ideal discourse".[9] Thus, ideal discourse becomes a hypothetical criterion of truth. According to the two-dimensional model, what is correct is what would be found to be correct in an ideal discourse.[10]

Second, ideal discourse serves as a standard for real discourses. Real discourse must comport with ideal discourse as far as possible. In this sense, Alexy understands "the regulative idea of absolute procedural correctness and with it the idea of an ideal discourse" as a "necessary condition of any reasonable argumentation" in

6 Whilst Habermas accounts for theoretical as well as practical discourse, Alexy confines himself to developing a theory of practical discourse. Thus, his definitions of the ideal and the real discourse refer solely to practical discourses.

7 Robert Alexy, "Problems of Discourse Theory", in *crítica* 20 (1988), 43–65, 48. On another occasion, Robert Alexy, "Diskurstheorie und Rechtssystem", in *Synthesis Philosophica* 5 (1988), 299–310, 304, points only to five ideal conditions of discourse: "Complete ideal conditions are on hand by means of five idealizations: (1) unlimited time, (2) unlimited participation, (3) complete linguistic-conceptual clearness, (4) complete information, and (5) complete freedom from prejudice". The condition of complete ability and willingness to change roles is missing here, as well as the complete freedom form constraints. Whether these conditions can be dispensed with in a world marked by the other five ideal conditions is impossible to determine, for there is no such world. See for specific doubts on the conceptual possibility of complete freedom from constraints Carsten Bäcker, *Begründen und Entscheiden: Kritik und Rekonstruktion der Alexyschen Diskurstheorie des Rechts*, 2nd ed. Baden-Baden 2012, 129, there n. 448.

8 Alexy, "Problems" (n. 7), 51. This is realized and criticized also by Ota Weinberger, "Basic Puzzles of Discourse Philosophy", in *Ratio Juris* 9 (1996), 172–181, 174, who, with an eye to the Habermasian discourse theory, holds ideal discourse to be impossible by definition: "Ideal discourse is not defined as the best possible discourse, but as an impossible discourse. It is not a normative ideal of a discourse, but an unreal, by definition impossible discourse".

9 For both quotations, see Alexy, "Problems" (n. 7), 51.

10 Skeptical of this function of the ideal discourse is Steffen Wesche, "Robert Alexys diskurstheoretische Menschenrechtsbegründung", in *Rechtstheorie* 30 (1999), 92: "If the ideal discourse is shaped normatively as superior as Alexy does, then it has no counterpart in reality. Real norms necessarily stem from distortions of the ideal discourse. Then, however, it is mistaken to lend its legitimatory force to any norm. […] At best, the ideal discourse may serve as a criterion for (real) discourses, but not for norms".

real discourses.[11] Thus, ideal discourse in the two-dimensional model draws on the "character of a goal to be achieved"[12] for real discourses.[13] In short, ideal discourse serves as a regulative idea for real discourses,[14] and, by the same token, as its standard and its justification. This function is reflected in Alexy's concept of real discourse.

B. Alexy's Concept of Real Discourse qua Real Dimension

Alexy begins with a negative definition of real discourses. It reads: "Real discourses are in no respect ideal discourses".[15] The positive definition of real practical discourses, according to Alexy, reads as follows:

> Real practical discourses are defined in terms of a search for an answer to a practical question under the conditions of limited time, limited participation, and incomplete freedom of constraints in the face of incomplete linguistic-conceptual clarity, incomplete empirical information, incomplete ability to change roles, and a lack of freedom from prejudice.[16]

This definition of real discourses[17] is distinguished from that of the ideal discourse only in that the unlimited conditions are changed to limited conditions.[18]

11 Both quotations are taken from Robert Alexy, "Idee und Struktur eines vernünftigen Rechtssystems", in *Rechts- und Sozialphilosophie in Deutschland heute*, R. Alexy, R. Dreier, and U. Neumann (eds.), ARSP-Beiheft 44, Stuttgart 1991, 30–44, 35.

12 Alexy (n. 11), 35.

13 See Robert Alexy, "Thirteen Replies", in *Law, Rights, and Discourse*, G. Pavlakos (ed.), Oxford 2007, 333–366, 361: "The participants of discourse are real persons in concrete historical situations who attempt to achieve correct moral judgments with respect to ideal rules of argumentation that never can be completely fulfilled. Under these conditions only an approximation to correctness is possible. For that reason, a consensus achieved in a *real* discourse cannot, indeed, be constitutive of correctness or objective validity. Such a consensus can never be more than an attempt to provide an answer to a practical question that meets correctness qua regulative idea to the extent possible".

14 See Alexy (n. 5), 157. Similarly Axel Tschentscher, "Der Konsensbegriff in Vertrags- und Diskurstheorien", in *Rechtstheorie* 33 (2002), 43–59, 58.

15 Alexy (n. 11), 35. This definition is accompanied by the following remark: "It is obvious that there are, alongside discourses that are ideal in all respects and discourses that are ideal in no respects, also in some respects ideal discourses", Alexy (n. 11), 35, there n. 24. – Discourses that are ideal in some respects may well be theoretically possible every bit as much as discourses that are ideal in all respects; actually existing discourses, however, need not be, under the conditions given, ideal in any respect. Thus, the (claimed) existence of discourses that are ideal in some respects is of no relevance to this enquiry.

16 Alexy (n. 11), 35.

17 The characterization of the real discourse by Ernst Zimmermann ought not to be followed, see his "Multideontische Logik, Prozedurale Rechtstheorie, Diskurs", in *Rechtstheorie* 30 (1999), 311–327, 321: "The real discourse is often carried out under the condition of limited time; it always has only a limited number of participants, and the condition of complete freedom from constraints is not always satisfied". Zimmermann claims, with this characterization, that a real discourse under the conditions of unlimited time and complete freedom of constraints would be possible. This is unsubstantiated, given the conditions of the world as we know it.

18 If one is prepared to leave out of account the missing element in one's willingness to change roles in the definition of the real discourse.

The introduction of a real discourse is necessary in the two-dimensional model in order to provide the actually impossible ideal discourse with an actually possible discourse, that is to say, a real discourse. Not unlike the ideal discourse,[19] the real discourse faces a number of problems. The main problem of real discourses arises, according to Alexy, from the "relativity of the concept of correctness"[20], corresponding to the concept of discursive possibility.[21] The concept of correctness is relative to "(1) the discourse rules, (2) the degree of their fulfillment, (3) the participants and (4) the points of time".[22]

C. Problems of the Two-Dimensional Model

The two-dimensional model faces severe challenges and puzzles; a goodly number of these have already been pointed out by critics[23] and even by Alexy himself. Not all of these problems are of significance; some may well lend themselves to resolution. At least three challenges and puzzles lead, however, to major doubts.

The first and most significant challenge consists in the question of the *Letztbegründbarkeit* of the ideal discourse.[24] The function of the ideal discourse as a crite-

19 On the problems of the concept of an ideal discourse out of the perspective of the two-dimensional model, see Bäcker (n. 7), 117–120; for a solution to these problems from the perspective of the one-dimensional model, see 153–156.

20 Alexy, "Problems" (n. 7), 61.

21 The concept of discursive possibility stems from the observation that, at any rate in real discourses, it will not always be the case that precisely one answer to any practical question is recognized to be correct. Although there are in real discourses discursive necessities as well as discursive impossibilities, it is nevertheless possible that several propositions, even inconsistent, will likewise have to be seen as discursively possible. On Alexy's categorical use of the concepts of discursive possibility, necessity, and impossibility, see Alexy (n. 3), 17, and Alexy, "Problems" (n. 7), 60. For these concepts as mere discursive modalities, see Bäcker (n. 7), 222–224.

22 Alexy, "Problems" (n. 7), 61. These four relativizations sum up the concept of relative procedural correctness, which Alexy distinguishes from the concept of absolute procedural correctness that is to be achieved in ideal discourses. With this comparison, Alexy suggests that the hypothetical correctness of the ideal discourse as provided by the two-dimensional model would not be relative. Thus, the problem of relative correctness would only affect real discourses. In fact, in the ideal discourse in Alexy's model, correctness is already relativized, for even an absolute procedural correctness is a correctness relative to the procedure, see Bäcker (n. 7), 124f. Therefore, there is also in the two-dimensional model no absolute correctness but only relative correctness.

23 The most determined critics of the common discourse theory as the basis of a discourse theory of law are Gril (n. 1) and Armin Engländer, *Diskurs als Rechtsquelle? Zur Kritik der Diskurstheorie des Rechts*, Tübingen 2002. Both works take up primarily the discourse theories of Habermas and Alexy. The more rewarding critics include, furthermore, Hain, Hilgendorf, Neumann, and Weinberger.

24 The familiar discourse theories attempt to arrive at a definitive justification (*Letztbegründetheit*) of the concept of an ideal discourse by appeal to transcendental philosophy. Apel choses a transcendental-pragmatic approach, followed by Habermas with his universal-pragmatism. Alexy undertakes a weak transcendental-pragmatism. – All of these approaches share a common ground: they rely on a meta-theoretic argumentative existence of the human-being, a kind of "discursive life form" that is significant for the human being and from which he cannot escape. According to Jürgen Habermas, "Diskursethik – Notizen zu einem Begründungsprogramm", in *Moralbewußtsein und kommunikatives Handeln*, Frankfurt a.M. 1983, 53–125, 112, taking a decision against discourse must end in "schizophrenia and suicide", and for Karl-Otto Apel,

rion of truth shows that the concept of the ideal discourse is taken to be absolutely correct and, in this sense, definitively justified. It remains less than clear, however, how an absolutely correct concept of an ideal discourse can be ascertained by means of the merely performable and, thus, actual possible real discourses.

The second challenge – rather, a puzzle – emerges as soon as one examines more closely the function of the ideal discourse as a standard of real discourses. The question arises as to how an inaccessible ideal can ever serve as a manageable tool for measuring actual performed discourses. To speak of a regulative ideal does not answer this question.

The third challenge stems from the fact that the two-dimensional conception turns on the concept of an absolute correctness, at least as a regulative ideal, although even in Alexy's discourse theory, only relative correctness can prevail.[25] The alternative that comes immediately to mind is to dispense with the concept of absolute correctness, be it merely a regulative ideal, and to recognize and accept relative correctness as all that can be achieved.[26] With this move, however, the function of the ideal discourse as the, albeit merely hypothetical, criterion of the correctness of propositions will also have to be abandoned.

The one-dimensional model to be presented is in a position to respond to these problems. The strategy consists in dispensing altogether with every absolutely correct ideal dimension of discourse, and in introducing discourse principles.

Part Two: The One-Dimensional Three-Staged Model of Discourse

The adumbrated strategy hints at the differences between the one-dimensional and two-dimensional models. First, it dispenses with the ideal dimension that is connected to the claim to absolute correctness or a definitive justification of the concept of an ideal discourse. This difference is categorical, it changes the theory to a one-dimensional model. By dispensing with any ideal dimension, both the first and the third challenges are met. For the claim to a definitive justification, implied in the

"Das Apriori der Kommunikationsgemeinschaft und die Grundlagen der Ethik. Zum Problem einer rationalen Begründung der Ethik im Zeitalter der Wissenschaft", in *Transformationen der Philosophie: Das Apriori der Kommunikationsgemeinschaft*, Frankfurt a. M. 1973, 358–435, 414, it leads to the loss of "any possibility of self-understanding and of self-identification", resulting in "self-destruction". Robert Alexy, "Discourse Theory and Human Rights", in Ratio Juris 9 (1996), 209–235, 217, terms discursive *performance* "the most general form of life of human beings"; and the human-being, referring to Brandom, as "discursive creature" that undergoes "a kind of self-destruction" should it decide to act against its nature, Robert Alexy, "Discourse Theory and Fundamental Rights", in *Fundamental Rights through Discourse*, A. J. Menéndez, E. O. Eriksen (eds.), Oslo 2004, 35–51, 43. For doubts about these approaches, especially Alexy's, see Bäcker (n. 7), 44–53.

25 See above, n. 22.

26 This has been stressed by Ota Weinberger, "Der Streit um die praktische Vernunft. Gegen Scheinargumente in der praktischen Philosophie", in *Rechtssystem und praktische Vernunft*, R. Alexy and R. Dreier (eds.), ARSP Beiheft 51, Stuttgart 1993, 30–46, 43: "The absolute character of correctness serves as the author's justification by constituting the end as a regulative idea that, in turn, makes it possible to determine the one right answer to practical questions". Such "a claim does not [help], if we know that it is not realizable".

presentation of an ideal discourse, vanishes along with the assumption of absolute correctness as a criterion of truth, be it merely hypothetical.

Second, the model to be presented here ascribes to discourse principles the measure of discourses. This is the answer to the second challenge, for the concept of discourse principles provides a measure for actual discourse that is retained in the real dimension.

These two major differences mark the three stages of the one-dimensional discourse model. These are: (I) the discourse ideal, (II) discourse principles, and (III) actual discourses.

A. The Stage of the Discourse Ideal

The design of the first stage takes its departure from the most significant puzzle of the function of the ideal discourse in the two-dimensional model. This puzzle, found in the common model of discourse, consists in understanding the ideal discourse as a criterion for correctness or truth, although this is only intelligible, not realizable.

The ideal discourse, according to Alexy, is characterized by an ideal situation of discourse, in which ideal results under ideal conditions are to be achieved. Thus, the ideal discourse takes place by definition under, as Alexy himself puts it, "not-real conditions"[27]. It stems from the world of thought.

The reason for this is no mystery. Plainly, our world is not a world, in which all discourse-relevant conditions are perfectly given.[28] A glimpse into the situation adds clarity to this report. The actual participants can only be, at present, we human beings.[29] We do not, however, have unlimited time for our discussions. We are not able to communicate with an unlimited number of participants, let alone to communicate with them simultaneously.[30] Complete freedom from constraints must remain a utopia, for the satisfaction of our basic needs is to be guaranteed.[31] What is more, where practical questions relevant here are concerned, there will never exist complete linguistic-conceptual clarity, due to our limited capacity to perceive the

27 Robert Alexy, "Ota Weinbergers Kritik der diskurstheoretischen Deutung juristischer Rationalität", in *Institution und Recht. Grazer Symposion zu Ehren von Ota Weinberger*, P. Koller, W. Krawietz, and P. Strasser (eds.), Rechtstheorie Beiheft 14, Berlin 1994, 143–157, 149.

28 Alexy, "Problems" (n. 7), 49, leaves the question unanswered as to "whether or not the described state [the fulfillment of the ideal conditions] is conceptually possible at all". There are reasons to assume that at least the satisfaction of all conditions at one and the same time is conceptually impossible.

29 This virtual impossibility of any realization of the ideal conditions of discourse could well be what prompted Ota Weinberger, "Grundlagenprobleme des Institutionalistischen Rechtspositivismus", in *Institution und Recht. Grazer Symposion zu Ehren von Ota Weinberger*, P. Koller, W. Krawietz, and P. Strasser (eds.), Rechtstheorie Beiheft 14, Berlin 1994, 173–284, 259 f., to term the ideal discourse a non-human discourse, a "discourse of angels".

30 On the limitation of time and the number of participants likewise Robert Alexy, "A Theory of Practical Discourse", transl. by D. Frisby, in *The Communicative Ethics Controversy*, S. Benhabib and F. Dallmayr (eds.), Cambridge, Mass. 1990, 151–190: "On factual grounds, it is impossible that everyone discuss everything without restriction; time is short".

31 Robert Spaemann, "Die Utopie der Herrschaftsfreiheit", in *Merkur* 26 (1972), 735–752, accounts in a similar way for the "utopia of reignlessness", with an eye to Habermas.

world around us.[32] We will never arrive at a complete roster of empirical data, we will never be completely able or, indeed, willing to change roles, and, finally, we shall never be completely free from prejudice.

Thus, human beings as real or actual existing participants in a discourse possess, on the basis of what we know, only capacities that are limited, never unlimited.[33] As long as the capacities of human beings as discourse participants are limited in this way, the realization of the ideal conditions of ideal discourses is, as Alexy states, "not actually possible in fact".[34] This is to say that the ideal conditions of the ideal discourse are neither jointly nor severally realizable in fact. Thus, the performance of an ideal discourse is impossible in our actual world; the notion exists solely in the world of thought.

That realizability is lacking is, to be sure, clear to Alexy as well as to Habermas. The puzzle of the common discourse theory amounts, in the end, to this: Why has the concept of ideal discourse been sustained? Why has it not been banished to the realm of unrealizable ideas? Instead of banishment, the realizability of the ideal discourse has been adopted "counterfactually" – with consequences for the real world.[35] The ideal discourse provides nothing less than the metaphysical foundation of the familiar discourse theory. In Alexy's work, this counterfactual assumption is reflected both in the functions of the ideal discourse as a hypothetical criterion of truth and as a regulative ideal of real discourses, as we have seen above.

Neither Alexy's concept of an ideal discourse nor Habermas's ideal speech situation can provide, however, for more than a description of a world in which a discourse, following our imagination, would be perfect. Precisely this, no more and no less than a description of our imagination of an ideal discourse, marks the restriction

32 Our limited capacity to perceive our world leads to the so-called defeasibility of those concepts with which we describe our world. Our concepts are necessarily relative to our knowledge of the objects being conceptualized. That is why, as Immanual Kant, *Critique of Pure Reason*, transl. by P. Guyer and A. W. Wood, Cambridge 1998, A 727, B 755, puts it, "an empirical concept cannot be defined at all but only explicated". The attributes of any concept may change owing to new empirical knowledge. Kant asserts: "One makes use of certain marks only as long as they are sufficient for making distinctions; new observations, however, take some away and add some, and therefore the concept never remains within secure boundaries", A 728, B 756. Complete linguistic-conceptual clarity is, therefore, achievable only in logic, mathematics or a closed linguistic system, like the rules of chess. Kant has seen this as well: "Mathematical definitions can never err. For since the concept is first given through the definition, it contains just that which the definition would think through it", A 731, B 759.

33 Alexy, "Problems" (n. 7), 49, concedes this when he asserts that the ideal conditions of the ideal discourse will be realized only if "participants in the ideal discourse undergo a nearly total change from real and actually existing into ideal and constructed participants".

34 Alexy, "Problems" (n. 7), 49. This is not to say that real circumstances are necessarily non-ideal. It is not to be excluded that we may one day live in a world that is ideal in at least some respects relevant to discourses. For as long as this is not the case, however, the ideal discourse is simply impossible.

35 The ideal speech situation, according to Jürgen Habermas, "Wahrheitstheorien", in *Wirklichkeit und Reflexion. Walter Schulz zum 60. Geburtstag*, H. Fahrenbach (ed.), Pfullingen 1973, 211–265, 258, is "neither an empirical phenomenon nor a mere construction, but a reciprocal allegation being unavoidable". The ideal speech situation serves, moreover, as the "fundament of any linguistic communication", for it belongs to "the structure of human speech" to "behave, counterfactually, as if the ideal speech situation were not merely fictitious, but real, while carrying out our speech acts".

that must be imposed on the function of the concept of an ideal discourse. By restricting the ideal discourse to this function, the ideal discourse becomes a *discourse ideal* that no longer floats about in an ideal dimension. The discourse ideal does not specify a discourse of angels, who may well be perfect at all times and under all conditions. Rather, it specifies a historically and culturally contingent idea[36] of an ideal discourse of human beings. The discourse ideal, in contrast to the ideal discourse, lies entirely in the real world.

Thus, the application of Alexy's concept of an ideal discourse in the one-dimensional model is restricted to the task of clarifying the concept and the conditions of an – always disputable[37] – ideal of discourse. In dispensing with the concept of an ideal discourse along with its claim to be definitively justified, be it in the course of a transcendental-pragmatic justification as in Apel, a universal-pragmatic justification as in Habermas, or even a weak transcendental-pragmatic justification as in Alexy,[38] the problem of justification is defused. The discourse ideal cannot serve as a condition of truth – not even as a hypothetical condition, for it grants its historico-cultural contingency.

A question remains, however, with reference to the one-dimensional model: Is the discourse ideal, say, Alexy's concept of an ideal discourse, really the actually prevailing discourse ideal? This, however, is a meta-theoretical question that is not answered by the model.

36 The objection of the historico-cultural contingency stems from Engländer (n. 23), 55, who objects in discussing Alexy's proposal of a transcendental-pragmatic justification of discourse theory with an eye to the "*nichthintergehbaren Bedingungen*" of the speech act of assertion assumed by Alexy that this assumption would be "– if anything – an account of the current, 'normal' and historically contingent rules of giving assertions".

37 The Alexyian discourse ideal is not to be understood as the one and only discourse ideal. It is simply one discourse ideal that, given a progressive debate, can be modified or even replaced. It is dependent on the actual imagination of a specific cultural area. In this way, the three-stage-model is capable of explaining that there have been and still are very different ideas for acting correctly in other cultural areas, when compared to ours. – A further reason for these differences that can only be mentioned here is the theory-internal weakness of all models of discourse: the lack of result-definiteness. On the inevitability of this weakness in the common model and in the one presented here, see Bäcker (n. 7), 162–164. This weakness gives rise, among other things, to the "open" character of the discourse vis-á-vis the various possible answers to a practical question even after the discourse is completed. That phenomenon of the discursive possibilities of various solutions may be encountered only with decisions. Therefore, in one cultural area at a given point in time there may be significantly different, even incompatible solutions to a whole set of questions, even substantial questions. This diversity is reflected in the distinct character of legal cultures, even in those European states that belong to a strongly related cultural area.

38 For a criticism of Apel's and Habermas's attempts at a justification from the perspective of legal philosophy, see Eric Hilgendorf, *Argumentation in der Jurisprudenz. Zur Rezeption von analytischer Philosophie und kritischer Theorie in der Grundlagenforschung der Jurisprudenz*, Berlin 1991, 131–157 (Apel), 158–185 (Habermas). For a criticism of Alexy's effort to arrive at a justification, see Bäcker (Fn. 3), 53–113.

B. The Stage of Discourse Principles

The second stage links the first stage, that of the imagination of an ideal discourse, summarized in the discourse ideal, to the third stage, that of actual discourses. This link presupposes the introduction of discourse principles. The concept of discourse principle is tied to that of a legal principle, as developed in the principles theory of fundamental rights by Alexy and his school.[39] Thus, discourse principles are the normative and regulative links between the ideal of discourse and the discourses performed in reality, the actual discourses.

According to principles theory, principles demand the realization of a given goal or ideal to the greatest extent possible by means of optimizing a state of conditions. In the model of discourse, the discourse ideal represents the ideal to be realized to the greatest extent possible. An approximation to this relative ideal is the maximum that is achievable in our world, characterized by limiting conditions. Thus, discourse principles embody the command to realize the ideal of discourse to the greatest extent possible. They command an optimal realization of the idealized conditions of the imagined ideal discourse in the discourse ideal relative to the given circumstances. By the same token, any single discourse principle commands the realization of a single ideal condition of discourse. According to the Alexyian ideal of discourse, there are at least seven[40] conflicting discourse-principles.[41]

Consequently, discourse principles connect the imagined (and therefore relative) ideality, the ideal of discourse, to the given reality, the actual conditions of discourse. However, discourse principles as such do not offer immediately workable discourse rules. Rather, discourse rules stem from the application of discourse principles to the given circumstances in a concrete discourse situation. This application takes place at the third stage, that of actual discourses.

C. The Stage of Actual Discourses

Discourse principles demand the realization of their objects to the greatest extent possible by way of optimizing discursive situations relative to its given circumstances. Thus, they command not an absolute but an optimal realization of their objects.[42] The adherence to this command, the realization of those conditions of dis-

39 For a short discussion of the concept of principles in principles theory, see Bäcker (n. 7), 131–146.

40 Imaginable, furthermore, is the possibility that there are only five discourse principles, following the lines of Alexy's narrower concept of an ideal discourse as per his description, see above, n. 7. For the three-dimensional conception of the model, however, this number is without relevance, as well as the material content of the discourse principles in general.

41 It is an open question whether these material principles of discourse need to be accompanied by formal or procedural principles. One can consider the six principles of rationality that Alexy named in an earlier work, written together with Aarnio and Peczenik, see Aulis Aarnio, Robert Alexy, and Aleksander Peczenik, "Grundlagen der juristischen Argumentation", in *Metatheorie juristischer Argumentation*, R. Alexy and W. Krawietz (eds.), Berlin 1983, 9–87, 45 f.

42 A complete realization of all objects would only be possible under ideal conditions. Ideal conditions of discourse, however, do not exist in our world, as noted above. If they existed, discourse principles would be unnecessary, for under ideal conditions all objects of discourse principles

course that are taken to be ideal, takes place on the third stage, that of actual discourses, by applying discourse principles to the circumstances given.

It is therefore imperative that the discursive situation at issue, as constituted by the given circumstances, be shaped in a way that it is consistent to the greatest extent possible with the ideal of discourse as facilitated by the discourse principles. The result of a successful application of discourse principles would be an optimal discourse. Taking the Alexyian ideal discourse as the basis of the ideal of discourse, the discursive situation at stake should provide for a maximum of time, participants, freedom of constraints by way of achieving incomplete linguistic-conceptual clarity, empirical data, willingness to change roles, and freedom from prejudice. The concrete possible maximum, however, depends on the circumstances of the situation.

Following the idea of the one-dimensional model, discourse principles offer a measure, a scale for actual discourses. In this way, they not only offer a criterion for developing new discourse rules but also a criterion for evaluating institutionalized discourses. Moreover, discourse principles make it possible to create general or typical discourse rules as well as concrete or specialized ones. The first kind of discourse rule occurs in applying discourse principles to general or typical discourse situations, the second in applying them to concrete or special situations. General discourse rules provide a measure for special discourse rules on their part.

The application of discourse principles with an eye to creating discourse rules basically follows the lines drawn in the discussion on the application of legal principles to create legal rules. The comprehension of the discourse model introduced here, however, does not presuppose a full-fledged understanding of this discussion in all its details, for it has achieved a remarkable complexity.[43] As an outline, it suffices to know the central axiom of principles theory concerning the genesis of rules via principles: Rules can be understood as stemming from a collision of principles, by determining the circumstances of the collision *qua* condition (*Tatbestand*) of the rule and the appropriate result of the balancing *qua* consequence.[44]

The many difficulties that arise with the application of discourse principles in their procedural dimension – for example, the issue of how single principles in the case of a collision are to be weighed – are not examined here. Instead, this difficulty

would be given. However, there are doubts regarding even the conceptual possibility of the realization of all objects of all discourse principles at the same time. This seems to hold true also for Alexy, see above, n. 28.

43 In particular, Jan-R. Sieckmann, *Recht als normatives System. Die Prinzipientheorie des Rechts*, Baden-Baden 2009, pursues a further arrangement of the principles theory in several publications. In this book, Sieckmann provides a *résumé* of his ideas on principles theory that not infrequently contradicts Alexy's theory of principles. Sieckmann's contributions, however, lend to principles theory a new level of complexity. The increasing complexity counts as a theoretically extremely demanding saturation of the material, and is not everywhere appreciated. For example, Jan Henrik Klement, "Vom Nutzen einer Theorie, die alles erklärt. Robert Alexys Prinzipientheorie aus der Sicht der Grundrechtsdogmatik", *JuristenZeitung* 2008, 756–763, criticizes "especially with an eye to Sieckmann's theory of principles" (757, there n. 17) that "complicating the theory [...] marks an end of some basic assumptions rather than a gradual perfectionization of the theory".

44 This has been described, in a rather early stage of the development of principles theory, as the law of competing principles. It reads, in its untechnical formulation: "The circumstances under which one principle takes precedence over another constitute the conditions of a rule which has the same legal consequences as the principle taking precedence", Robert Alexy, *A Theory of Constitutional Rights*, transl. by J. Rivers, Oxford 2002, 54.

may serve as an example of one of the many open questions that will have to be pursued further.[45]

Concluding Remark

The first stage of the relativistic model of discourse is about determining a preliminary ideal of discourse. This discourse ideal shifts the foundation of the whole discourse-theoretic system. Accordingly, any change in the ideal of discourse, be it very slight, can lead to earthshaking consequences for the system.

Discourse principles provide the ideal of discourse as a normative guideline for developing discursive subsystems. These stem, in the end, from an application of the discourse principles to given discourse situations. As an intermediate step, general discourse rules may be developed that empower us to find specialized discourse rules for concrete discourse situations with less effort. Every special discourse rule that has been generated from general discourse rules needs, however, to be reconnected to the discourse principles. Discourse principles remain, then, as the only measure for all discourse rules.

Result: Strengthening the Discourse Theory of Law

Every new theory needs to address the question of the advantages it provides over the existing theories. The presented relativistic variant of discourse theory seems to offer only disadvantages, when compared to the common discourse theories. Precisely the renunciation of any idealistic claim leads to a significant weakening of discourse theory.

The claim to offer a criterion of truth vanishes without any replacement; a historico-culturally contingent ideal of discourse can never augur truth. Likewise, the relativistic discourse theory dispenses with claims as to a definitive justification for even the most fundamental material propositions, by understanding them to be contingent in the same way as the discourse ideal. Thus, contributions of discourse theory for a foundation and justification of universal human rights, for example, give rise to doubts.

These severe disadvantages are inescapable, however, when discourse theory seeks to answer its critics. In fact, the abundance of the ideal dimension is the consequence of the propositions and assumptions of discourse theory. The relativistic discourse theory grants that present knowledge is something other than absolutely correct cognition. If this assumption is true, the supposed weakening of discourse theory can be rendered as a strengthening. For it is only without an ideal dimension

45 A notion of the possibilities that come with the application of the new model to concrete legal questions may be achieved when the discursive character of a trial is assessed. The thesis that a trial is a discourse, central to the acceptability of any discourse theory of law, has been the object of some well-founded criticism. The three-stage model shows, however, that even the discursively restricted trials of a criminal court may be reconstructed in accordance with the measures of discourse principles, see Bäcker (n. 7), 277–285. The possible objection that simply everything could be named "a discourse" in accordance to the three-stage model underestimates the capability of a measurement grounded on discourse principles. Optimization is not arbitrary.

that we are able to realize the unavoidable relativity of our own cognition; and this awareness makes it possible to concentrate on the task at hand: optimizing the means of cognition.[46]

On the basis of the relativistic conception presented here, the theory of legal argumentation is able to escape the very central and fundamental skepticism concerning the absolute assumptions of the common discourse theory – that would otherwise affect the theory of legal argumentation. Two consequences for the theory of rational discourse as theory of legal justification arise from this.

First, the reconstruction of a legal system in a relativistic discourse-theoretic model of law requires an adequate tie between the argumentative procedures for *justifying* and the competences for *deciding*. The legislator needs to be able to decide those remaining questions in the actual practical discourse by means of his power, just as the judge has to be able to decide those questions that remain unanswered in the actual legal discourse in court.[47] The relativistic discourse theory provides all that is needed to justify this systemic necessity of a legislator and a judge as decision-makers on the basis of the weaknesses of the procedures of discourse itself.[48]

Second, the one-dimensional model requires that attention be focussed on rationality as optimality. This, in the framework of the relativistic discourse theory, is the flip side of the ability of relative cognition. That focus is achieved, in the one-dimensional model, by the postulate to optimize the discursive circumstances. This postulate is inherent in the discourse principles.[49] By way of the discourse principles with their postulate to optimize the discursive circumstances, a scale of rationality is brought into the theory of legal argumentation, a scale of rationality that is adequate to the reality of legal discourses – for it is realizable: A legal judgment is correct if and only if it is a discursively possible result of an optimal legal discourse.

In this way, the familiar scale of rationality provided by discourse theory, the ideal discourse *qua* never achievable regulative ideal, is displaced. Rationality without ideality emerges.

46 Thus, the relativistic theory of discourse comports with one of Weinberger's (n. 26), 39, main demands: One shall "strive to optimize real discourses and to enforce them thereby, and to keep the deceptive construction of an ideal discourse out of the game".

47 Central to this discourse-theoretical model of law is Alexy's four-stage procedural model of law, see Alexy (n. 44), 370f., Carsten Bäcker, "Recht als institutionalisierte Vernunft?", in *Archiv für Rechts- und Sozialphilosophie* 97 (2011), 346–359.

48 See Bäcker (n. 7), 260–263.

49 See Bäcker (n. 7), 173f. The postulate reads: "If an optimum of rationality is to be achieved, everything is to be focused on optimizing the circumstances of the actual discourses according to the discourse principles".

Gonzalo Villa Rosas*

A Matter of Interest

On Robert Alexy's Justification of Practical Discourse

Introduction

Tugendhat has rightly pointed out the need for a philosophical answer to the underlying tension, characteristic of our times, between the claim to universal validity that we spontaneously attach to our practical statements and the necessary historical and social relativity of them.[1] This answer should be based both on the impossibility to appeal again to the authority of tradition, and on the rejection of nihilism.[2] However, a justification of our practical statements that would be a result of a rational discussion would be faced by the requirement of an ultimate justification of its rules. This justification poses a risk for itself, since it leads to an infinite regress that can only be avoided either by means of an unjustified decision which breaks the chain of thoughts, or by means of the resigned approval of a circular justification.[3]

Among the various attempts to justify the norms of the practical discourse should be considered especially the universal pragmatic theory of Habermas[4] and the transcendental-pragmatic ultimate justification of Apel[5]. Although Alexy avoided[6] carrying out such a task in his *Theorie der juristischen Argumentation* (1976)

* My thanks and gratitude to my gracious host Professor Dr. George Pavlakos at the Centre for Law and Cosmopolitan Values, Antwerp University (May-September, 2014). I should like to thank Andrej Kristan for his help and advice on matters of language.

1 Ernst Tugendhat, *Vorlesung über Ethik* (Frankfurt am Main: Suhrkamp Verlag, 1993), 14.

2 Ibid. 13.

3 Hans Albert, *Traktat über kritische Vernunft* (first publ. 1968), (Tübingen: Mohr Siebeck, 1991), 15; Robert Alexy, *Theorie der juristischen Argumentation. Die Theorie des rationalen Diskurses als Theorie der juristischen Begründung* (Frankfurt am Main: Suhrkamp Verlag, 1983), 223.

4 See Jürgen Habermas, 'Diskursethik-Notizen zu einem Begründungsprogramm', in Jürgen Habermas, *Moralbewußtsein und kommunikatives Handeln* (Frankfurt am Main: Suhrkamp Verlag, 1983), 52–125; Jürgen Habermas, 'Was heißt Universalpragmatik?' (first publ. 1976), in Jürgen Habermas, *Vorstudien und Ergänzungen zur Theorie des kommunikativen Handelns*, (Frankfurt am Main: Suhrkamp Verlag, 1995), 353–440.

5 Karl-Otto Apel, 'Das Apriori der Kommunikationsgemeinschaft und die Grundlagen der Ethik. Zum Problem einer rationalen Begründung der Ethik im Zeitalter der Wissenschaft', in *Transformation der Philosophie*, 2nd. vol.: *Das Apriori der Kommunikationsgemeinschaft*, ed. Karl-Otto Apel (Frankfurt am Main: Suhrkamp Verlag, 1973), 358–435; Karl-Otto Apel, 'Sprechakttheorie und transzendentale Sprachpragmatik zur Frage ethischer Normen' (first publ. 1976), in *Auseinandersetzungen. In Erprobung des transzendentalpragmatischen Ansatzes* (Frankfurt am Main: Suhrkamp, 1998), 281–411. See, too, Wolfgang Kuhlman, *Reflexive Letztbegründung: Untersuchungen zur Transzendentalpragmatik* (Freiburg: K. Alber Verlag, 1985); Dietrich Böhler, *Rekonstruktive Pragmatik: Von der Bewußtseinphilosophie zur Kommunikationsreflexion. Neubegründung der praktischen Wissenschaften und Philosophie* (Frankfurt am Main: Suhrkamp Verlag, 1985).

6 Indeed, according to Alexy, "[d]aß nicht nur nach begründeten Regeln vorgegangen wird, ist nicht unvernünftig. Da dies nicht möglich ist und da es vernünftig ist, überhaupt mit dem Diskutieren anzufangen, ist es vernünftig, zunächst auch auf der Grundlage nicht begründeter Regeln zu beginnen." (Robert Alexy, *Theorie der juristischen Argumentation. Die Theorie des rationalen*

– in which he ruled out numerous strategies of justification[7] – he put forward his proposal in his *Nachwort* (1991)[8] for the first time. He developed the justification of discourse norms in his articles *Eine diskurstheoretische Konzeption der praktischen Vernunft* (1993)[9] and *Diskurstheorie und Menschenrechte* (1995)[10] in a more detailed and extensive way. Alexy has responded to a systemic requirement of his own theory of argumentation with his strategy.[11]

That is why Alexy's proposal takes on characteristics of its own.[12] On the one hand, Alexy has accepted the restrictions of the transcendental-pragmatic argument,[13] and hence, in this line, he has avoided imposing practical requirements at the pragmatic level of justification that emerge from the search of an ultimate justification of the constitutive norms of discourse.[14] On the other hand, Alexy has renounced the transcendental feature that Habermas has given to the universal task of understanding developed by our communicative practices.[15] According to Alexy,

Diskurses als Theorie der juristischen Begründung (n. 3), 233. See, too, Robert Alexy, 'Eine Theorie des praktischen Diskurses', in *Materialien zur Normendiskussion*, ed. Willi Oelmüller, vol. 2: *Normenbegründung – Normendurchsetzung* (Padeborn: Ferdinan Schöningh, 1978), 22–58, at 35.

7 Robert Alexy, *Theorie der juristischen Argumentation. Die Theorie des rationalen Diskurses als Theorie der juristischen Begründung* (n. 3), 225–233. See, too, Robert Alexy, 'Eine Theorie des praktischen Diskurses' (n. 6), 22–58, at 26–34.

8 Robert Alexy, 'Nachwort (1991): Antwort auf einige Kritiker', in *Theorie der juristischen Argumentation. Die Theorie des rationalen Diskurses als Theorie der juristischen Begründung* (Frankfurt am Main: Suhrkamp Verlag, 1983), 399–435.

9 Robert Alexy, 'Eine diskurstheoretische Konzeption der praktischen Vernunft', in *Rechtssystem und praktische Vernunft. Verhandlungen des 15. Weltkongresses der Internationalen Vereinigung für Rechts und Sozialphilosophie (IVR) in Göttingen, August 1991*, vol. 1, ed. Robert Alexy *et al.* (Stuttgart: Franz Steiner, 1993), 11–29.

10 Robert Alexy, 'Diskurstheorie und Menschenrechte', in *Recht, Vernunft, Diskurs. Studien zur Rechtsphilosophie*, ed. Robert Alexy (Frankfurt am Main: Suhrkamp, 1995), 127–162, republ. in 'Discourse Theory and Human Rights', *Ratio Juris*, 9 (1996), 209–233. The following quotations were taken from the English version.

11 As stated by Alexy: "Die Theorie des rationalen Diskurses ist eine normative Diskurstheorie. Damit stellt sich in ihr das Problem, wie die Regeln des rationalen Diskurses begründet werden können" (Robert Alexy, *Theorie der juristischen Argumentation. Die Theorie des rationalen Diskurses als Theorie der juristischen Begründung* (n. 3), 225.)

12 In contrast, Hilgendorf has pointed out that since the publication of Nachwort (1991) Alexy's theory should be counted as an example of Apel's transcendental-pragmatic thinking. See Eric Hilgendorf, 'Zur traszendentalpragmatischen Begründung von Diskursregeln', *Rechtstheorie*, 27, 1995, 183–200, at 185, 190.

13 Alexy has made explicit the commitments of the theory of rational discourse with the political liberalism and has accepted the fallibility of the transcendental argument from the point of view of its practical validity. (Robert Alexy, 'Discourse Theory and Human Rights' (n. 10), 209–233, at 212.)

14 In this regard, Habermas has written: "Eine Letztbegründung der Ethik is weder möglich nicht nötig." (Jürgen Habermas, 'Erläuterungen zur Diskursethik', in *Erläuterungen zur Diskursethik*, ed. Jürgen Habermas (Frankfurt am Main: Suhrkamp Verlag, 1991), 119–226, at 195.

15 In this vein, Habermas has stated "der verständigungsorientierte Sprachgebrauch [ist] der *Originalmodus*, zu dem sich die indirekte Verständigung, das Zu-verstehen-geben oder das Verstehen-lassen, parasitär verhalten" (Jürgen Habermas, *Theorie des kommunikativen Handelns*, vol. 1: *Handlungsrationalität und gesellschaftliche Rationalisierung* (first publ. 1981), (Frankfurt am Main: Suhrkamp, 1991), 388. See, too, Jürgen Habermas, 'Sprechakttheoretische Erläuterung zum Begriff der kommunikativen Rationalität', *Zeitschrift für philosophische Forschung*, 50, 1, 1996, 65–91, at 72; Jürgen Habermas, 'Erläuterungen zum Begriff des kommunikativen Handelns', in Jürgen

this transcendental feature has led Habermas to overestimate the transcendental-pragmatic argument for the justification of practical discourse.[16] As a result, Habermas has not taken into consideration the distinction between motivation and moral obligation.[17] This Kantian distinction takes on an essential meaning in the Alexyan proposal. Indeed, this distinction allows Alexy to define the subjects participating in the discourse practice on the basis of their cognitive abilities related to the possibility of making judgments and action. Consequently, Alexy has left the subjects free to perform behaviors directed towards mutual understanding.[18] This non-idealized definition of the subjects lays the foundations of the free expression of discourse participants' opinions, desires and needs,[19] i. e. it lays the foundations of the free expression of discourse participants in accordance with their real and concrete situation.[20] This form of participation fits with the definition not only of balancing and recognition of participating subjects' interests,[21] but also of a communication structure as necessary conditions for the correctness of practical statements.[22]

However, from the point of view of the practical validity, the distinction between motivation and moral obligation also entails the fallibility of the transcen-

Habermas, *Jürgen Habermas: Vorstudien und Ergänzungen zur Theorie des kommunikativen Handelns* (Frankfurt am Main: Suhrkamp, 1995), 571–606, at 595–598; Jürgen Habermas, 'Vorlesungen zu einer sprachtheoretischen Grundlegung der Soziologie' (1970–1971), in Jürgen Habermas, *Jürgen Habermas: Vorstudien und Ergänzungen zur Theorie des kommunikativen Handelns* (Frankfurt am Main: Suhrkamp, 1995), 11–126, at 73; Jürgen Habermas, 'Replik auf Einwände' (1980), in Jürgen Habermas, Jürgen Habermas: Vorstudien und Ergänzungen zur Theorie des *kommunikativen Handelns* (Frankfurt am Main: Suhrkamp, 1995), 475–570, at 497; Jürgen Habermas, *Faktizität und Geltung. Beiträge zur Diskurstheorie des Rechts und des demokratischen Rechtsstaats* (first publ. 1992), (Frankfurt am Main: Suhrkamp, 1994), 18; Jürgen Habermas, *Theorie des kommunikativen Handelns*, vol. 1: *Handlungsrationalität und gesellschaftliche Rationalisierung* (first publ. 1981), (Frankfurt am Main: Suhrkamp, 1991), 387–388. Jürgen Habermas, 'Handlungen, Sprechakte, sprachlich vermittelte Interaktionen und Lebenswelt', in Jürgen Habermas, *Nachmetaphysisches Denken. Philosophische Aufsätze* (Frankfurt am Main: Suhrkamp, 1988), 63–104, at 75; Jürgen Habermas, 'Dialektik der Rationalisierung', in Jürgen Habermas, *Die neue Unübersichtlichkeit* (Frankfurt am Main: Suhrkamp, 1985), 167–208, at 173; Jürgen Habermas, 'Diskusionsbeitrag', in *Transzendentalphilosophische Normenbegründung. Materialien zur Normendiskussion*, vol. 1, ed. Willi Oelmüller (Paderborn: Schöningh Verlag, 1978), 123–159, at 156.

16 Robert Alexy, 'Discourse Theory and Human Rights' (n. 10), 209–233, at 212–213.

17 Robert Alexy, 'Nachwort (1991): Antwort auf einige Kritiker' (n. 8), 399–435, at 407.

18 Peter Gril, *Die Möglichkeit praktischer Erkenntnis aus Sicht der Diskurstheorie. Eine Untersuchung zu Jürgen Habermas und Robert Alexy* (Berlin: Dunckler & Humbolt, 1998), 140.

19 See third normative component of the second rationality rule (Robert Alexy, *Theorie der juristischen Argumentation. Die Theorie des rationalen Diskurses als Theorie der juristischen Begründung* (n. 3), 240.)

20 Manuel Atienza, *Las razones del derecho. Teorías de la argumentación jurídica* (México: Universidad Nacional Autónoma de México, 2005), 155.

21 Robert Alexy, 'Eine diskurstheoretische Konzeption der praktischen Vernunft' (n. 9), 11–29, at 17; Robert Alexy, 'Problems of Discourse Theory', *Crítica, Revista Hispanoamericana de Filosofía*, vol. XX, 58, april, 1988, 43–65, at 58.

22 Robert Alexy, 'Eine diskurstheoretische Konzeption der praktischen Vernunft' (n. 9), 11–29, at 17; Robert Alexy, 'Nachwort (1991): Antwort auf einige Kritiker' (n. 8), 399–435, at 404–410.

dental argument.[23] This possibility has led Alexy to complement the transcendental-pragmatic argument with an argument stemming from a practical level of justification. In other words, Alexy has chosen to complement the transcendental-pragmatic argument with reasons showing the universal validity of the constitutive norms of discourse – and specifically, of the rationality principles – based on their motivating power.[24] Notwithstanding, Alexy has recognized that only empirical reasons can prove the existence of this motivation or interest. Accordingly, Alexy has pointed out that although the pragmatic level of justification of the constitutive discourse norms is fundamental, the necessity of an argument, which stems from a practical level of justification and it is empirical in nature, makes his justification a weak version of the transcendental-pragmatic argument.[25]

Thus, the Alexyan justification of the constitutive norms of discourse is composed of two levels: A first necessary level directed towards the justification of their universal validity from the pragmatic point of view,[26] and a second complementary level directed towards the justification of their universal validity from the practical perspective.[27] Consequently, these remarks on the Alexyan strategy of discourse justification will be addressed in three parts. The first one will be devoted to the presentation of the theory of rational practical discourse, and the other two parts will deal respectively with the pragmatic and the practical level of justification.

Elsewhere Paulson has rightly said that "[i]f we tap into the desiderata of genius in philosophy, one of the many things that come to mind is a corpus of writings rich enough to sustain an array of readings, reflecting different philosophical interest and persuasion."[28] The thoughts expressed in these pages are that and nothing more, a possible critical reading of the justification of the constitutive norms of discourse undertaken by Robert Alexy.

23 Robert Alexy, 'Menschenrechte ohne Metaphysik?', *Deutsche Zeitschrift für Philosophie*, 52, 2004, 15–24, at 20.

24 Robert Alexy, 'Nachwort (1991): Antwort auf einige Kritiker' (n. 8), 399–435, at 419. Carsten Bäcker, *Begründen und Entscheiden: Kritik und Rekonstruktion der Alexyschen Diskurstheorie des Rechts*, 2nd edn. (Baden-Baden: Nomos Verlagsgesell schaft, 2012), 47.

25 Robert Alexy, 'Nachwort (1991): Antwort auf einige Kritiker' (n. 8), 399–435, at 420.

26 Pragmatics is a very contested concept (see *i. a.* Stephen C. Levinson, *Pragmatics* (Cambridge: Cambridge Universitiy Press, 2009), 1–35; Dan Sperber and Deirdre Wilson, 'Pragmatics', in *Oxford Handbook of Contemporary Analytic Philosophy*, eds. Frank Jackson and Michael Smith (Oxford: Oxford University Press, 2005), 354–388. See, too, Gerald Gazdar, *Pragmatics: Implicature, Presupposition, and Logical Form* (New York: Academic Press, 1979), 4–5, Jerrold Jacob Katz, *Propositional Structure and Illocutionary Force: A Study of the Contribution of Sentence Meaning to Speech Acts* (Cambridge (Mass.): Harvard University Press, 1977, 14,19.) In this regard, for the sake of clarity I should like to allude to well known Stalnaker's definition: "Syntax studies sentences, semantics studies propositions. Pragmatics is the study of linguistic acts and the contexts in which they are performed." (Robert Stalnaker, 'Pragmatics', in *Semantics of Natural Language*, ed. Gilbert Harman and Donald Davidson (Dordrecht & Boston: D. Reidel, 1972), 380–397, at 383.)

27 According to Kant, "[m]it dem praktischen Gebrauche der Vernunft verhält es sich schon anders [als mit dem Gebrauche der theoretischen Vernunft]. In diesem beschäftigt sich die Vernunft mit Bestimmungsgründen des Willens, welcher ein Vermögen ist, den Vorstellungen entsprechende Gegenstände entweder hervorzubringen, oder sich selbst zu Bewirkung derselben (das physische Vermögen mag nun hinreichend sein, | oder nicht), d. i. seine Kausalität zu bestimmen." (Immanuel Kant, *Kritik der praktischen Vernunft*, <29>, <30>.)

28 Stanley L. Paulson, 'The Weak Reading of Authority in Hans Kelsen's Pure Theory of Law', *Law and Philosophy*, 19, 2000, 131–171, at 171.

Part One: A Theory of Rational Practical Discourse

As is known, Alexy has described the perspective of his own theory of argumentation as normative-analytic.[29] In an enlightening paper, Coleman and Leiter have alluded to this distinction of philosophical theories[30] arguing that while those analytical are aimed to provide explanations of human practices – particularly in relation to their conceptual and theoretical commitments[31] – those normative seek to clarify the commitments of our practices by defining the conditions under which these practices could be justified or defended.[32] The Alexyan theory of argumentation responds to these analytical and normative purposes. This theory aims not only to penetrate the structure of arguments and rules of our argumentative practices,[33] but also to define criteria for distinguishing the valid arguments from the invalid ones[34] in order to assess the statements targeted to govern our possible courses of action.[35]

In this vein, a necessary objective assumption of rational discourse theory is the existence of a certain discursive practice which cannot only be described, but also assessed.[36] Rescorla has alluded to the particular nature of the practices in contrast

29 Aulis Aarnio, Robert Alexy and Aleksander Peczenik, 'The Foundation of Legal Reasoning', *Rechtstheorie. Zeitschrift für Logik, Methodenlehre Kybernetik und Soziologie des Rechts*, 12, 1981, 257–279, at 260.

30 Jules L. Coleman and Brian Leiter, 'Determinacy, Objectivity, and Authority', in *Law and Interpretation. Essays in Legal Philosophy*, ed. Andrei Marmor (Oxford: Clarendon Press, 1997), 203–278, at 207.

31 Ibid. 207.

32 Ibid. 208.

33 Manuel Atienza, *Las razones del derecho. Teorías de la argumentación jurídica* (n. 20), 150; Aulis Aarnio, Robert Alexy and Aleksander Peczenik, 'The Foundation of Legal Reasoning' (n. 29), 257–279, at 260.

34 Robert Alexy, *Theorie der juristischen Argumentation. Die Theorie des rationalen Diskurses als Theorie der juristischen Begründung* (n. 3), 222; Aulis Aarnio, Robert Alexy, Aleksander Peczenik, 'The Foundation of Legal Reasoning' (n. 29), 257–279, at 260.

35 Alexy has defined normative statements as judgments of value and judgements of duty. In this regard, see Robert Alexy, *Theorie der juristischen Argumentation. Die Theorie des rationalen Diskurses als Theorie der juristischen Begründung* (n. 3), 221.

36 Indeed, Alexy has stated that a suitable discourse theory cannot abandon the assumption of a discourse practice. In regards to the analysis of the possible ways of justification of the constitutive norms of discourse, Alexy has held that a suitable justification not only has to take in consideration their empirical justification, but also – even more important – has to take into account that the discussion on the possible justification of these norms involves itself a discourse practice that can be considered as a theoretical meta-discourse. But not only that, the functions that Alexy confers to his theory would make no sense without assuming the existence of a real discourse practice. Alexy has held that a discourse theory has four basic functions. The discourse theory is an instrument for criticisms construction; it serves as a criterion for the correction of hypothetical practical statements; it allows to explain the claim to truth and correctness; and it allows to define a workable ideal based on the factual and institutional cirumstances at stake (see Robert Alexy, 'Eine Theorie des praktischen Diskurses' (n 6), 22–58, at 35, 52–58; Robert Alexy, *Theorie der juristischen Argumentation. Die Theorie des rationalen Diskurses als Theorie der juristischen Begründung* (n. 3), 232–233.) Regarding the Law, Bernal has also spoken about this necessary ontological assumption for the interpretation of Alexy's legal theory. He has written: "[T]he claim that the Law institutionalizes reason, justice, morality or correctness, or ought to do it, makes sense only if understood as the claim that the legal practice actually does it or ought to do it." (Carlos Bernal, 'In Search of the Ontological Structure of Law', *Analisi e diritto*, 2012, 59–76, at 67.)

to the mere activities.[37] Indeed, although both are forms of action, unlike the mere activities, the practices are associated with internal normative evaluation standards which are coded by means of norms. These norms govern how to run a practice correctly.[38] In this way, unlike the mere activities regarding which it is only possible to differentiate between actions which belong to the activity from those which do not,[39] every practice allows a threefold division of actions. According to this division, it is possible to distinguish besides the actions which belong to the practices, those actions which are correctly performed.[40] This threefold division involves the special relationship that one sort of norms has with the practice, due to the fact that this sort of norms allows one not only to identify some actions as precedents belonging to the practice, but also to assess the singular actions as correct or incorrect. From the observer's point of view, this group of norms is a necessary condition for the identification of the practice. From the participant's point of view, meeting this group of norms is a necessary condition for achieving the aim associated with the practice.[41] Due to their features, the norms belonging to this group can be called constitutive.[42]

37 According to Rescorla: "[…] sample practices include: dances, like the waltz or the tango; religious ceremonies, like weddings; fraternity initiation rites; performing Beethoven's Fifth Symphony." Sample mere activities are "jumping, bathing, or holding hands" (Michael Rescorla, 'Assertion and its constitutive norms', *Philosophy and Phenomenological Research*, vol. LXXIX, 1, 2009, 98–130, at 101.)

38 Ibid. 101. Regarding the function of internal sanction see Robert Brandom, *Making It Explicit. Reasoning, Representing and Discourse Commitment* (Cambridge (Mass.): Harvard University Press, 1998), 42–46.

39 Michael Rescorla, 'Assertion and its constitutive norms' (n. 37), 98–130, at 101.

40 Rescorla has written: "The norms for performing Beethoven's Fifth Symphony demand that musicians play the notes of Beethoven's score at roughly the indicated tempo. The norms for dancing the waltz demand that dancers move in time with the music, selecting their movements from a fixed repertoire of dance steps. Agents who violate a practice's norms do not implement the practice correctly, but they may still implement the practice. A devious gambler might repeatedly cheat during a poker game. He plays poker incorrectly, but he plays poker nonetheless." Ibid. 101.)

41 Since the aim associated with the practice can be expressed as a prescriptive norm, from the internal point of view there is a necessary connection between constitutive and prescriptive norms. This relation is compatible with the means-end relationship of participant's action. On the thesis of connection between constitutive and prescriptive norms in linguistic practice see Matthias Klatt, *Making the Law Explicit. The normativity of Legal Argumentation* (Oxford: Hart Publishing, 2008), 109–115.

42 On the distinction between constitutive and regulative norms, see *i. a.* John Rawls, 'Two Concepts of Rules', *The Philosophical Review*, 64, 1955, 3–32; Geoffrey Charles John Midgley, 'Linguistic Rules and Language Habits', *Supplementary Volume of the Aristotelian Society*, XXIX, 1955, 185–213; Geoffrey Charles John Midgley, 'Linguistic Rules', *Proceedings of the Aristotelian Society*, LIX, June, 1959, 271–290; John R. Searle, *Speech Acts. An Essay in the Philosophy of Language* (first publ. 1969), (New York: Cambridge University Press, 2009), 33–42, 50–53; Joseph Ransdell, 'Constitutive Rules and Speech-Act Analysis', *The Journal of Philsosophy*, 68, 1971, 385–400; Christopher Cherry, 'Regulative Rules and Constitutive Rules', *The Philosophical Quarterly*, 23, 93, October 1973, 301–315; Gertrude Elizabeth Margaret Anscombe, 'On Brute Facts', in *The Collected Papers of G. E. M. Anscombe* (Oxford: Basil Blackwell, 1981), Vol. 3, 22–25; Eerik Lagerspetz, *The Opposite Mirrors. An Essay on the Conventionalist Theory of Institutions* (Dordrect: Kluwer, 1995); John R. Searle, *The Construction of Social Reality*, 1995, 31–57; Timothy Williamson, 'Knowing and Asserting', *The Philosophical Review*, 105, 4, 1996, 489–523; Dick W. P. Ruiter, A

Alexy has developed the description of an ideal discursive practice in order to lay the foundations of practical knowledge[43].[44] This ideal discursive practice aims to justify practical statements on the basis of the universal consent of its participants,[45] namely on the basis of a situation in which the consequences of the general observance of these statements "for the satisfaction of everyone's interest can be accepted by all."[46] This condition for correct practical statements can be termed principle of universalization or UA.[47] The definition of this principle as a correctness criterion

Basic Classification of Legal Institutions, *Ratio Juris*, 10, 4, 1997, 357–371; Kathrin Glüer and Peter Pagin, 'Rules of Meaning and Practical Reasoning', *Synthese*, 117, 1999, 207–227; Guido Boella and Leendert van der Torre, 'Constitutive Norms in the Design of Normative Multiagent Systems', in *Computational Logic in Multi-Agent Systems. Lecture Notes in Computer Science Volume 3900* (Berlin Heidelberg: Springer Verlag, 2006) 303–319; Frank Hindriks, 'Constituve Rules, Language, and Ontology', *Erkenntnis*, 71, 2009, 253–275.

43 In this vein, according to Wimmer the cognitive nature of discourse ethics lies in the fact that ethic issues can be decided on the basis of reasons. See Reiner Wimmer, *Universalisierung in der Ethik. Analyse, Kritik und Rekonstruktion ethischer Rationalansprüche* (Frankruft am Main: Suhrkamp, 1980), 21.)

44 Atienza has rightly pointed out the differences between the approaches, which nurtured MacCormick's and Alexy's theories of argumentation. According to Atienza, MacCormick developed his theory on the basis of justifications of decisions as actually taking place in the Courts. The analysis of these decisions constituted the ground for the development of a theory of legal argumentation, which MacCormick considered as part of a general theory of practical argumentation. In contrast, Alexy developed a general theory of practical argumentation, which he expanded on the field of Law (Manuel Atienza, *Las razones del derecho. Teorías de la argumentación jurídica* (n. 20), 149) Two strategies can be used in order to achieve a general theory of practical argumentation. According to the first one, one might consider some cases which are accepted as a standard forms of practical argumentation. In this way, one might establish their common and distinctive features in order to determine what practical argumentation is about. According to the second one, one might try to characterize what a practical argumentation is about from the ideal point of view in order to reveal the basic characteristics which must obey all argumentation aimed at assessing statements targeted to govern possible courses of action. This second approach was the one adopted by Alexy. This approach enable him not only to assess other theories of argumentation as those developed by Toulmin and Baier, but also to critically accept the influence of those theories developed by Habermas, Perelman and the School of Erlangen (see Robert Alexy, *Theorie der juristischen Argumentation. Die Theorie des rationalen Diskurses als Theorie der juristischen Begründung* [n. 3].)

45 According to Alexy the ideal discourse is "defined by searching for an answer to a practical question under the conditions of unlimited time, unlimited participation, and complete freedom of constraints by way of achieving complete linguistic-conceptual clearness, complete empirical information, complete ability and willingness to change roles and complete freedom from prejudice." (Robert Alexy, 'Problems of Discourse Theory' (n. 21), 43–65, at 48.) On contrast, a real practical discourse can be characterized by restricted conditions for searching an answer to a practical question. (Robert Alexy, 'Problems of Discourse Theory' (n. 21), 43–65, at 60–61; Robert Alexy, 'Hauptelemente einer Theorie der Doppelnatur des Rechts', in *Archives for Philosophy of Law and Social Philosophy* (Stuttgard: Franz Steiner Verlag, 2009), vol. 95, 2, 151–166, 157).

46 Robert Alexy, 'Discourse Theory and Human Rights' (n. 10), 209–233, at 211.

47 This principle of universalization, which plays the role of a regulative idea (Immanuel Kant, *Kritik der reinen Vernunft*, <A 509, 644; B 537, 672>) in the purview of the Kantian discourse theories, expresses that only those practical statements against which has not been raised any single valid objection can be called 'correct'. (see Niels Gottschalk-Mazouz, *Diskursethik. Theorien, Entwicklungen, Perspektiven* (Berlin: Akademie Verlag, 2000), 243.) As is well known, this universalization ideal involves in its turn the necessary distinction between the ideal and the

of the discursive practices distinguishes the theory of rational discourse as a Kantian theory.[48]

This description of the ideal argumentative practices consists of five sets[49] of norms[50] – which are complemented by two argumentative forms[51] – that determine the procedure for the justification of correct practical statements[52] – i. e., those statements that are a result from the discursive procedure[53] – by means of the

real practical discourse. (See Robert Alexy, 'Hauptelemente einer Theorie der Doppelnatur des Rechts' (n. 45), 151–166, 157.)

48 Bäcker has argued the failure of the Alexian justification of the rationality principles, and therefore, he has held the impossibility of the ideal discourse. Building on these foundations and based on the logical structure of the rationality principles, Bäcker has proposed an one-dimensional model of discourse in opposition to Alexy's two-dimensional model (see Carsten Bäcker, *Begründen und Entscheiden: Kritik und der Alexyschen Rekonstruktion Diskurstheorie des Rechts* (n. 24), 37–38; 90–91; 115–186.) Notwithstanding, the consequences of the abandonment of the ideal discourse remain uncertain in Bäcker's theory. If this abandonment involves identifying a different correction criterium from that defined by the principle of universalization (UA), then Bäcker's theory cannot be considered a Kantian theory of argumentation.

49 These groups of norms are the following: The basic rules, the rational rules, the rules for allocating the burden of argument, the justification rules, and the transition rules (see Robert Alexy, *Theorie der juristischen Argumentation. Die Theorie des rationalen Diskurses als Theorie der juristischen Begründung* (n. 3), 233–255; 361–367).

50 Although Alexy uses the word 'rules' in order to name the constitutive norms of discourse, even in his most recent writings (see *i. a.* Robert Alexy, 'Discourse Theory and Human Rights' [n. 10]), I shall prefer the term 'norms'. This is due to the fact that Alexy himself has accepted that some of the constitutive norms of discourse exhibit the structure of principles (see *i. a.* Robert Alexy, 'Eine Theorie des praktischen Diskurses' (n. 6), 22–58, at 51.) From the perspective of the analysis of Alexy's theory, the use of the term 'rules' for naming the constitutive norms of discourse is not meaningless. This terminological use shows a temporal asymmetry of Alexian theoretical development. Indeed, the development of Alexy's theory of discourse is prior to the development of his theory of legal principles. (see *i. a.* Robert Alexy, 'Zum Begriff des Rechtsprinzips', in *Argumentation und Hermeneutik in der Jurisprudenz*, *Rechtstheorie*, Beiheft 1, 1979, 59–87, at 63–82; Robert Alexy, *Theorie der Grundrechte* (1985), (Frankfurt am Main: Suhrkamp, 1994), 71–104.) On some discourse rules *qua* principles according to Alexy's discourse theory see Carsten Bäcker, *Begründen und Entscheiden: Kritik und Rekonstruktion der Alexyschen Diskurstheorie des Rechts* (n. 24), 170–174.

51 See Robert Alexy, *Theorie der juristischen Argumentation. Die Theorie des rationalen Diskurses als Theorie der juristischen Begründung* (n. 3), 245–250.

52 As written by Gril: "Die Diskurse gemäß dieser Regeln und Formen können ein dreifaches Ergebnis haben: Normen oder normative Aussagen erweisen sich entweder als diskursiv notwendig, als diskursiv unmöglich oder als diskursiv möglich. Diskurs notwendig bzw. diskursiv unmöglich heißen diejenigen Normen bzw. normativen Aussagen, die 'durch die Diskursregeln zwingend gefordert bzw. zwingend ausgeschlossen' werden. […] In vielen Fällen legen die Diskursregeln allein das Ergebnis des Diskurses aber nicht eindeutig fest. Das bedeutet, dass verschiedene Diskursteilnehmer auch noch am Ende des Argumentationsverfahrens verschiedene Überzeugungen haben, ein Konsens also nicht erzielt wurde. Wenn die verschiedenen Überzeugungen aufgrund eines Verfahrens gewonnen wurden, das die Diskursregeln eingehalten hat, so kann jede normative Aussage bzw. jede Norm, die Inhalt der diskursiv gebildeten Überzeugung ist, richtig genannt werden." (Peter Gril, *Die Möglichkeit praktischer Erkenntnis aus Sicht der Diskurstheorie* (n. 18), 126).

53 In this vein, Alexy has written: "Die Diskurstheorie ist eine prozedurale Theorie. Nach ihr ist eine Norm genau dann richtig, wenn sie das Ergebnis der durch die Diskursregeln definierten Prozedur sein kann." (Robert Alexy, 'Ota Weinbergers Kritik der diskurstheoretischen Deutung juristischer Rationalität', in *Institution und Recht. Grazer Internationales Symposium zu Ehren von Ota*

interpretation and balancing of participating subjects' interests.[54] In this way, while Alexy's discourse theory is based on a non-idealized conception of participating subjects,[55] his proposal assumes that those subjects have cognitive abilities regarding both the possibility of action, and the possibility of making judgments.[56]

With regard to the ability to judgment, Alexy has pointed out that his theory assumes that the subjects are generally capable of distinguishing between good and bad reasons for substantive propositions.[57] Nevertheless, Alexy has argued that this ability is not strong enough to replace the need for the discursive practice.[58] This ability shows a transcendental status in terms of general requirements of rationality. It is for this reason that these general requirements of rationality are prior to the discursive practice.[59] The ability to make judgments lays the foundations not only of the possibility of the monological assessment of practical statements,[60] but also of the connection between the universal consent or agreement under ideal conditions, and the concept of moral correctness or validity.[61]

Regarding the possibility of action, Alexy's theory assumes that the participants in the discursive practice are capable of following rules. This competence underlies not only the possibility of communication between participants, but also participants' ability of applying discourse norms. In response to the possibility of a mono-

Weinberger, ed. Peter Koller *et al.* (Berlin: Duncker und Humbolt, 1994), Rechtstheorie-Beiheft, 14, 143–157, at 143)

54 Robert Alexy, 'Problems of Discourse Theory' (n. 21), 43–65, at 58; Robert Alexy, 'Eine diskurstheoretische Konzeption der praktischen Vernunft' (n. 9), 11–29, at 17).

55 Manuel Atienza, *Las razones del derecho. Teorías de la argumentación jurídica* (n. 20), 154.

56 This distinction is that between *principium diiudicationis* and *principium executionis* which Alexy has expressly adopted in his *Nachwort* (1991) (see Robert Alexy, 'Nachwort (1991): Antwort auf einige Kritiker' (n. 8), 399–435, at 407, 420) As Allison has argued (see Henry E. Allison, *Kant's Theory of Freedom* (first publ 1990), (Cambridge. Cambridge University Press, 1995), 66–67) Kant introduced the distinction between the principle of moral obligation and the principle of action or execution – along with the distinction between subjective and objective practical necessitation – in order to address the problem of freedom. With this distinction Kant alluded to the fact that one issue is to consider that a moral principle is justified – and valid in this sense – and one quite different issue is to be motivated to act in accordance with it (Robert Alexy, 'Normativity, Metaphysics and Decision', in *New Essays on the Normativity of Law*, ed. George Pavlakos and Stefano Bertea (Oxford: Hart Publishing, 2011), 219–228, at 221. See Dieter Schönecker, *Kants Begriff transzendentaler und praktischer Freiheit. Eine entwicklungsgeschichtliche Studie unter Mitarbeit von Stefanie Buchenau und Desmond Hagen* (Berlin, New York: Walter De Gruyter, 2005), 113–134; Günther Patzig, 'Principium diiudicationis und Principium executionis', in *Handlungstheorie und Transzendentalpragmatik*, ed. Gerold Prauss (Frankfurt am Main: Vittorio Klostermann, 1986), 204–218; Immanuel Kant, *Vorlesungen über Moralphilosophie: Moralphilosophie Collins, in Kant's gessammelte Schriften. Herausgeben von der Akademie der Wissenschaften der DDR und der Akademie der Wissenschaften zu Göttingen*, vol. XXVII, 1, (Berlin: Walter de Gruyter & Co., 1974) 252–278.)

57 Robert Alexy, 'Problems of Discourse Theory' (n. 21), 43–65, at 56.

58 Ibid. 56.

59 Alexy has written: "The conditions of rational practical argumentation can be summed up in a system of discourse rules. Some of these rules formulate general demands of rationality which are also valid independently of discourse theory. They include freedom from contradictions, universability in the sense of a consistent use of the predicates employed, linguistic-conceptual cleiarness, empirical truth, consideration of consequences, and weighing." (Robert Alexy, 'Discourse Theory and Human Rights' (n. 10), 209–233, at 211.)

60 Robert Alexy, 'Discourse Theory and Human Rights' (n. 10), 209–233, at 211.

61 Robert Alexy, 'Problems of Discourse Theory' (n. 21), 43–65, at 48–59.

logical justification of the practical statements proposed by Tugendhat,[62] Alexy has held that the communication is a necessary condition for correctness.[63] Indeed, Alexy stated that, if it is intended that the practical statements' construction meets the claim to rationality, then this construction must necessarily be embedded in a communication structure.[64]

Against Habermas,[65] Alexy has noted that the construction of practical statements does not aim at finding common or shared interests,[66] but on the contrary, what should be the central focus of this construction is interpreting and balancing the discourse participants' interests.[67] In consequence, for Alexy, ideal discourse practice is only possible on the basis of the argumentation about the relative weight or justification of the conflicting interests involved.[68] This discursive condition, along with the need to take seriously the mutual acknowledgment of the participants as persons, makes the communication structure necessary for the rational construction of practical statements.[69]

Gril[70] has rightly argued that, due to the fact that Alexy has supported the construction of practical statements on the basis of interpreting and balancing the discourse participants' interests, he has renounced the universal task of mutual understanding developed by our communicative practices.[71] As is known, Habermas has interpreted this task as a transcendental coercion imposed on anyone who can use her argumentative competence.[72] In contrast, Alexy has replaced this existential

62 Ernst Tugendhat, 'Zur Entwicklung von moralischen Begründungsstrukturen im modernen Recht', in *Archives for Philosophy of Law and Social Philosophy. Argumentation und Recht*, ed. Winfried Hassermer *et al.* (Stuttgard: Franz Steiner Verlag, 1980), ARSP-Beiheft 14, 1980, 1–20, at 6; in a similar vein, see David A. Richards, 'Robert Alexy, A Theory of Legal Argumentation: The Theory of Rational Discourse as Theory of Legal Justification', *Ratio Juris*, vol. 2, no. 3, 1989, 304–317, at 311.

63 According to Alexy, "if the correctness of the results of discourse depends on the correctness of the interpretation of interest, and if the correctness of interpretation of interest is a matter of argumentative investigation, the discourse is *essentially non-monological*" (Robert Alexy, 'Problems of Discourse Theory' (n. 21), 43–65, at 52.)

64 Robert Alexy, 'Eine diskurstheoretische Konzeption der praktischen Vernunft' (n. 9), 11–29, at 17.

65 Jürgen Habermas, 'Diskursethik-Notizen zu einem Begründungsprogramm' (n. 4), 52–125, at 83 (at n. 27).

66 From a different perspective, some criticism has been raised by Brandom against Habermas' position. See Robert Brandom, 'Facts, Norms and Normative Facts: A Reply to Habermas', *European Journal of Philosophy*, 2000, 8, 3, 356–374, at 363–364.

67 According to Alexy, "[...] answers to practical questions rest not only, but essentially on the interpretation and weighing of interest" (Robert Alexy, 'Problems of Discourse Theory' (n. 21), 43–65, at 58).

68 Robert Alexy, 'Eine diskurstheoretische Konzeption der praktischen Vernunft' (n. 9), 11–29, at 17.

69 Ibid.18.

70 Peter Gril, *Die Möglichkeit praktischer Erkenntnis aus Sicht der Diskurstheorie* (n. 18), 140–143.

71 See n. 15 above.

72 As is known, the social action types that Habermas has distinguished – that is, the communicative action and the strategic action (see *i. a.* Jürgen Habermas, 'Zur Kritik der Bedeutungstheorie', in Jürgen Habermas, *Nachmetaphysisches Denken. Philosophische Aufsätze* (Frankfurt am Main: Suhrkamp, 1988), 105–135, at 130) – are completely unavailable to the individual decision. Indeed, according to Habermas, "[d]ie Möglichkeit, zwischen kommunikativem und strategi-

goal with mutual understandings restricted to certain subjects under certain circumstances.[73] Consequently, since Alexy lays the foundations of subjects' definition on the basis of their abilities and since he has renounced the universal task of our communicative practice, Alexy has left the subjects free to perform behaviors directed towards mutual understanding.[74] Consistently, Alexy has asserted: "From the fact that someone has the ability to solve conflicts of interests by means of argument, and that he has at least a minimal or rudimentary practice with reference to this ability does not follow that he must make use of this ability in every conflict of interests and against everyone possibly concerned."[75]

Notwithstanding, from the fact that Habermas has endorsed the need for a pragmatic justification of discourse based on the transcendental task of mutual un-

schen Handeln zu wählen, ist abstrakt, weil sie nur aus der zufälligen Perspektive des einzelnene Aktors gegeben ist. Aus der Perspektive der Lebenswelt, der der Aktor jeweils angehört, stehen diese Modi des Handelns nicht zu freien Disposition" (Jürgen Habermas, 'Diskursethik-Notizen zu einem Begründungsprogramm' (n. 4), 52–125, at 111; Jürgen Habermas, 'Replik auf Einwände' (1980) (n. 15), 475–570, at 488). For Habermas, the priority of the communicative action over the strategic one in the lifeworld shows up due to the language function. The language is tied immanently to the understanding. (Jürgen Habermas, 'Vorbereiten der Bemerkungen zu einer Theorie der kommunikativen Kompetenz', in *Theorie der Gesellschaft oder Sozialtechnologie – Was leistet die Systemforschung?*, ed. Jürgen Habermas and Niklas Luhmann (Frankfurt am Main: Suhrkamp Verlag, 1971), 101–141, at 114; Thomas McCarthy, *Kritik der Verständigungsverhältnisse. Zur Theorie von Jürgen Habermas* (Frankfurt am Main: Suhrkamp Verlag, 1989), 326) This immanent and original relationship is imposed on all participants in a communicative practice, and hence, in this line, it is not available to their individual decision. (According to Habermas, "[n]o matter how the intersubjectivity of mutual understanding may be deformed, the design of an ideal speech situation is necessarily implied with the structure of potential speech; for every speech, even that of intentional deception, is oriented towards the idea of truth (and understanding)" [Jürgen Habermas, 'Towards a Theory of Communicative Competence', in *Recent Sociology. No. 2: Patterns of Communicative Behaviour* (New York: MacMillan, 1970), 115–148, at 144].) In this way, since the communication directed towards mutual understanding allows the comprehension of other forms of communication, this form of communication takes normative precedence over them. Accordingly, since the various forms of communication, by means of which the participants aim at getting mutual influence, require from the participants the coordination of their interests, these forms of communication maintain a parasitic existence regarding the communication directed towards mutual understanding (Jürgen Habermas, *Theorie des kommunikativen Handelns*, vol. 1: *Handlungsrationalität und gesellschaftliche Rationalisierung* (n. 15), 388; Jürgen Habermas, 'Erläuterungen zum Begriff des kommunikativen Handelns' (n. 15), 595–598.) Therefore, from the point of view of the individual any attempt to break the immanent relationship that the language has with the understanding will lead him to his self-destruction. (In this vein, Habermas has stated: "Deshalb steht auch den Einzelnen, die ihre Identität nicht anders als über die Aneignung von Traditionen, über die Zugehörigkeit zu sozialen Gruppen und über die Teilnahme an sozialisatorischen Interaktionen erwerben und behaupten können, die Wahl zwischen kommunikativ emund strategischen Handeln nur in einem abstrakten Sinne, d.h. von Fall zu Fall, offen. Die Option für einen langfristigen Ausstieg aus Kontexten verständigungsorientierten Handelns haben sie nicht. Dieser würde den Rückzug in die monadische Vereinsamung strategischen Handelns – oder in Schizophrenie und Selbstmord bedeuten" [Jürgen Habermas, 'Diskursethik-Notizen zu einem Begründungsprogramm' (n. 4), 52–125, at 112, 110].)

73 Peter Gril, *Die Möglichkeit praktischer Erkenntnis aus Sicht der Diskurstheorie* (n. 18), 140.

74 Ibid. 140.

75 Robert Alexy, 'Discourse Theory and Human Rights' (n. 10), 209–233, at 218.

derstanding,[76] Gril deduces the lack of justification for the use of a pragmatic level in the Alexyan proposal.[77] Gril's argument is reinforced by the fact that Alexy has acknowledged the possibility of the monological assessment of practical statements.[78] This possibility has however been misinterpreted.[79] It is true that due to the fact that the general requirements of rationality are necessary conditions for the monological assessment of practical statements, for Alexy, acknowledging monological assessment of practical statements implies in its turn acknowledging the transcendental status of the general requirements of rationality.[80] However, as noted above, in his response to Tugendhat's criticism, Alexy has made clear that a communication structure is a necessary condition for the correctness of practical statements.[81] This necessary communication structure involves, on the one hand, the subordinate nature of the monological assessment of practical statements to the communicative discursive practice,[82] and on the other hand, the justification of the use of the pragmatic level for laying the foundations of the constitutive norms of rational practical discourse.

Indeed, Alexy addresses the problem of the justification of the constitutive norms of rational practical discourse through the distinction between a pragmatic and a practical level of justification.[83] This distinction reflects the two aspects of the claim to universality which is shown by these norms. A first aspect of this claim refers to its content. As Alexy has argued, the content of these norms is universal, because they seek equal rights for all participants in the discourse.[84] A second aspect of this claim refers to their validity. As Alexy has stated, the question is whether

76 Jürgen Habermas, 'Zur Kritik der Bedeutungstheorie' (n. 72), 105–135, at 123–135.

77 Indeed, Gril has pointed out that: "Die Frage ist aber, warum Argumentation nicht als Folge von Sätzen, die whar oder falsch sind, verstanden werden kann, sondern als eine Reihe von Sprechhandlungen zwischen Kommunikationsteilnehmern aufgefaßt werden muß. Habermas konnte auf der Grundlage seiner Prämisse, daß das Telos der Sprache Verständigung sei, wenigstens plausibel machen, warum die pragmatische Ebene berücksichtigt werden müsse. [...] Gerade weil nach Habermas Verständigung eine für den Menschen nicht hintergehbare Aufgabe ist, diese aber nur unter Einbeziehung der pragmatischen Ebene zureichend formuliert und gelöst werden kann, ist die Pragmatik unverzichtbar. Wie gesehen gibt aber Alexy genau diese Prämisse auf. Eine Begründung dafür, daß für die Bestimmung der Kernbedeutung des Begriffs 'Behauptung' pragmatische Regeln konsititutiv sein müssen, bleibt er damit schuldig." (Peter Gril, *Die Möglichkeit praktischer Erkenntnis aus Sicht der Diskurstheorie* (n. 18), 146.)

78 Peter Gril, *Die Möglichkeit praktischer Erkenntnis aus Sicht der Diskurstheorie* (n. 18), 152; Robert Alexy, 'Problems of Discourse Theory' (n. 21), 43–65, at 51–52.

79 See Carsten Bäcker, *Begründen und Entscheiden: Kritik und Rekonstruktion der Alexyschen Diskurstheorie des Rechts* (n. 24), 83–86.

80 Robert Alexy, 'Discourse Theory and Human Rights' (n. 10), 209–233, at 211.

81 Robert Alexy, 'Problems of Discourse Theory' (n. 21), 43–65, at 52; Robert Alexy, 'Nachwort (1991): Antwort auf einige Kritiker' (n. 8), 399–435, at 407.

82 Carsten Bäcker, *Begründen und Entscheiden: Kritik und Rekonstruktion der Alexyschen Diskurstheorie des Rechts* (n. 24), 85 (at n. 248).

83 See Robert Alexy, 'Discourse Theory and Human Rights' (n. 10), 209–233, at 211–220; Robert Alexy, 'Eine diskurstheoretische Konzeption der praktischen Vernunft' (n. 9), 11–29, at 18–24; Robert Alexy, 'Nachwort (1991): Antwort auf einige Kritiker' (n. 8), 399–435, at 417–426.

84 Robert Alexy, 'Eine diskurstheoretische Konzeption der praktischen Vernunft' (n. 9), 11–29, at 19.

this universal content of the constitutive norms of discourse can claim to be applied with regard to every practical statement.[85]

Alexy aspires with his justification of the constitutive norms of rational practical discourse to dissolve the underlying tension between, on the one hand, the claim to universal validity that his theory confers on the aim of the ideal discursive practice – and therefore, on both the constitutive discourse norms, and the correct practical statements – and on the other hand, the historical and cultural relativity of rational discourse which has been alleged by the critics.[86] Indeed, based on the postmodern thought and the communitarianism it is possible to argue that the rationalist conception which is defended by the Alexyan theory of discourse is an expression of a certain form of life, and hence, it is also possible to argue that Alexy's theory can only claim universal validity in an illegitimate manner.[87]

Due to the need for a communication structure for correctness of practical statements, and due to the restrictions of the justification method chosen by Alexy,[88] he undertakes the justification of the constitutive norms of the rational practical discourse by focusing on a privileged subset of these norms.[89] This privileged subset is composed of norms which, firstly, do not play any role in monological discourses – that is, they do not have to be applied in argumentative procedures that a subject carries out in order to assess and justify practical statements adopted in exercise of her autonomy – and secondly, are targeted to ensure the impartiality of the discourse by means of the guarantee of freedom and equality of its participants.[90] As noted by Bäcker, these norms have the structure of principles,[91] and therefore, they require the optimal achievement of the ideal discourse.[92] In other words, the optimal achievement of these norms is a sufficient condition for reaching the aim of the ideal discursive practice which is defined by the principle of univer-

85 Ibid. 19.

86 Tungendhat has interpreted this tension in terms of a general challenge of our current practical rationality. He has written: "Wenn das moralische Urteilen ein unvermeidliches Ingredients unseres Lebens ist, müßte sich ein Dilemma ergeben, wenn moralisches Urteilen einerseits Allgemeingültigkeit impliziert und es sich andererseits als historisch und sozial relativ herausstellen sollte. Kann man moralisch urteilen, ohne an das Begründetsein seines Urteilen zu glauben? Wäre aber eine solche absolute Begründung, auf die das hinauszulaufen schiene, nicht eine Basis, die uns heute unglaubhaft erscheinen muß?" (Ernst Tugendhat, *Vorlesung über Ethik* (n. 1), 14.)

87 Robert Alexy, 'Eine diskurstheoretische Konzeption der praktischen Vernunft' (n. 9), 11–29, at 18–19.

88 Indeed, Alexy has accepted the limitations of transcendental arguments use in *Theorie der juristischen Argumentation* (1978). He has stated: "Eine solche Begründung wird allerdings nur für relativ wenige grundlegende Regeln möglich." (Robert Alexy, *Theorie der juristischen Argumentation. Die Theorie des rationalen Diskurses als Theorie der juristischen Begründung* (n. 3), 232.)

89 Robert Alexy, 'Nachwort (1991): Antwort auf einige Kritiker' (n. 7), 418.

90 Robert Alexy, 'Discourse Theory and Human Rights' (n. 10), 209–233, at 211. That is why Alexy claims that the rationality principles – i. e. the rationality rules – "[stehen] im Zentrum des Problems der universellen Geltung." (Robert Alexy, 'Nachwort (1991): Antwort auf einige Kritiker' (n. 8), 399–435, at 418.)

91 Carsten Bäcker, *Begründen und Entscheiden: Kritik und Rekonstruktion der Alexyschen Diskurstheorie des Rechts* (n. 24), 143–145.

92 Ibid. 131.

salization.[93] That is why we can affirm the fundamental status of these norms in comparison with other constitutive norms of the rational practical discourse. This assertion implies in its turn that the normative system proposed by Alexy shows a hierarchical structure.[94] These privileged norms should be named rationality principles[95] and are formulated as follows:

"1. Everyone who can speak may take part in discourse.
2. (a) Everyone may question any assertion.
   (b) Everyone may introduce any assertion into the discourse.
   (c) Everyone may express his or her attitudes, wishes, and needs.
3. No speaker may be prevented from exercising the rights laid down in (1) and (2) by any kind of coercion internal or external to the discourse."[96]

93 Indeed, Alexy wrote: "If [the most important rules] are valid, that is, if everyone can decide freely and equally about what she is willing to accept, the following condition of universal agreement or consent is necessarily valid: (U) A norm only find universal agreement in a discourse if the consequences of its general observance for the satisfaction of everyone's interest can be accepted by all" (Robert Alexy, 'Discourse Theory and Human Rights' (n. 10), 209–233, at 211.) In this way, "the connection between agreement under ideal condtions and the concept of correctness and moral validity can be formulated as follows: (D) Correct and therefore valid are exactly those norms that in an ideal discourse would be judged correct by everyone" (Robert Alexy, 'Discourse Theory and Human Rights' (n. 10), 209–233, at 212.)

94 Carsten Bäcker, *Begründen und Entscheiden: Kritik und Rekonstruktion der Alexyschen Diskurstheorie des Rechts* (n. 24), 131. This hierarchical order of the rules of discourse explains in its turn the argumentative structure which is presented by Alexy in his essay "Discourse Theory and Human Rights". Indeed, Alexy has held in this essay that "[t]he basis for discourse theoretical justification of human rights consequently has to face two tasks: On the first level it must substantiate the rules of practical discourse in order to justify, on a second level, the human rights on these grounds". (Robert Alexy, 'Discourse Theory and Human Rights' (n. 10), 209–233, at 210–211) This hierarchical order that governed the discourse rules according to Alexy's theory of argumentation involves a normative unity on the basis of the coherence principle. This claim to normative unity has not been taken into account by Atienza when called into question Alexy's position about the claim to universality of constitutive norms of discourse on the basis of the claim to universality of rationality principles, Atienza has held that: "[N]o queda claro hasta qué punto las reglas del discurso racional tienen o no un carácter universal. Puesto que el discurso de teoría del discurso parte de las convicciones realmente existentes de los participantes, la existencia de diversas formas de vida parece llevar también a que quepa formular diversos sistemas de reglas. Dicho de otra manera, algunas de las reglas del discurso racional formuladas por Alexy serían contingentes, esto es, culturalmente dependientes, mientras que otras tendrían un valor universal (cfr. Aarnio-Alexy-Peczenik, 1981, pp. 371–372). Pero, ¿cuáles serían contingentes y cuáles no? Supongamos que cabe aceptar – como Alexy lo hace – que las reglas de razón tienen un carácter universal. Pero, ¿qué pasa con las otras? Si fuera racional también dejar de seguir alguna de estas, entonces no es ya que pueda existir más de una respuesta correcta (esto es, más de una respuesta que se mantenga dentro de los límites marcados por las reglas del discurso), sino que podría ser correcta también una respuesta dada en infracción de alguna de estas reglas. Pero entonces, ¿sigue teniendo sentido sostener que las reglas del discurso suministran un criterio de corrección objetivo?" (Manuel Atienza, *Las razones del derecho. Teorías de la argumentación jurídica* (n. 20), 189.)

95 These privileged norms are named "rationality rules", according to Alexy's terminological use. See above n. 50.

96 Robert Alexy, 'Discourse Theory and Human Rights' (n. 10), 209–233, at 211; Robert Alexy, *Theorie der juristischen Argumentation. Die Theorie des rationalen Diskurses als Theorie der juristischen Begründung* (n. 3), 240.

Based on the distinction between the pragmatic and the practical level of justification,[97] Alexy seeks a complementary strategy to those perspectives that have nurtured the positions of Habermas and Nino.[98] From the practical point of view, Alexy has made explicit the commitment of his theory with a liberal philosophical political position which underlies the definition of the rational discourse theory within the Kantian tradition.[99] From this perspective, Alexy has argued that Nino is right, when he holds that a contingent social practice can only justify itself under threat of falling into an infinite regress.[100] In this way, from the subjective practical point of view, a justification of a moral discourse goes beyond the limits of our possible knowledge.[101] However, the skeptical position about a possible justification of practical discourse leads Nino to underestimate the use of the pragmatic analysis and to estimate only a possible explanation about the moral discourse in evolutionary terms.[102]

Notwithstanding, the omission of the practical level of justification weakens Habermas's position. For Alexy, Habermas overestimated the transcendental-pragmatic argument scope, when he held that this kind of argument is necessary and sufficient for justifying the practical discourse.[103] Indeed, the transcendental status that Habermas has given the universal task of our communicative practices[104] has prevented him from taking into account the distinction between motivation and moral obligation.[105] This omission has led Habermas to overestimate the pragmatic

97 See above n. 83.

98 See Robert Alexy, 'Discourse Theory and Human Rights' (n. 10), 209–233, at 212–213.

99 Ibid. 212.

100 Ibid. 212.

101 In this vein, according to Nino, "[s]i asumimos en forma optimista que la determinación de ciertos aspectos estructurales subyacentes a nuestra práctica del discurso moral puede arrojar algunos criterios que permitan justificar principios sustantivos como los que generan derechos humanos, todavía cabría preguntarse cuál es la relevancia de tal justificación. Ésta es una justificación relativa a ciertas reglas y presupuestos de una práctica social contingente y, suponiendo que ellas sean constitutivas de cualquier fenómeno que sea razonable calificar de moral, ésta sería una justificación moral. Pero se podría decir que ella es de por sí irrelevante, ya que, en todo caso, tal justificación depende de la justificación de las reglas constitutivas del razonamiento moral: la justificación moral dependería de la justificación moral." (Carlos Santiago Nino, Ética y Derechos Humanos. Un ensayo de fundamentación (Barcelona: Editorial Ariel S.A., 1991), 125.)

102 Nino wrote: "Lo que sí puede darse es, por supuesto, una explicación de por qué una sociedad desarrolla una cierta práctica de discurso moral y por qué buena parte de los individuos tienden a participar en ese discurso. Probablemente – como ha sido muchas veces señalado – intervengan en esta explicación consideraciones relacionadas con teorías evolucionistas (aunque es importante aislarlas de toda implicación justificatoria)" (Ibid. 127.)

103 Indeed, according to Habermas, "[d]er im schwachen Sinne transzendentale Nachweis, wenn wir ihn denn, was ich mit Apel annehme, führen können, genügt freilich, um den universalistischen, nämlich für alle sprach- und handlungsfähigen Subjekte verbindlichen Geltungsanspruch eines prozedural gefaßten Moralprinzips zu begründen" (Jürgen Habermas, 'Erläuterungen zur Diskursethik' (n. 14), 119–126, at 194.)

104 See above n. 72.

105 See above n. 56.

level and to lose sight of the need to add arguments stemming from the practical level of justification.[106]

The following sections are devoted to the analysis, interpretation, and criticism of the pragmatic and of the practical level of justification of rationality principles undertaken by Robert Alexy.

Part Two: The Pragmatic Level of Justification of Rationality Principles

Alexy has held that balancing is one of the general requirements of rationality.[107] Consistently, as noted above, he has defined balancing and recognition of subjects' interests as necessary conditions for correctness of practical statements.[108] In addition, based on this basis, Alexy has stated that a communication structure is a necessary condition for the construction of correct practical statements.[109] In consequence, Alexy has thrown out the transcendental status that Habermas has assigned to the universal task of our communicative practices directed towards mutual understanding. By keeping a distance from Habermas's proposal, Alexy not only has introduced the Kantian distinction between motivation and moral obligation,[110] but also has preferred the term "transcendental pragmatics" in his *Nachwort* (1991)[111] – over the term "universal pragmatics"[112] that he has used in his *Theorie der juristischen Argumentation* (1976)[113] – in order to describe the justification strategy of rationality principles at the pragmatic level. According to Alexy, this expression refers to a variant of the transcendental argument.[114]

A transcendental argument can be defined by virtue of its aim or goal rather than by virtue of its form.[115] A transcendental argument so defined may take the

106 Robert Alexy, 'Nachwort (1991): Antwort auf einige Kritiker' (n. 8), 399–435, at 419. Carsten Bäcker, *Begründen und Entscheiden: Kritik und Rekonstruktion der Alexyschen Diskurstheorie des Rechts* (n. 24), 47.

107 Robert Alexy, 'Discourse Theory and Human Rights' (n. 10), 209–233, at 211.

108 Robert Alexy, 'Problems of Discourse Theory' (n. 21), 43–65, at 58; Robert Alexy, 'Eine diskurstheoretische Konzeption der praktischen Vernunft' (n. 9), 11–29, at 17.)

109 Robert Alexy, 'Eine diskurstheoretische Konzeption der praktischen Vernunft' (n. 9), 11–29, at 17. Robert Alexy, 'Nachwort (1991): Antwort auf einige Kritiker' (n. 8), 399–435, at 404–410.

110 Robert Alexy, 'Nachwort (1991): Antwort auf einige Kritiker' (n. 8), 399–435, at 407.

111 Ibid. 418.

112 According to Habermas, "[d]ie Universalpragmatik hat die Aufgabe, universale Bedingungen möglicher Verständigung zu identifizieren und nachzukonstruieren. In anderen Zusammenhängen spricht man auch von allgemeinen Kommunikationsvoraussetzungen; ich spreche lieber von allgemeinen Voraussetzungen kommunikativen Handelns" (Jürgen Habermas, 'Was heißt Universalpragmatik?' (n. 4), 353. See, too, George Pavlakos, 'The Special Case Thesis. An Assessment of R. Alexy's Discoursive Theory of Law', *Ratio Juris*, 11, 1998, 126–154, at 129, n. 3.

113 Robert Alexy, *Theorie der juristischen Argumentation. Die Theorie des rationalen Diskurses als Theorie der juristischen Begründung* (n. 3), 231.

114 Robert Alexy, 'Nachwort (1991): Antwort auf einige Kritiker' (n. 8), 399–435, at 418.

115 In this line, Stroud has written: "I think that what makes it transcendental is not its logical form or its subject matter, but its aim or goal. We might speak rather of a transcendental strategy or project, of a transcendental enterprise this brings it closer to Kant's 'transcendental philosophy'. Particular arguments put forward to achieve that goal, or advance or promote that project, might be good or bad, sound or unsound, or even of different logical forms, without losing the label 'transcendental'. What they are meant to do is what counts. [...] Understanding what tran-

form of a contradiction[116] by means of which some practical normative content could be shown as a necessary or ultimate condition[117] for thinking mediated by

scendental arguments are, or are meant to do, means understanding this special transcendental status, and seeing the point of trying to establish that certain things have it." (Barry Stroud, 'The Goal of Transcendental Arguments', in *Transcendental Arguments. Problems and Prospects*, ed. Robert Stern (Oxford: Clarendon Press, 2000), 155–172, at 157.)

116 In this regard, Apel has written: "Unter letzterem [transzendentalpragmatischen Selbstwiderspruch] verstehe ich einen performativen Widerspruch zwischen dem Inhalt einer Proposition und dem selbstbezüglichen – impliziten oder performativ expliziten – intentionalen Inhalt des Aktes des Vorbringens der Proposition im Rahmen eines argumentativen Diskurses" (Karl-Otto Apel, 'Die Vernunftfunktion der kommunikativen Rationalität. Zum Verhältnis von konsensual-kommunikativer Rationalität, strategischer Rationalität und Systemrationalität', in *Die eine Vernunft und die vielen Rationalitäten*, ed. Karl-Otto Apel and Matthiar Kettner (Frankfurt am Main: Suhrkamp Verlag, 1996), 17–42, 22.) As stated by Apel, this refutation model is rooted in Aristotelian philosophy (see Karl-Otto Apel, 'Sprechakttheorie und transzendentale Sprachpragmatik zur Frage ethischer Normen' (n. 5), 281–411, at 400.) Indeed, Aristotle held that the law of non-contradiction is constitutive of all reasoning, and therefore, this law is a condition even for its contradiction. In this way, this law cannot be proven, but it can just be revealed. Aristotle wrote: "There are some, however, as we have said, who both state themselves that the same thing can be and not be, and say that it is possible to hold this view. Many even of the physicists adopt this theory. But we have just assumed that it is impossible at once to be and not to be, and by this means we have proved that this is the most certain of all principles. Some, indeed, demand to have the law proved, but this is because they lack education; for it shows lack of education not to know of what we should require proof, and of what we should not. For it is quite impossible that everything should have a proof; the process would go on to infinity, so that even so there would be no proof. If on the other hand there are some things of which no proof need be sought, they cannot say what principle they think to be more self-evident. Even in the case of this law, however, we can demonstrate the impossibility by refutation, if only our opponent makes some statement. If he makes none, it is absurd to seek for an argument against one who has no arguments of his own about anything, in so far as he has none; for such a person, in so far as he is such, is really no better than a vegetable. And I say that proof by refutation differs from simple proof in that he who attempts to prove might seem to beg the fundamental question, whereas if the discussion is provoked thus by someone else, refutation and not proof will result." (Aristotle, *Metaphysics*, <4.1005b–4.1006a>) The Sophist's contradiction alluded by Aristotle does not occur neither due to the structure of the linguistic constructions, nor due to the grammatical properties and their relations, but instead due to the implicatures that underlie the relation between speaker's performance and her audience. Such a contradiction was analysed by Hintikka in his paper about *cogito ergo, sum*. As is well known, Hintikka pointed out that "[t]he inconsistency (absurdity) of an existentially inconsistent statement can in a sense be said to be of performatory (performative) character. It depends on an act or 'performance,' namely on a certain person's act of uttering a sentence (or of otherwise making a statement); it does not depend solely on the means used for the purpose, that is, on the sentence which is being uttered. The sentence is perfectly correct as a sentence, but the attempt of a certain man to utter it assertively is curiously pointless. If one of these days I should read in the morning paper, 'There is no De Gaulle any more,' I could understand what is being said. But no one who knows Charles de Gaulle could help being puzzled by these words if they were uttered by De Gaulle himself; the only way of making sense of them would be to give them a nonliteral meaning." (Jaakko Hintikka, 'Cogito, Ergo Sum: Inference or Performance?', *The Philosophical Review*, vol. 71, 1, 1962, 3–32, at 12.)

117 As is well known, Apel has proposed a practical rule as foundation for the illocutionary force of speech acts. This rule is based on the fact that a cooperative behavior of the participants is a necessary condition for the felicitous performance of these acts. This rule refers to the requirement of mutual recognition of all members of the communication community as participants in the

language.[118] This contradiction could be found in the fact that even those who argue against that normative content must assume it.[119] However, such an argument would raise the discourse theory at the level of a theory of rationality. In this way, this theory would impose practical requirements on the pragmatic level, by interpreting the weak coercion in which this level lies in a strong moral sense.[120]

With different purposes than those pursued by Kant,[121] Strawson introduced in his *Individuals: An Essay in Descriptive Metaphysics* (1959) as well as in his *The Bounds of Sense: An Essay on Kant's Critique of Pure Reason* (1966) various transcendental arguments aimed at arguing against the skeptic who raises doubts about the existence of the external world. In response to the criticisms raised by Stroud,[122] Strawson has

discussion with equal rights. From the point of view of the ideal communication community, all beings able to communicate should be recognized as potencial participants in the discussion. (See Karl-Otto Apel, 'Das Apriori der Kommunikationsgemeinschaft und die Grundlagen der Ethik. Zum Problem einer rationalen Begründung der Ethik im Zeitalter der Wissenschaft' (n. 5), 358–435, at 400.)

118 Karl-Otto Apel, *Diskurs und Verantwortung. Das Problem des Übergangs zur postkonventionellen Moral* (Frankfurt am Main: Suhrkamp Verlag, 1988), 35.

119 According to Apel, "[d]ie einschlägige Letztbegründungsfrage [...], ob Vernunft überhaupt sein solle [...] übersieht m.E. die merkwürdige Tatsache, dass derjenige, der argumentiert – und das heißt: derjenige, der auch nur ernshaft die Frage nach der Möglichkeit einer Begründung der Ethik stellt – notwendigerweise die Verbindlichkeit der Vernunft schon anerkannt hat". (Ibid. 253)

120 In this respect, Habermas has written: "Appels Theoriearchitektonik stützt sich, wenn ich recht sehe, auf zwei problematische Grundannahamen. Die *erste Prämisse*, nämlich die fundamentalphilosophische Auszeichnung der Diskursethik, erkauft sich Apel mit einer Gleichsetzung von kommunikativer und praktischer Vernunft. [...] Diese [kommunikative Vernunft] hat einen nur im weiteren Sinne normativen Gehalt insofern, als sich der kommunikativ Handelnde auf pragmatischer Voraussetzungen kontrafaktischer Art einlassen muß. Er muß Idealisierungen vornehmen – z.B. Ausdrücken identischer Bedeutungen zuschreiben, für Außerungen einen kontextüberschreitenden Geltungsanspruch erheben, dem Adressaten Zurechnungsfähigkeit unterstellen usw. Dabei steht der kommunikativ Handelnde unter dem »Muß« einer Handlungsregel zu begegnen – ob sich dieses nun deontologisch auf die Sollgeltung eines moralischen Gebots, axiologisch auf eine Konstellation bevorzugter Werte oder empirisch auf die Wirksamkeit eines technischen Imperativs zurückführen läßt. Die kommunikative Vernunft ist nicht wie die praktischer Vernunft per se eine Quelle für Normen des richtigen Handelns." (Jürgen Habermas, 'Erläuterungen zur Diskursethik' (n. 14), 119–226, at 190–191.)

121 As rightly stated Grundmann, the Cartesian skepticism about the existence of the external world has just played a secondary role in regards to concerns related with Kant's use of transcendental arguments in the Critique of Pure Reason. Such arguments have been directed especially towards a different kind of skeptic. Contrary to Descartes and Strawson, Kant faced the arguments of the empiricist who was not convinced about the existence of the *a priori* conditions for our representations. (Thomas Grundmann, 'Was ist eigentlich ein transzendentales Argument?', in *Warum Kant heute?*, ed. Dieter H. Heidemann and Kristina Engelhard (Berlin: Walter de Gruyter & Co., 2003), 44–75, at 46. See, too, Patricia Kitcher, 'Kant's Epistemological Problem and Its Coherent Solution', *Noûs*, 33, 3, 1999, 415–441, at 418–420.)

122 As is known, Stroud stated the sufficiency of the self-conscious experience against the realistic claim of the transcendental arguments proposed by Strawson. (See Barry Stroud, 'Transcendental Arguments', *Journal of Philosophy*, 65, 1968, 141–256; Barry Stroud, 'Kantian Argument, Conceptual Capacities, and Invulnerability', in *Kant and Contemporary Epistemology*, ed. Paolo Parrini, (Dordrecht: Kluwer Academic Publishers – The University of Western Ontario Series in Philosophy v. 54, 1994), 231–251.)

held a weak form of transcendental argument[123] in his book *Skepticism and Naturalism* (1985).[124] This argument does not aim to show the existence of a external structured world in a certain way,[125] but rather to prove some form of interdependence between our cognitive abilities and beliefs – as necessary conditions for self-conscious thinking and experience.[126] By ruling out the possibility of an ultimate justification of the practical reason,[127] Habermas refers to this weak form of transcendental argument. He regards this form of transcendental argument as sufficient for supporting the claim to universal validity, namely as binding on all subjects capable of speech and action.[128]

This weak form of transcendental argument seems appropriate to make explicit participants' common beliefs which determine implicit normative contents constituting the practice in which they are involved. In other words, this weak form of transcendental argument seems appropriate to make explicit necessary normative conditions for the existence of a practice – i. e. for its existence in an independent manner from the mental states of its participants individually considered. Specifically, this weak form of transcendental argument seems suitable to explore necessary normative pragmatic assumptions of our speech practices, and hence, of our speech acts individually considered.[129] By means of this weak form of argument, Alexy has developed the pragmatic justification of rationality principles.[130]

However, Alexy has pointed out that the transcendental pragmatic argument he used in the justification of the rationality principles is not only weak in the fallibilist sense attributed by Strawson – and used by Habermas – but also weak in the sense of having restricted practical validity.[131] As shown, the background for this remark comes from the fact that Alexy has left the subjects free to perform behaviors directed towards mutual understanding. Consequently, at the practical level of analysis, Alexy has waived the justification of the subjective validity of rationality princi-

123 Barry Stroud, 'Kantian Argument, Conceptual Capacities, and Invulnerability' (n. 122), 231–251, at 241.

124 Peter Frederick Strawson, *Skepticism and Naturalism: Some Varieties* (New York: Columbia University Press, 1985), 21.

125 Thomas Grundmann and Catrin Misselhorn, 'Transcendental Arguments and Realism', in *Strawson and Kant*, ed. Hans-Johan Glock (Oxford: Oxford University Press, 2003), 205–218, at 205.

126 In this vein, Strawson has claimed that "even if we have a tenderness for transcendental arguments, we shall be happy to accept the criticism of Stroud and others that either such arguments rely on an unacceptably simple verificationism or the most they can establish is a certain sort of interdependence of conceptual capacities and beliefs: e. g. [...] in order for self-conscious thought and experience to be possible, we must take it, or believe that we have knowledge of external physical objects or other minds." (Peter Frederick Strawson, *Skepticism and Naturalism: Some Varieties* (n. 124), 21.)

127 Jürgen Habermas, 'Erläuterungen zur Diskursethik' (n. 14), 119–226, at 194.

128 Ibid. 194.

129 Robert Alexy, 'Discourse Theory and Human Rights' (n. 10), 209–233, at 213.

130 Ibid. 213. This outcome reveals the weakness of Hilgendorf's interpretation, who has proposed the discontinuity thesis. According to this thesis since the publication of Nachwort (1991) Alexy's theory has shifted towards the Apelian transcendental-pragmatic thinking. (See Eric Hilgendorf, 'Zur traszendentalpragmatischen Begründung von Diskursregeln' (n. 12), 183–200, 185, 190.)

131 Robert Alexy, 'Discourse Theory and Human Rights' (n. 10), 209–233, at 213.

ples.[132] This waiver has led Alexy to accept a restricted scope of the transcendental argument regarding subjects' motivations.[133] From the subjective practical point of view, this restriction makes the transcendental argument fallible.[134]

On the other hand, throwing out the most ambitious ontological claim of transcendental arguments has led to defining them by emphasizing their form. In this way, e. g. Chisholm has held that transcendental arguments can be understood as a result from a procedure – a "transcendental procedure."[135] In the same vein, Alexy has termed transcendental arguments those arguments "which consist of at least two premises with the following structure: The first premise identifies the argument's starting point, which consists of things like perceptions, thoughts or speech acts, and claims that this starting point is necessary in some sense. The second premise then says that some categories or rules are necessary if the matter or issue chosen as starting point is meant to be possible. The final conclusion is that these categories or rules are necessarily valid."[136]

Notwithstanding, this weak way of defining transcendental arguments should not lead to removal of all ontological claim, in a way that could be possible to define transcendental arguments only by virtue of their structure. As stated by Stroud, such a way of defining trivializes this kind of arguments.[137] Nevertheless, claiming that transcendental arguments maintain a certain ontological claim implies the assertion that transcendental arguments are targeted to make explicit the conditions of what we assume as true.[138]

132 Alexy wrote: "[Rationality] rules, furthermore, have categorical validity from the ideal point of view of correctness." (Ibid. 218.)

133 According to Alexy, "[b]ut no transcendental argument can generate interests or motivations. Under the aspect of reality or facticity the transcendental argument therefore leads only to a hypothetical validity of the discourse rules: It shows what is valid if there is an interest in moral correctness and if therefore the ideal point of view of correctness is taken up." (Ibid. 218–219.)

134 As stated by Alexy: "Dass es notwendig ist, den anderen im Diskurs als gleichberechtigt zu behandeln, impliziert nicht, dass es notwendig ist, ihn auch im Bereich des Handelns als Freien und Gleichen anzuerkennen." (Robert Alexy, 'Menschenrechte ohne Metaphysik?' (n. 23), 20.)

135 Roderick Chisholm, 'What is a Transcendental Argument?', in *Zur Zukunft der Transzendentalphilosophie*, Neue Hefte für Philosophie, 14, 1978, 19–22, 19. In the same vein, see too Stanley L. Paulson, 'Läßt sich die Reine Rechtslehre transzendental begründen?', *Rechtstheorie. Zeitschrift für Logik, Methodenlehre Kybernetik und Soziologie des Rechts*, 21, 1990, 155–179, at 172.

136 Robert Alexy, 'Discourse Theory and Human Rights' (n. 10), 209–233, at 213.

137 In this vein, Stroud has stated that: "[S]ince every argument in which one thing is deduced from another proves that one thing is a necessary condition of another that would make all valid deductions transcendental. [...] That gets closer to the transcendental, but it is still too general. We eat bananas and drive automobiles, for example, so there must be such things as bananas and automobiles. Is this a transcendental argument for the existence of such things? If so, we could transcendental prove the existence of all those things that are required for all the practices we engage in." (Barry Stroud, 'The Goal of Transcendental Arguments' (n. 115), 155–172, 158.)

138 In this way, Paulson has stated that: "Wenn man die Struktur eines 'transzendentalen Arguments' im allgemeinen betrachtet, so handelt es sich dabei um ein Argument, demzufolge ein Satz 'P', der als wahr angenommen wird, nur dann wahr sein kann, wenn ein anderer Satz 'Q' ebenfalls wahr ist." (Stanley L. Paulson, 'Läßt sich die Reine Rechtslehre transzendental begründen?' (n. 135), 155–179, at 172.)

Strawson has stressed that the task of transcendental arguments is characteristically to argue against skeptical arguments.[139] Based on this task, Stern has distinguished two kinds of transcendental arguments.[140] While those transcendental arguments directed towards the truth are intended to respond to epistemic objections, those transcendental arguments directed towards beliefs are intended to respond to doxastic objections.[141] The latter ones aim to show the need for a prior belief for the possibility of a belief at issue.[142] As has been argued by Sacks, a transcendental argument of this kind is targeted to prove that it is justified to believe that a certain proposition is true, but only in terms of our normative doxastic contents.[143] In contrast, the epistemic skeptic seeks to contest our possibility to know either in general terms, or regarding some particular object.[144] This skeptic may not dispute propositions concerning beliefs, but concerning the external world.[145] Due to their task concerning the argument against skeptical arguments, transcendental arguments – both those aimed to respond to an epistemic doubt, and those aimed to respond to an doxastic doubt – are restricted in scope. Indeed, transcendental arguments require that their starting point – or better said, their first premise – be accepted as true by the skeptic.[146] For this reason, these arguments are not effective against radical forms of skepticism.[147]

The transcendental argument used by Alexy for the justification of the discourse constitutive norms at the pragmatic level assumes the claim to contest that non-radical skeptic who not only raises doubts about the possibility of rationality principles, but instead is willing to accept that assertion[148] is the most widespread

139 Peter Frederick Strawson, *Skepticism and Naturalism: Some Varieties* (n. 124), 10.

140 Robert Stern, 'On Kant's Response to Hume: The Second Analogy as Transcendental Argument', in *Transcendental Arguments. Problems and Prospects*, ed. Robert Stern (Oxford: Clarendon Press, 2000), 47–66, at 51.

141 Mark Sacks, 'Transcendental Arguments and the Inference to Reality: A Reply to Stern', in *Transcendental Arguments. Problems and Prospects*, ed. Robert Stern (Oxford: Clarendon Press, 2000), 67–82, 70.

142 Robert Stern, 'On Kant's Response to Hume: The Second Analogy as Transcendental Argument' (n. 140), 47–66, 51.

143 Mark Sacks, 'Transcendental Arguments and the Inference to Reality: A Reply to Stern'(n. 141), 67–82, 70.

144 Robert Stern, 'On Kant's Response to Hume: The Second Analogy as Transcendental Argument' (n. 140), 47–66, 48.

145 Mark Sacks, 'Transcendental Arguments and the Inference to Reality: A Reply to Stern'(n. 141), 67–82, 71.

146 Robert Stern, 'Transcendental Arguments', in *The Stanford Encyclopedia of Philosophy (Summer 2013 Edition)*, ed. Edward N. Zalta (Stanford: Center for Study of Language and Information – Stanford University), <URL=http://plato.stanford.edu/archives/sum2013/entries/transcendental-arguments/>

147 Ibid.

148 In this way, according to Alexy, "[t]he speech acts of asserting, arguing, and asking are of special importance for the justification of discourse rules. As a starting point for that version of a transcendental-pragmatic argument I intend to suggest here, I choose the speech act of assertion. I shall strart with some these about the necessary preconditions of assertions." (Robert Alexy, 'Discourse Theory and Human Rights' (n. 10), 209–233, at 214.)

communicative practice[149] – or in Alexy's words, a practice belonging to the most general form of life of human beings.[150] This kind of practice allows in its turn the communication between different forms of life,[151] and therefore, it can be interpreted as necessary in a existential sense from the participant's point of view.[152] According to Alexy, "[w]hoever never in his life makes an assertion [...] and never puts forward an argument [...] does not take part in the most general form of life of human beings."[153]

As is well known, the argument of the existential coercion has also been developed by Apel[154], and Habermas[155]. On the one hand, by making explicit the commitments of the rational discourse theory with a liberal philosophical political position, and by undertaking the justification of rationality principles based on two levels of analysis, Alexy has waived the possibility of an ultimate justification of practical discourse. On the other hand, as shown above, Alexy has contested the transcendental task of mutual understanding that Habermas has attributed to our communicative practices. These reasons explain the weakness that shows the existential coercion of discourse alluded to by Alexy.[156] The weakness of the argument becomes more evident, however, when one considers the fact that its foundations

149 As claimed by Alexy: "[...] the transcendental argument does not consist of deducing norms from facts, but of the reconstruction of a practice, from the point of view of a participant, in which everyone takes part at least rudimentarily" (Robert Alexy, 'Discourse Theory and Human Rights' (n. 10), 209–233, at 218 (at n. 10).)

150 Ibid. 217.

151 As stated by Alexy: "The thesis about the most general form of life of human beings does not disregard the fact that there are vey different concrete forms of life. It says, however, that all human forms of life necessarily include universals of argumentation, which can be expressed by the discourse rules. [...] The discourse rules therefore do not define any particular form of life, but something that is shared by all human forms of life, notwithstanding the fact that it is of vastly different importance in each of them" (Ibid. 218.)

152 As claimed by Alexy: "Assertions, and the arguments connected with them would not be necessary at all if one could do without them at will." (Ibid. 217.)

153 Ibid. 217.

154 For Apel, abandoning the communication community (Kommunikationsgemeinschaft) means for the subject losing her ability of self-understanding and self-identification to such an extent that it would be clinically demonstrable as a psychopathology (see Karl-Otto Apel, 'Das Apriori der Kommunikationsgemeinschaft und die Grundlagen der Ethik. Zum Problem einer rationalen Begründung der Ethik im Zeitalter der Wissenschaft (n. 5), 414 (at n. 87).)

155 For Habermas the abandonment of all everyday communicative practice leads the subject to schizophrenia or suicide (see Jürgen Habermas, 'Diskursethik-Notizen zu einem Begründungsprogramm' (n. 4), 52–125, at 112.)

156 Indeed, Alexy has stated: "The transcendental argument is radically weakened in this way. It does not establish an argumentative obligation against everyone. In order to take part in the most general form of life of human beings it is not necessary to make assertions and to give reasons to everyone who demands them; it is sufficient to do this at all in some context and to someone. The stronger one does not have to justify what he wants to burden the weaker one with. He can utter a plain order and enforce it by violence, and still take part in the most general human form of life by exchanging assertions and arguments with members of his own group." (Robert Alexy, 'Discourse Theory and Human Rights' (n. 10), 209–233, at 217.)

lie in an empirical argument – and that this kind of foundations makes it, therefore, defeasible. Indeed, according to Alexy, "[a]part from extremely unusual circumstances, such as growing up in total isolation, it is probably factually impossible to opt out of the most general form of life of human beings by never making any assertion at all however trivial, never putting forward any kind of justification, and never asking the question 'why?'."[157] In a patent manner, the skeptic does not accept this argument because it is true, but because it is plausible.[158] As has been argued by Gril, "*dieser Ausganspunkt ist aber zu schwach, um ein transzendentalpragmatisches Argument tragen zu können.*"[159]

Against Alexy's position, Gril has argued that based on the same assumptions and through a reasoning supported on empirical arguments could be concluded that, like the practice of assertion, other practices such as deceit, lies, and manipulation belong to the most general form of life of human beings.[160] According to Gril, if Alexy would want to hold that this general form of life is composed only by practices directed towards mutual understanding, then he should expressly introduce an additional premise in that regard. Notwithstanding, Alexy has not done so. Therefore, according to Gril, Alexy's justification has obstructed the achievement of the specific aim of the transcendental-pragmatic argument, that is, showing that there is no other alternative than to accept the justification regarding certain rules of thinking and action.[161] Nevertheless, while it is true that Alexy had to face the fallibility of the transcendental argument from the subjective practical point of view by means of the introduction of an empirical argument,[162] Gril's criticism ignores the epistemic privileged feature that assertion shows in comparison with other kinds of speech acts. Indeed, although we need the act of assertion for identifying practices such as deceit, lies, and manipulation, we cannot identify an assertion by means of these practices.

157 Ibid. 218.

158 As noted above, although the more ambitious ontological claim of the transcendental argument has been thrown out and the abandonment of this claim has led to emphasize the form of this kind of argument in order to achieve its suitable definition, the abandonment of this claim should not involve removal of the ontological aim to such an extent that it would be possible to define the transcendental argument only by virtue of its structure. As stated by Stroud, a reading in this sense would have the effect of making the transcendental argument a trivial one (in this regard, see Barry Stroud, 'The Goal of Transcendental Arguments' (n. 115), 155–172, 158.) For, preserving a restricted ontological claim depends on the definition of the transcendental argument's first premise, a trivial reading would result from the definition of the first premise of this argument on the basis of the alethic modality of possibility.

159 Peter Gril, *Die Möglichkeit praktischer Erkenntnis aus Sicht der Diskurstheorie* (n. 18), 142.

160 Ibid. 143.

161 Ibid. 143.

162 Ibid. 143.

As is well known, like Kant,[163] Frege,[164] and Wittgenstein,[165] Brandom[166] has identified the propositional content of utterances as the unit of meaning. In this vein, Brandom has identified assertions as the basic linguistic practices on which the others depend.[167] This identification is a result from his theory of meaning that he has defined in opposition to representationalism.[168]

The term 'representationalism' refers to those numerous theoretical variants which attribute to certain mental objects capable of representing the environment the central role that explains the relationship of the mind with it.[169] From the semantic point of view, representationalism refers to the set of theoretical approaches that assume as a least common thesis that, by virtue of which the function of the

163 According to Kant, "[b]egriffe gründen sich also auf der Spontaneität des Denkens, wie sinnliche Anschauungen auf der Rezeptivität der Eindrücke. Von diesen Begriffen kann nun der Verstand keinen andern Gebrauch machen, als daß er dadurch urteilt. Da keine Vorstellung unmittelbar auf den Gegenstand geht, als bloß die Anschauung, so wird ein Begriff niemals auf einen Gegenstand unmittelbar, sondern auf irgend eine andre Vorstellung von demselben (sie sei Anschauung oder selbst schon Begriff) bezogen. Das Urteil ist also die mittelbare Erkenntnis eines Gegenstandes, mithin die Vorstellung einer Vorstellung desselben. In jedem Urteil ist ein Begriff, der für viele gilt, und unter diesem Vielen auch eine gegebene Vorstellung begreift, welche letztere denn auf den Gegenstand unmittelbar bezogen wird. […] Wir können aber alle Handlungen des Verstandes auf Urteile zurückführen, so daß der Verstand überhaupt als ein Vermögen zu urteilen vorgestellt werden kann." (Immanuel Kant, *Kritik der reinen Vernunft*, <A69/B93>; <A69/B94>.)

164 According to Frege, "I start out from judgements and their contents, and from concepts […] I only allow the formation of concepts to proceed from judgements" (Gottlob Frege, 'Boole's logical Calculus and the Concept-script', in *Gottlob Frege. Posthumous Writtings*, ed. Hans Hermes *et al.* (Oxford, Basil Blackwell, 1979), 9–46, at 16.) In the same vein, Frege stated, "I begin by giving pride of place to the content of the word 'true', and then immediately go on to introduce a thought as that to whith the question 'Is it true?' is in principle applicable. So I do not begin with concepts and put them together to form a thought or judgement; I come by the parts of thought by analysing the thought." (Gottlob Frege, 'Notes for Ludwig Darmstadter', in *Gottlob Frege. Posthumous Writtings*, ed. Hans Hermes *et al.* (Oxford, Basil Blackwell, 1979), 253–257, at 253.)

165 According to Wittgenstein, "[a] proposition shows how things stand if it is true. And it says that they do so stand." (Ludwig Wittgenstein, Tractatus Logico-Philosophicus, <4.022>.) In the same vein, Wittgenstein wrote: "'[T]rue' and 'false' are not accidental properties of a proposition, such that, when it has meaning, we can say it is also true or false: on the contrary, to have meaning means to be true or false: the being true or false actually constitutes the relation of the proposition to reality, which we mean by saying that it has meaning (*Sinn*)." (Ludwig Wittgenstein, 'Notes Dictated to G.E. Moore in Norway', in *Notebooks, 1914–1916*, ed. Georg Henrik von Wright and Gertrude Elizabeth Margaret Anscombe, 2nd ed. (Oxford: Basil Blackwell, 1979), 108–119, at 112–113.)

166 Robert Brandom, *Making It Explicit. Reasoning, Representing and Discourse Commitment* (n. 38), 79–85.

167 Brandom has written: "By contrast to Wittgenstein, the inferential identification of the conceptual claims that language (discourse practice) has a *center*; it is not a motley. Inferential practices of producing and consuming *reasons* are *downtown* in the region of linguistic practice. Suburban linguistic practices utilize and depend on the conceptual contents forged in the game of giving and asking for reasons, are parasitic on it." (Brandom, *Articulating Reasons: An Introduction to Inferentialism* (Cambridge (Mass.): Harvard University Press, 2000, 14.)

168 Robert Brandom, *Making It Explicit. Reasoning, Representing and Discourse Commitment* (n. 38), 93–94.

169 George Pavlakos, *Own Knowledge of the Law* (Oxford: Hart Publishing, 2007), 24.

true statements is to represent states of affairs.[170] In other words, the representationalist theories of meaning hold the conceptual independence of semantics from pragmatics.[171]

In contrast to representationalism, the term 'inferentialism' refers to a part of those theoretical approaches[172] that hold the conceptual dependency of semantics on pragmatics.[173] According to MacFarlane,[174] Brandom has argued that the fundamental semantic concepts can be explained in terms of the properties needed to perform certain actions used to draw conclusions from premises. Accordingly, inferring is the fundamental action that determines the meaning.[175] In this way, Brandom embraces Sellars' view, according to which the linguistic meaning of a statement lies in the inferential relations with other statements.[176] Thus, as stated by Klatt,[177] understanding the meaning of a statement depends on understanding its

170 Huw Price, 'Two Readings of Representationalism', Descartes Lectures 2008 and Workshop on Pragmatism and Naturalism. Tilburg University. On 8th of May, 2008 <URL = http://philsci-archive.pitt.edu/4430/2/Tilburg2.pdf>

171 In that regard, see John MacFarlane, 'Pragmatism and Inferentialism', in *Reading Brandom. On Making It Explicit*, ed. Bernhard Weiss and Jeremy Wanderer (New York: Routledge, 2010), 81–95, at 83.

172 See *i. a.* Paul Horwich, *Reflections on Meaning* (Oxford: Oxford University Press, 2005); Christopher Peacocke, *A Study of Concepts (Representation and Mind)* (fisrt publ. 1992), 2nd ed., (Cambridge (Mass.): Massachussetts Insitute of Technology, 1999); Ned Block, 'Conceptual Role Semantics', in *Routledge Encyclopedia of Philosophy*, ed. Edward Craig (New York: Routledge, 1998), 242–256; Paul A. Boghossian, 'Does an Inferential Role Semantics Rest Up on a Mistake?', in *Mind and Language*, 8, 1, 1993, 27–40; Gilbert Harman, '(Non-solipsistic) Conceptual Role Semantics', in *New Directions in Semantics*, ed. Ernest LePore (London: Academic Press, 1987); Barry H. Loewer, 'The Role of 'Conceptual Role Semantics'', in *Notre Dame Journal of Formal Logic*, 23, 1982, 305–315; Robert Brandom, *Making It Explicit. Reasoning, Representing and Discourse Commitment* (n. 38). On some references, see Jaroslav Peregrin, 'What is Inferentialism?', in *Inference, Consequence, and Meaning. Perspectives on Inferentialism* (Newcastle upon Tyne: Cambridge Scholars Publishing, 2012), 3–18.

173 For example, Brandom has stated regarding the relations between pragmatics and semantics that: "One of the fundamental methodological commitments governing the account presented here is *pragmatism* about the relations between semantics and pragmatics. Pragmatism in this sense is the view that what attributions of semantic contentfulness are *for* is explaining the normative significance of intentional states such as beliefs and of speech acts such as assertions." (Robert Brandom, *Making It Explicit. Reasoning, Representing and Discourse Commitment* (n. 38), 143.)

174 John MacFarlane, 'Pragmatism and Inferentialism' (n. 171), 86.

175 Brandom has written: "*Inferring* is accordingly the key concept linking semantic content and pragmatic significance. For not only can propositional semantic contents be understood as inferential roles, but properties of inference can be made sense of pragmatically, and specifically assertional significance can be understood in terms of them" (Robert Brandom, *Making It Explicit. Reasoning, Representing and Discourse Commitment* (n. 38), 190.)

176 Robert Brandom, *Making It Explicit. Reasoning, Representing and Discourse Commitment* (n. 38), 89.

177 Matthias Klatt, *Making the Law Explicit. The normativity of Legal Argumentation* (n. 41), 123. According to Brandom, "[o]ne immediate consequence of such an inferential demarcation of the conceptual is that one must have may concepts in order to have any. For grasping a concept involves mastering the properties of inferential moves that connect it to many other concepts: those whose applicability follows from the applicability of the concept in question, those from whose applicability the applicability of the target concept follows, those whose applicability precludes or is precluded by it. One cannot have just one concept." (Robert Brandom, *Making It Explicit. Reasoning, Representing and Discourse Commitment* (n. 38), 89.)

inferential role in a statements' network. In this vein, the semantic content of an utterance in inferential terms is necessarily holistic.[178] By developing a tradition introduced by Frege and continued by Sellars, Brandom argues that determining the correctness of the possible inferences consists in determining their material inferences, i.e. determining non-logical but pragmatic inferences.[179] Accordingly, for Brandom, while material inferences have elementary validity, the logic makes explicit those inferences whose correctness underlies implicitly the meaning of non-logical concepts.[180]

The holistic understanding of a statement's meaning is possible, if there is a conceptual practice by means of which the statement's meaning is attributed.[181] Since this fundamental practice depends on assertion, then accordingly, assertion must be understood as a privileged speech act on which the other speech acts depend. As written by Price: "Brandom does not claim that making assertions is the only game we can play with language, of course, but he does claim that the assertoric game is both central and indispensable. Contrasting his own view to Wittgenstein's, he explains that his view requires that language 'has a downtown' – that assertion is a fundamental linguistic activity, on which others depend."[182]

Although Alexy has acknowledged the significance of assertion in regards to the discourse practice, and particularly for the justification of the rationality principles,[183] his position – like Gril's criticism – has overlooked the epistemic privileged feature that assertion shows when compared with other kinds of speech acts, according to a general theory of meaning. From an inferentialist point of view, assertion is necessary for determining meaning, and therefore, for communication.[184] In this vein, one cannot throw this practice overboard and "still engage in those forms of behavior we consider characteristically human."[185] By overlooking this privileged feature of assertion, Alexyan strategy has turned to an empirical argument for the

178 Ibid. 89–91.

179 Ibid. 132–133.

180 Ibid. 102.

181 According to Sellars, "[t]he essential point is that in characterizing an episode or a state as that of knowing, we are not giving an empirical description of that episode or state; we are placing it in the logical space of reasons, of justifying and being able to justify what one says" (Wilfrid Sellars, 'Empicirism and the Philosophy of Mind', in *Science, Perception and Reality*, ed. Wilfrid Sellars (London: Routledge and Kegan Paul, 1963), 127–196, 169.)

182 Huw Price, 'Two Readings of Representationalism', Descartes Lectures 2008 and Workshop on Pragmatism and Naturalism. Tilburg University. On 8th of May, 2008 <URL = http://philsci-archive.pitt.edu/4430/2/Tilburg2.pdf>

183 Robert Alexy, 'Discourse Theory and Human Rights' (n. 10), 209–233, at 214; Robert Alexy, *Theorie der juristischen Argumentation. Die Theorie des rationalen Diskurses als Theorie der juristischen Begründung* (n. 3), 231.

184 In this vein, Klatt has commented on Brandom's work: "[the] propositional content is picked out by the pragmatic property of being *assertible*" (Matthias Klatt, *Making the Law Explicit. The normativity of Legal Argumentation* (n. 41), 127.)

185 John R. Searle, *Speech Acts. An Essay in the Philosophy of Language* (n. 42), 186 (at n. 1).

justification of the transcendental-pragmatic argument's first premise.[186] This starting point does not seem strong enough to sustain the ontological claim required for making explicit the constitutive norms of our discursive practices.[187]

This criticism reveals that although the Alexyan transcendental-pragmatic justification of rationality principles assumes a theory of assertion institutional in nature,[188] and although Alexy has highlighted the relationship between the ideal discursive practice described by him and the game of giving and asking for reasons described by Brandom,[189] Alexy's theory does not seem willing to accept the consequences that draw from an inferentialist normative interpretation of the institutional feature of assertion.

As we have seen, the transcendental-pragmatic argument used in Alexyan justification of rationality principles requires that the skeptic accepts that assertion is the most widespread communicative practice.[190] According to Alexy, such a practice is constituted[191] by a singular rule which defines the necessary and sufficient conditions for the speech act of assertion.[192] This constitutive rule is termed claim to truth or correctness.[193] For Alexy, this claim implies in its turn a *prima facie* obligation to

186 Indeed, as shown above this argument is formulated by Alexy as follows: "Apart from extremely unusual circumstances, such as growing up in total isolation, it is probably factually impossible to opt out of the most general form of life of human beings by never making any assertion at all however trivial, never putting forward any kind of justification, and never asking the question 'why?'" (Robert Alexy, 'Discourse Theory and Human Rights' (n. 10), 209–233, at 218.)

187 Peter Gril, *Die Möglichkeit praktischer Erkenntnis aus Sicht der Diskurstheorie* (n. 18), 142.

188 Peter Pagin, 'Assertion', in *The Stanford Encyclopedia of Philosophy (Spring 2014 Edition)*, ed. Edward N. Zalta (Stanford: Center for Study of Language and Information – Stanford University), <URL= http://plato.stanford.edu/archives/spr2014/entries/assertion/>.)

189 See Robert Alexy, 'Menschenrechte ohne Metaphysik?' (n. 23), 20.

190 Robert Alexy, 'Discourse Theory and Human Rights' (n. 10), 209–233, at 217.

191 As noted above, constitutive norms are the kind of norms which allows to differentiate practices from mere activities. (See Michael Rescorla, 'Assertion and its constitutive norms' (n. 37), 98–130.)

192 With this statement, Alexy joins a number of authors who have recognized the conventional attribute or rule-governed feature of the illocutionary acts, among them – and predominantly – the act of assertion. (See *i. a.* Michael Dummett, *Frege. Philosophy of Language,* 2nd ed. (Cambridge (Mass.): Harvard University Press, 1981), 302, 311; John R. Searle, *Speech Acts. An Essay in the Philosophy of Language* (n. 42), 29–71; John L. Austin, *How To Do Things With Words*, 2nd ed. (Oxford: Oxford University Press, 1975), 103.) However, this is not a unique position. Some authors have claimed that a convention is not a necessary condition for performing assertions. (See *i. a.* Peter Frederick Strawson, 'Intention and Convention in Speech Acts', in *Logico-linguistic Papers* (London: Methuen, 1971), 149–169, at 153–154; Robert J. Stainton, 'In Defense of Non-Sentential Assertion', in *Semantics vs. Pragmatics*, ed. Zolán Gendler Szabó (Oxford: Clarendon Press, 2005), 383–457; Robert J. Stainton, 'What Assertion is Not', *Philosophical Studies*, 85, 1997, 57–73.) In contrast, some others have stated that a convention is a necessary, but not a sufficient condition for performing assertions. (See *i. a.* Donald Davidson, 'Moods and Performances', in *Meaning and Use. Papers presented at the Second Jerusalem Philosophical Encounter, April 1976*, ed. Avishai Margalit (Dordrecht: D. Reidel Publishing Company, 1979), 9–20; Donald Davidson, 'Communication and Convention', in *Inquiries into Truth and Interpretation, ed. Donald Davidson (New York: Clarendon Press, 1984)*, 265–280; Kent Bach and Robert M. Harnish, *Linguistic Communication and Speech Acts* (Cambridge (Mass.): Massachussetts Insitute of Technology, 1979), 122–127.)

193 Robert Alexy, 'Discourse Theory and Human Rights' (n. 10), 209–233, at 214. Against this definition could be argued that the claim to truth or correctness characterizes not only the as-

justify[194] by one who has performed an assertion in case of being asked by her audience. Thus, according to Alexy, "[s]he who claims that her assertion is true or correct, and at the same time says that there are absolutely no reasons for what she asserts, does perhaps not even make a genuine assertion."[195] Alexy has held that rationality principles are necessary conditions for this *prima facie* obligation, because "[w]hoever gives justifying reasons for something raises claims to equality, freedom from force, and universality, at least as far as the justification is concerned."[196] In this vein, according to the Alexyan justification, the transcendental-pragmatic argument makes explicit the rationality principles. Since these norms are necessary conditions for assertion, such norms must be accepted by everyone who agrees that the assertion is a practice, in some sense, necessary.

Understanding this argument requires to make explicit the complex normative structure underlying it. Alexy has somehow linked the ideal discursive practice described by him with the game of giving and asking for reasons described by Brandom.[197] Brandom has held that the statement meaning is attributed according to the possible material inferences associated with the speech act performance in which the

sertion, but also some other acts like assumptions, presumptions, and conjectures. In some way, however, these acts cannot be defined as assertions. (Peter Pagin, 'Assertion', in *The Stanford Encyclopedia of Philosophy (Spring 2014 Edition)*, ed. Edward N. Zalta (Stanford: Center for Study of Language and Information – Stanford University), <URL= http://plato.stanford.edu/archives/spr2014/entries/assertion/>) If this criticism were true, then the claim to truth or correctness would not only characterize the act of assertion, and hence, the thesis of singularity defended by Alexy would be false. Two strategies should be combined in facing this criticism. On the one hand, it should be settled, how the claim to truth or correctness should be understood according to Alexy's theory – if his theory is understood as a system. On the other hand, it should be established how the claim to truth or correctness defended by Alexy should be understood according to general theories on the relation between assertion and truth. Although this analysis exceeds our goals, it could be stated that a plausible interpretation of the claim to truth or correctness defended by Alexy would link this claim with the rule of knowledge if understood as constitutive singular rule of the act of assertion. (On the rule of knowledge as constitutive rule of assertion, see Manuel García-Carpintero, 'Assertion and the Semantics of Force-Markers', in *The Semantics/Pragmatics Distinction*, ed. Claudia Bianchi (Stanford: CSLI Lecture Notes, The University of Chicago Press – Stanford, 2004), 133–166; Keith DeRose, 'Assertion, Knowledge and Context', *The Philosophical Review*, 111, 2002, 167–203; Timothy Williamson, *Knowledge and its Limits* (Oxford: Oxford University Press, 2002), 249–269; Timothy Williamson, 'Knowing and Asserting' (n. 42); Michael Slote, 'Assertion and Belief', in *Papers on Language and Logic: Proceedings of the Conference on the Philosophy of Language and Logic held at the University of Keele in April, 1979*, ed. Jonathan Dancy (Keele: Keele University Library, 1980), 177–190; Peter Unger, *Ignorance: The Case for Skepticism*, (Oxford: Clarendon Press, 1975).)

194 Alexy has taken up the defeasible feature of assertion's justifiability claim. He has written: "That assertions raise a claim to justifiability does not mean that anyone at any time must justify every assertion to everyone. Quite often, the addressee of an assertion already disapproves of the assertion as such and under no circumstances wants to be bothered with reasons for it. On the other hand someone who has made an assertion might have sound reasons for denying a substantiation" (Robert Alexy, 'Discourse Theory and Human Rights' (n. 10), 209–233, at 215.)

195 Ibid. 215.

196 Ibid. 216.

197 Indeed, Alexy has claimed: "Das Argument beginn mit einer Analyse der diskursiven Praxis, die als Praxis des Behauptens, des Fragens und des Anführens von Gründen verstanden wird. [...] Diese Praxis entspricht dem, was Robert Brandom als 'practices of giving and asking for reasons bezeichnet'." (Robert Alexy, 'Menschenrechte ohne Metaphysik?' (n. 23), 20.)

statement is involved.[198] This thesis corresponds to a strong version of inferentialism,[199] and it is correlated with the kind of relation between semantics and pragmatics defended by Brandom.

As argued by MacFarlane,[200] two different versions of pragmatism are defended with regard to the relation between semantics and pragmatics. A weak version of pragmatism is stated, when it is argued that semantic concepts are not conceptually independent from pragmatics. In other words, when it is affirmed that those concepts are meaningful, due to the fact that they acquire their meaning from their relation with pragmatic concepts. However, a strong version of pragmatism is stated, when it is argued that semantic concepts can be only defined in pragmatic terms. Accordingly, Brandom's theory should be considered a strong version of pragmatism, since it attempts to reduce semantics to the norms governing a privileged practice by means of which the meaning is attributed.[201] Making explicit the norms which govern that privileged practice is a necessary condition for achieving such an attempt.[202]

Indeed, as noted above, since according to the inferentialist theory of meaning the meaning of a statement is attributed based on the possible material inferences associated with the speech act performance, the statement meaning depends on a

198 See Robert Brandom, *Making It Explicit. Reasoning, Representing and Discourse Commitment* (n. 38), 97.

199 According to Brandom, "[t]here are three different ways in which one might take inference to be of particular significance for understanding conceptual content. The weak inferentialist thesis is that inferential articulation is *necessary* for specifically *conceptual* contentfulness. The strong inferentialist thesis is that broadly inferential articulation is *sufficient* for specifically conceptual content than its broadly inferential articulation. [...] For strong inferentialism as it is worked out in the rest of this project is not committed to the hyperinferentialist thesis, which maintains that *narrowly* inferential articulation is sufficient for conceptual contentfulness of all sorts." (Robert Brandom, *Making It Explicit. Reasoning, Representing and Discourse Commitment* (n. 38), 131.)

200 John MacFarlane, 'Pragmatism and Inferentialism' (n. 171), 89–90. On the distinction between pragmatism and inferentialism see, too, Robert Brandom, 'Inferentialism and Some of its Challenges', *Philosophy and Phenomenological Research*, 74, 3, May, 2007, 651–676.

201 Brandom has written: "In this way a suitable pragmatic theory can ground an inferentialist semantic theory; its explanations of what it is in practice to treat inferences as correct are what ultimately license appeal to material properties of inference, which can then function as semantic primitives. [...] the strategy is to start with properties of inference and to elucidate the notion of conceptual content in terms of those properties." (Robert Brandom, *Making It Explicit. Reasoning, Representing and Discourse Commitment* (n. 38), 134.)

202 In this way, Brandom continues the tradition defended by Wittgenstein. This tradition is characterized by searching of intelligibility of our practices. As noted by Pavlakos, the idea of intelligibility underlies to the precedence of the logic over the ontology which is defended by Wittgenstein in Tractatus Logico-Philosophicus (1922) (See George Pavlakos, *Own Knowledge of the Law* (n. 169), 36.) Intelligibility is a Wittgenstein's constant concern. The search of making our practices intelligible survives the terminology changes and the dissatisfaction with the role of logic which characterized the Wittgensteinian work. Wittgenstein replaced the use of the word "logic" for the use of the word "grammar" in Philosophical Grammar (1933.) Moreover, in Philosophical Investigations (1945), Wittgenstein replaced the use of the word "grammar" for concepts like "form of life", "practice", and "language game". Notwithstanding, the substance is the same, i. e. the idea of a network of rules which allows to determine the meaning-bearers.

conceptual practice by means of which the statement meaning is attributed.[203] Brandom has held that this conceptual practice is normative in nature.[204] He has noted

203 According to Brandom, "[…] because the activity through which the norms get their grip on conceptual contents is construed as inference, it is specifically propositional contents that in the first instance count as conceptually articulated. Inferential relations hold, in the paradigm case, between contents that are expressed explicitly by declarative sentences. The premises of inferences, and in the central cases their conclusions as well, must be understood to have a propositional form. Insofar as an independent theoretical grip is possible on the notion of inference, propositional contents can be picked out by appeal to his property. […] So on an inferential rendering of the conceptual, the sort of doing that inferring is yields in a natural way the priority of propositional conceptual contents." (Robert Brandom, *Making It Explicit. Reasoning, Representing and Discourse Commitment* (n. 38), 91–92.)

204 As is known, on the basis of Sellars' concept of "pattern-govern behavior" (see Ruth Garrett Millikan, 'The Father, The Son, and The Daughter. Sellars, Brandom, and Millikan', in *The Pragmatics of Making It Explicit*, ed. Pirmin Stekeler-Weithofer (Amsterdam: John Benjamins Publishing Co., 2008), 53–64. Particularly see Sellars Wilfrid Sellars, 'Language, Rules and Behavior', in *John Dewey: Philosopher of Science and Freedom*, ed. Sidney Hook (New York: The Dial Press, 1949), 289–315; Wilfrid Sellars, 'Some Reflections on Language Games', *Philosophy of Science*, 21, 3, July, 1954, 204–228) Brandom has addressed the definition of linguistic rules by means of the opposition to the regulism – i. e. the reduction of the norms either to natural events or to ideal platonic entities (Robert Brandom, *Making It Explicit. Reasoning, Representing and Discourse Commitment* (n. 38), 18–20) – and to the regularism – i. e. the reduction of the norms to descriptive terms, under which the distinction between regular and irregular performance corresponds to the distinction between correct and incorrect (Robert Brandom, *Making It Explicit. Reasoning, Representing and Discourse Commitment* (n. 38), 26–30.) On the one hand, according to Wittgenstein's criticism, the intellectualist conception is inadequate to explain the normative phenomenon, because it cannot explain the essential feature of this phenomenon, that is the possibility of following rules (see Wittgenstein, *Philosophical Investigations*, <201>.) According to Brandom, "the intellectualist model will not do as an account of the nature of the normative as such. For when applied to the norms governing the application of rules and principles, it generates a regress, which can be halted only by acknowledging the existence of some more primitive form of norm" (Robert Brandom, *Making It Explicit. Reasoning, Representing and Discourse Commitment* (n. 38), 23.) On the other hand, Brandom argues that the regularism is based on a fiction (*rectius*: gerrymandering argument. See Robert Brandom, *Making It Explicit. Reasoning, Representing and Discourse Commitment* (n. 38), 28.) The problem is that "any particular set of performances exhibits many regularities." (Robert Brandom, *Making It Explicit. Reasoning, Representing and Discourse Commitment* (n. 38), 28) There is no obvious pattern or regularity in a set of past behaviors, which can be appealed to "in judging some candidate bit of future behavior as regular or irregular, and hence, on this line, as correct or incorrect." (Robert Brandom, *Making It Explicit. Reasoning, Representing and Discourse Commitment* (n. 38), 28) In this way, the regularism is based on the selection of a criterion which allows the definition of a set of past behaviors in order to show them as privileged performances. These privileged performances are shown as the regularities which should govern the practice (Robert Brandom, *Making It Explicit. Reasoning, Representing and Discourse Commitment* (n. 38), 28.) However, the definition of this criterion leads to input by smuggling of elitist normative notions, which specify what should count as communitarian. This situation, Brandom has argued,"may take the form of specifying a subclass of community members whose assessments are imbued with communal authority and so have the status of official or experts assessments" (Robert Brandom, *Making It Explicit. Reasoning, Representing and Discourse Commitment* (n. 38), 45.) Moreover, on the basis of the anti-reductionist supervenience condition it has been argued that the correctness conditions cannot be reduced to empirical description, because by doing they lose their normative status. (In this vein, Boghossian has written: "[W]e have reason to believe that there could not be naturalistically specifiable conditions under which a subject will be disposed to apply an

that the practice of giving and asking for reasons is made of deontic statutes which govern the behavior of the participants in this privileged practice. These deontic statutes correspond to doxastic commitments and entitlements.[205] The doxastic commitments are distinguished by the fact that they can be required by other participants who are entitled to do it. In this way, a consequential relationship is generated by means of changes in the deontic statutes of each participant. Each change is brought about as a result from an assertion performance.[206]

On the other hand, Brandom has reminded us that for Kant the distinction between facts and rules is itself not a factual but a normative difference.[207] This distinction is that between acting according to rules and acting according to conceptions of rules. Thus, according to Brandom, "[w]hat is distinctive about us as normative creatures is the *way* in which we are subject to norms (for Kant, in the form of rules). As natural beings, we act according to rules. As rational beings, we act according to our *conceptions* of rules. It is not being bound by necessity, acting according to rules, that sets us apart; it is being bound not just by natural but by rational necessity."[208]

According to Brandom, the Kantian practical philosophy – and particularly his *Kritik der praktischen Vernunft* – is devoted to examining these two different ways of relating to rules.[209] With regard to the particular human way of relating to them, Kant's position explains two key features. On the one hand, his position clarifies the link with the rules by means of normative modalities in terms of "ought".[210] This explanation allows one to distinguish between causal relations, and obedience relations. The first ones refer to relations between natural entities. The second ones refer to relations between intentional agents. On the other hand, his position illustrates the human link with the rules through the analysis of normative coercion.[211] This second approach refers to the distinction between motivation and moral obligation. According to Brandom's Kantian interpretation, with regard to us – as humans – the normative coercion is mediated by our attitude toward the rules. In this vein, the tension involving the distinction between motivation and moral obligation is settled by means of the conclusion according to which "[w]hat makes us act as we do is not the rule or norm itself but our acknowledgment of it."[212]

expression only to what it means; and, hence, that no attempt at specifying such conditions can hope to succeed" [Paul A. Boghossian, 'The Rule-Following Considerations', *Mind*, 98, 392, 1989, 507–549, at 537]). On the anti-reductionist supervenience condition see Jaegwon Kim, 'Concepts of Supervenience', *Philosophy and Phenomenological Research*, XLV, 2, December, 1984, 153–176; Thomas Grimes, 'Supervinience, Determination, and Dependency', *Philosophical Studies*, 62, April, 1991, 81–92; Thomas Grimes, 'The Myth of Supervenience', *Pacific Philosophical Quarterly*, 69, 1988, 152–160.)

205 Robert Brandom, *Making It Explicit. Reasoning, Representing and Discourse Commitment* (n. 38), 142–143.

206 Ibid. 142.

207 Ibid. 58.

208 Ibid. 30.

209 Ibid. 30.

210 Ibid. 31.

211 Ibid. 31.

212 Ibid. 31. According to the Enlightenment tradition, our own acknowledgment of a rule is "the source of its authority over us." (Ibid. 51.) In this way, Brandom has pointed out, "our normative statuses such as obligation are institute by our normative attitudes." (Ibid. 51.) Brandom

Brandom has stated that his proposal is a Hegelian work in some sense.[213] On this basis, Brandom has argued that acknowledgment helps to explain the self-conscious process of a linguistic community regarding its own authority concerning the constitution of the necessary discursive procedures not only for attributing meaning, but also for the constitution of subjects. The latter, is a normative process in nature, due to the fact that subjects are understood in terms of deontic statutes, i. e. in terms of responsibility and authority.[214] This Hegelian approach to acknowledg-

has explained that this statement should not be understood in the sense of the normative status effect upon our everyday behavior, but it should be understood according to the fact that we are exposed to a moral judgement under the rule that expresses its rational necessity. (Ibid. 51–52.) Notwithstanding, once we endorse a rule – Brandom has argued – "it is not up to us what it demands – there is some fact of the matter as to what we have thereby obliged ourselves to do" (Ibid. 52.)

213 Robert Brandom, 'Facts, Norms and Normative Facts: A Reply to Habermas' (n. 66), 356–374, at 360–362.

214 In this regard, Brandom has stated: "Hegel takes over Kant's fundamental idea that to call something a self, to treat it as an 'I,' is to take up an essentially *normative* attitude toward it. It is to treat it as the subject of *commitments*, as something that can be *responsible* – hence as a potential knower and agent." (Robert Brandom, 'Some Pragmatist Themes in Hegel's Idealism', in Tales of the Mighty Dead, 2002, 210–234, 216.) Moreover, Brandom has pointed out that the constitution of the subject and the constitution of the community are a result from the same mutual recognition process. Thus, according to Brandom, "[a]t the same time and by the same means that selves, in this normative sense, are synthesized, so are communities, as structured wholes of selves all of whom recognize and are recognized by one another. Both selves and communities are normative structures instituted by reciprocal recognition. This is a social theory of selves in the sense that selves and communities are products of the same process, aspects of the same structure. [...] This account of what it is to be a good chess player, in the various senses that term can take – and more generally, what it is to have some specific normative status – gives the candidate a certain sort of authority: the authority to constitute a community by recognizing individuals as members of it. But doing that is also ceding another sort of authority to those one recognizes: the authority to determine whether or not the candidate qualifies as a member of the community so constituted by the standards to which I have subjected myself. Having a normative status in this sense is an essentially social achievement, in which both the individual self and the community must participate. And both the self and the community achieve their status as such only as the result of successful reciprocal recognition. So when we talk about the structure and unity of the 'I' or of self-conscious selves according to Hegel, we are talking about the structure and unity produced by this process of reciprocal recognition, by which normative communities and community members are simultaneously instituted. This is what the idealist thesis proposes to use as a model for understanding the structure and unity of concepts. Here is a hint, to be followed up below. In recognizing others, I in effect institute a community – a kind of universal common to those others, and if all goes well, to me too. If they recognize me in turn, they constitute me as something more than just the particular I started out as – a kind of individual (self), which is that particular (organism) as a member of the community, as characterized by that universal. The (recognizing) particular accordingly exercises a certain sort of authority over the universal, and the universal then exercises a certain sort of authority over the individual. It is at something like this level of abstraction that we find a common structure between the social institution of selves and communities by reciprocal recognition and the relation between concepts, as universals, and the particulars that fall under them, yielding the characterized individuals (particulars as falling under universals) that are presented by judgments." (Robert Brandom, 'Some Pragmatist Themes in Hegel's Idealism', in *Tales of the Mighty Dead*, (Cambridge (Mass.): Harvard University Press, 2002), 210–234, at 216–218.) However, de Vries has raised doubts about Brandom's account about the origin and nature of the mutual recognition as constituting substance of the community developed on the Hegelian basis. (See

ment allows one to answer one of the fundamental dilemmas shown by Brandom's account of discursive practice. According to Brandom, "[o]rdinarily the relation of an authorizing event to the performances it licenses requires at least that in the context of that event, performances become socially appropriate that otherwise would not be. For example purchasing a ticket entitles one to take a seat in the theater, which it would be inappropriate to do without the ticket. This observation presents a dilemma. If asserting a sentence is not a performance requiring prior authorization, then it seems one cannot understand the function of assertion as inferentially licensing further assertions. If, however, asserting is a performance requiring authorization, how does one become entitled to the original licensing assertion?"[215] The answer about the normative nature of the starting point of our discursive practices lies in the mutual acknowledgment by means of which subjects achieve their own constitutive status as normative entities. From the first person perspective, this acknowledgment involves a subject's universal doxastic commitment – as a member of the linguistic community – to acknowledge others as capable of making commitments and being accountable.[216] In other words, this universal commitment means that each linguistic community member should acknowledge with respect to others what he acknowledges of himself, that is, in general, the ability to follow rules, and specifically, the ability to follow linguistic rules – *rectius* linguistic competence. In this way, with regard to the privileged speech act of assertion, the acknowledgment commitment implies the addressee's doxastic commitment of assuming that the speaker is able to meet the rule of knowledge – as assertion's singular constitutive rule – when the speaker performs an assertion.[217]

In short, on the basis of the universal doxastic commitment – which entails the constitutive mutual acknowledgment of the subjects as members of a linguistic community – the speaker is entitled to perform an assertion. On the one hand, such speaker's entitlement corresponds in its turn to an addressee's acknowledgment particular commitment, that is, a commitment that refers in particular to the duty of abstention – in order to permit the assertion performance by the speaker – and the

Willem A. deVries, 'Brandom and the Spirit of Hegel', in *Robert Brandoms Expressive Vernunft: Historische und Systematische Untersuchungen*, ed. Christian Barth and Holger Sturm (Paderborn: Mentis Verlag, 2011), 159–174, at 159–169.)

215 Robert Brandom, *Making It Explicit. Reasoning, Representing and Discourse Commitment* (n. 38), 170–171.

216 Brandom has written: "The practical attitude of taking or treating something as able to undertake commitments and be responsible for its doings – in the sense articulated by concepts, that is, the sense in which at least part of what one is committed to or responsible for is being able to give reasons – Hegel calls 'recognition' [Anerkennung]. The core idea structuring Hegel's social understanding of selves is that they are synthesized by mutual recognition. That is, to be a self – a locus of conceptual commitment and responsibility – is to be taken or treated as one by those one takes or treats as one: to be recognized by those one recognizes. Merely biological beings, subjects and objects of desires, become spiritual beings, undertakers (and attributors) of commitments, by being at once the subjects and the objects of recognitive attitudes." (Robert Brandom, 'Some Pragmatist Themes in Hegel's Idealism' (n. 214), 210–234, 216–217.)

217 With regard to the rule of knowledge as constitutive rule of the act of assertion, see above n. 193. By performing an act of assertion, the speaker affirms at the same the fulfillment of the constitutive rule of assertion – that is, of the rule of knowledge. However, as stated by Williamson, the rule of knowledge is defeasible (Timothy Williamson, *Knowledge and its Limits* (n. 193), 249–269, esp. at 256.)

duty to assess such speaker's performance as an assertion – not as other kind of speech act. On the other hand – since the rule of knowledge is a singular constitutive rule of assertion – the speaker's entitlement to perform an assertion corresponds to the duty of justification[218] that every speaker has to meet in case of being asked by her addressee. In this way, the addressee's commitment to acknowledge is in its turn correlated with her entitlement to ask the speaker.[219] In this vein, on the basis of both a starting point – i. e., the universal commitment of acknowledgment – and an assertion performance, a deontic correlative positions system is brought about[220] – or better said, according to Brandom's terminology, a system of deontic correlative statutes corresponding to commitments and entitlements. Such a deontic dynamic system is shown by Alexy in order to justify the underlying static deontic system – or better said, a system of immunities – expressed by the rationality principles.

However, while the Alexyan transcendental-pragmatic justification of rationality principles assumes a theory of assertion institutional in nature, and while Alexy has somehow linked the ideal discursive practice described by him and the game of giving and asking for reasons described by Brandom,[221] Alexy's theory does not seem willing to accept the consequences that draw from an inferentialist normative interpretation of the institutional feature of assertion. In fact, as shown, although Alexy has noted that communication is a necessary condition for practical correctness,[222] his theory assumes the conceptual independence of semantics from pragmatics. In this way, while according to the normative inferentialist view logic makes explicit those inferences whose correctness underlies implicitly the meaning of

218 According to Brandom, "[i]n asserting a claim, one not only authorizes further assertions (for one self and for others) but undertakes a responsability, for one commits oneself to being able to vindicate the original claim by showing that one is entitled to make it" (Robert Brandom, *Making It Explicit. Reasoning, Representing and Discourse Commitment* (n. 38), 171.) In the same vein, Peirce also claimed: "[T]o assert a proposition is to make oneself responsible for its truth." (CP 5.543) (Charles Sanders Peirce, 'Belief and Judgment' (1902), in *Collected Papers of Charles Sanders Peirce*, ed. Charles Hartshorn and Paul Weiss, vol. V: Pragmatism and Pragmaticism and Scientific Metaphysics, book III: Unpublished Papers, ch. 4 (Cambridge (Mass.): Harvard University Press, 1931–1935), <CP 5.543>.)

219 Brandom has expanded his account by means of the introduction of four types of auxiliary speech acts. These are the following: deferrals, disavowals, queries, and challenges. (See Robert Brandom, *Making It Explicit. Reasoning, Representing and Discourse Commitment* (n. 38), 191–193.) Brandom has claimed the fundamentality of challenges over the rest of auxiliary speech acts. (See Robert Brandom, 'Facts, Norms and Normative Facts: A Reply to Habermas' (n. 66), 356–374, at 362.)

220 As can be inferred, this dynamic deontic system of correlative positions is evident from the fact that with regard to the speaker, an assertion performance involves two normative or institutional results at the same time – or more specifically, two changes in speaker's deontic statutes. On the one hand, by performing the assertion, the speaker and her addressee are entitled to assert what can be justifiably inferred from the first assertion. On the other hand, by performing the assertion, the speaker is committed with her addressee to justifying her assertion if asked. (See Peter Pagin, 'Assertion', in *The Stanford Encyclopedia of Philosophy (Spring 2014 Edition)*, ed. Edward N. Zalta (Stanford: Center for Study of Language and Information – Stanford University), <URL= http://plato.stanford.edu/archives/spr2014/entries/assertion/>.)

221 See Robert Alexy, 'Menschenrechte ohne Metaphysik?' (n. 23), 20.

222 Robert Alexy, 'Problems of Discourse Theory' (n. 21), 43–65, at 52.

non-logical concepts,[223] Alexy has held the existence of general requirements of rationality which are logical and pragmatic in nature and prior to the discourse practice.[224] But even more, Alexy has turned to the existence of a third world made of abstract or ideal entities postulated by Frege[225] in order to support his semantic-norm theory[226]. As argued by Dummett, the Fregean ontological claim of thought is independent of our ability not only to express it, but even to understand it.[227]

In this vein, the fact that Alexy's theory cannot take on the consequences that draw from an inferentialist normative interpretation of the institutional feature of assertion which underlies the Alexyan transcendental-pragmatic justification of rationality principles, has led Alexy to overlook the epistemic privileged feature that assertion shows according to a general theory of meaning. By overlooking this priv-

223 Robert Brandom, *Making It Explicit. Reasoning, Representing and Discourse Commitment* (n. 38), 102.

224 Robert Alexy, 'Discourse Theory and Human Rights' (n. 10), 209–233, at 67.

225 Gottlob Frege, 'Der Gedanke. Eine logische Untersuchung', in *Logische Untersuchungen*, ed. Günther Patzig (Göttingen: Vandenhoeck und Ruprecht, 1966), 30–53, at 43.

226 In this vein, Alexy has stated that: "Überträgt man die These Freges über die Existenz von Gedanken auf Normen, so entsteht der semantischer Normbegriff, mit dessen Hilfe sich sagen lässt, was als Norm vorhanden ist, wenn ein Menschenrecht gilt." (Robert Alexy, 'Menschenrechte ohne Metaphysik?' (n. 23), 23.) Alexy has acknowledged the roots of his position in Kelsen and the Neo-Kantian tradition. He has written that: "Die Norm aber sei ein 'Sinngehalt'. Als Sinngehalt gehöre die Norm nicht zu einer natürlichen, sondern zu einer geistigen Realität. Als Element einer geistigen Realität stehe die Norm, anders als alles in der Natur, 'nicht in Raum und Zeit'. Physische und psychische Phänomene, die mit der Norm verbunden seien, gehörten nicht zur Norm selbst, sondern seien nur 'Parallelphänomene in der Natur' [...] Diese Äußerungen Kelsens lassen deutlich das dreistufige Schema physisch-psychisch-geistig erkennen. Das legt es nahe, die Norm als Sinngehlat einem 'dritten Reich' im Sinne Freges, also einer Welt der abstrakten Entitäten zuzuordnen. Der Normbegriff des neukantischen Kelsens ist also ein semantischer Normbegriff. Dieser ist durch die Parallelität von Aussagesatz und Normsatz auf der einen und Assage und Norm auf der anderen Seite definiert. So wie Aussagesätze Aussagen oder – in Freges Terminologie – Gedanken ausdrücken, so drücken Normsätze Normen aus. Normen als 'Sinngehalte' im Sinne Kelsens haben demnach den ontologischen Status von Bedeutungsgehalten." (Robert Alexy, 'Hans Kelsens Begriff des relativen Apriori', in *Neukantismus und Rechtsphilosophie*, ed. Robert Alexy *et al.* (Baden-Baden: Nomos Verlagsgesellschaft, 2002), 179–202, at 182. On the semantic concept of norm see Robert Alexy, *Theorie der Grundrechte* (1985) (n. 49), 40–53.)

227 Dummett wrote: "Frege's choosing to take the thought as the possessor of truth-value and the sense as the possessor of reference is due in part to his conception of sense in general, and thoughts in particular, as existing independently of whether we have words to express them. Indeed he sometimes argues for the thesis that it is thoughts to which truth and falsity are primarily ascribe by urging that it would still be true that the Earth has only one (natural) satellite even if there were no human being to express the fact or recognize its truth. If what is true would still be true even if we were not able to express or grasp it, or did not even exist, then that which is true cannot be anything whose existence depend on us, as the existence of a sentence depends at least on the existence of the language to which it belongs, but must be something, like a thought which exists independently of us. Conversely, given that a thought is taken to be what is true or false, and given also that any true thought which does not relate to us would still be true if we did not exist, it follows that the existence of a thought cannot be dependent on our ability to express it or to grasp it. [...] [I]ndeed, it might seem natural to maintain that the price Frege paid for dispensing with facts from his ontology was precisely to have to regard thoughts in the way he does, as timeless or eternal entities whose existence is not dependent upon the existence in any actual language of sentences which express them, or even of beings capable of grasping them." (Dummett, *Frege. Philosophy of Language* (n. 194), 369.)

ileged feature of assertion, Alexy's account has turned to an empirical argument for the justification of the transcendental-pragmatic argument's starting point. This justification seems too weak to sustain the ontological claim required for making explicit the constitutive norms of our discursive practices.

Part Three: The Practical Level of Justification of Rationality Principles

However, even if it is assumed that rationality principles have been justified at the pragmatic level, their universal validity at the action level has not yet been demonstrated.[228] As discussed by Alexy: "*Man kann mit Sklaven diskutieren. Das zeigt, dass zusätzliche Prämissen erforderlich sind, wenn man von der Freiheit und Gleichheit in der luftigen Welt des Diskurses zur Freiheit und Gleichheit im engen Raum des Handelns übergehen will.*"[229]

As we have seen, Alexy has stated that balancing is one of the general requirements of rationality.[230] Consistently, he has defined the balancing and recognition of subjects' interests as necessary conditions for correctness of practical statements.[231] Moreover, Alexy has proven that a communication structure is a necessary condition for the construction of correct practical statements. Alexy has shown this necessary condition without turning to the transcendental task of mutual understanding that has been attributed to our communicative practices.[232] Throwing out this transcendental task has led Alexy to introduce the Kantian distinction between motivation and moral obligation.[233] This distinction has allowed Alexy to define the subjects participating in the discourse practice on the basis of their cognitive abilities related to the possibility of making judgments and action. Consequently, Alexy has left the participating subjects free to perform behaviors directed towards mutual understanding.[234] This participating subjects' definition has led Alexy to complement the pragmatic level of justification of rationality principles with arguments aimed to show their universal practical validity on the basis of their motivating power.[235]

228 As noted above, the foundations of the rationality principles' content have to be found at the pragmatic level. As has been argued by Alexy, the content of these norms is universal because they seek equal rights for all participants in discourse (Robert Alexy, 'Eine diskurstheoretische Konzeption der praktischen Vernunft' (n. 20), 19.) Notwithstanding, the foundations of the rationality principles at the pragmatic level do not imply the merits of their claim to universal validity at the practical level. In other words, the validity of these norms at the pragmatic level gives us no grounds for their necessity regarding the evaluation and justification of every single statement aimed to govern our possible future courses of action (Robert Alexy, 'Eine diskurstheoretische Konzeption der praktischen Vernunft' (n. 20), 19.)

229 Robert Alexy, 'Menschenrechte ohne Metaphysik?' (n. 23), 20.

230 Robert Alexy, 'Discourse Theory and Human Rights' (n. 10), 209–233, at 211.

231 Robert Alexy, 'Problems of Discourse Theory' (n. 21), 43–65, at 58; Robert Alexy, 'Eine diskurstheoretische Konzeption der praktischen Vernunft' (n. 20), 17.

232 See above (n. 15)

233 Robert Alexy, 'Nachwort (1991): Antwort auf einige Kritiker' (n. 8), 399–435, at 407.

234 Peter Gril, *Die Möglichkeit praktischer Erkenntnis aus Sicht der Diskurstheorie* (n. 18), 140.

235 In this way, Alexy has pointed out: "Es wird sich gezeigt, daß zur Begründung der Geltung der Diskursregeln das transzendentalpragmatische Argument um Erwägungen ergänzt werden muß, die auf Interesse abstellen. Die Existenz dieser Interessen ist eine empirische Tatsache.

In order to demonstrate the universal practical validity of rationality principles, Alexy has introduced the distinction in the field of speech between a subjective validity – which rests upon motivations – and an objective validity[236] – which refers to external behavior.[237] Regarding the first one, Alexy has held the categorical validity of rationality principles.[238] In doing so, he has implicitly recognized that from the subjective practical point of view, a justification of the moral discourse goes beyond the limits of our possible knowledge.[239] Regarding the second one, Alexy's account has to assume that rationality principles are hypothetical in nature, due to the fact that Alexy's account attempts to demonstrate the universal validity of these norms based on their motivational power. Indeed, according to Alexy, from the first person point of view, compliance with the rationality principles rests upon the maximization of individual utility under the condition of the existence of a majority of subjects with interest in correctness.[240] Due to the nature of the motivations or interests that lead the subject to compliance with the rationality principles, Alexy has held that only empirical arguments are acceptable in order to show the universal validity of these norms at the objective practical level.[241] As is known, empirical arguments are necessarily defeasible.

Insofern handeln es sich nicht um eine rein transzendentalpragmatische Begründung. Das transzendentalpragmatische Argument spielt aber in der gesamten Begründung eine notwendige Rolle. Es kann daher von einer «schwachen transzendentalpragmatischen Begründung» gesprochen werden." (Robert Alexy, 'Nachwort (1991): Antwort auf einige Kritiker' (n. 8), 399–435, at 419–420.) In the same vein, see too Eric Hilgendorf, 'Zur traszendentalpragmatischen Begründung von Diskursregeln' (n. 12), 198; Armin Engländer, Zur begrifflichen Möglichkeit des Rechtspositivismus. Eine Kritik des Richtigkeitsarguments von Robert Alexy, *Rechtstheorie*, 28, 1997, 437–485, at 451. On the contrary, Atienza has stated that the practical level of justification plays a main role in Alexy's justification, rather than a mere complementary one. (See Manuel Atienza, *Las razones del derecho. Teorías de la argumentación jurídica* (n. 20), 190.)

236 Robert Alexy, 'Discourse Theory and Human Rights' (n. 10), 209–233, at 220.

237 According to Alexy the distinction between objective and subjective validity corresponds to the Kantian distinction between morality and legality (see Robert Alexy, 'Discourse Theory and Human Rights' (n. 10), 209–233, at 220 (n. 12). In this regard, Kant wrote: "Man nennt die bloße Übereinstimmung oder Nichtübereinstimmung einer Handlung mit dem Gesetz ohne Rücksicht auf die Triebfeder derselben die Legalität (Gesetzmäßigkeit), diejenige aber, in welcher die Idee der Pflicht aus dem Gesezt zugleich die Triebfeder der Handlug ist, die Moralität (Sittlichkeit) derselben." (Immanuel Kant, *Metaphysik der Sitten*, in *Kant's gesammelte Schriften. Herausgeben von der Königlich Preußischen Akademie der Wissenschaften*, vol. VI, Erste Abtheilung: Werke, Sechter Band (Berlin: Druck und Verlag von Georg Reimer, 1907), 219.

238 See above n. 132.

239 According to Kant: "[a]uch ist das moralische Gesetz gleichsam als ein Faktum der reinen Vernunft, dessen wir uns a priori bewußt sind und welches apodiktisch gewiß ist, gegeben, gesetzt, daß man auch in der Erfahrung kein Beispiel, da es genau befolgt wäre, auftreiben konnte. Also kann die objektive Realität des moralischen Gesetzes durch keine Deduktion, durch alle Anstrengung der theoretischen, spekulativen oder empirisch untersützten Vernunft, bewiesen und | also, wenn man auch auf die apodiktische Gewißheit Verzicht tun wollte, durch Erfahrung bestätigt und so a posteriori bewiesen werden, und steht dennoch für sich selbst fest." (Immanuel Kant, *Kritik der praktischen Vernunft*, <81>, <82>.)

240 Robert Alexy, 'Discourse Theory and Human Rights' (n. 10), 209–233, at 219–220.

241 Robert Alexy, 'Nachwort (1991): Antwort auf einige Kritiker' (n. 8), 399–435, at 420.

Based on the defeasible nature of these arguments, several strategies aimed at showing the fallible nature of the Alexyan justification have been undertaken.[242] Notwithstanding, if it is true that Alexy's arguments which support the utility of applying the rationality principles are defeasible, so are the arguments used by his critics.[243] In this way, it seems preferable to focus the discussion on other matters often forgotten. As noted above, Alexy has developed the description of an ideal discursive practice. This ideal discursive practice aims to justify practical statements on the basis of the universal consent of its participants, namely on the basis of a situation in which the consequences of the general observance of these statements "for the satisfaction of everyone's interest can be accepted by all."[244] This condition for correct practical statements has been termed principle of universalization or UA. The definition of this principle as a correctness criterion of the discursive practices distinguishes the rational discourse theory as a Kantian theory. Alexy undertakes the justification of the constitutive norms of the rational practical discourse by focusing on a privileged subset of these norms. These norms are targeted to ensure the impartiality of the discourse by means of the guarantee of freedom and equality of its participants.[245] These norms have the structure of principles,[246] and therefore, they require the optimal achievement of the ideal discourse.[247] In other words, the optimal achievement of these norms is a sufficient condition for reaching the aim of the ideal discursive practice which is defined by the principle of universalization.[248] Due to the fact that the rationality principles are sufficient conditions for achieving this aim, the categorical or hypothetical feature that is attributed to these norms will be also attributed to the principle of universalization.[249] In this vein, according to Alexy's account the principle of universalization has a double nature. Indeed, from the subjective practical point of view, this principle has a categorical validity – in

242 For a summary on the criticisms against the utilitarian empirical argument used by Alexy in order to justify the rationality principles see Carsten Bäcker, *Begründen und Entscheiden: Kritik und Rekonstruktion der Alexyschen Diskurstheorie des Rechts* (n. 24), 91–115.

243 See Carsten Bäcker, *Begründen und Entscheiden: Kritik und Rekonstruktion der Alexyschen Diskurstheorie des Rechts* (n. 24), 91–115.

244 Robert Alexy, 'Discourse Theory and Human Rights' (n. 10), 209–233, at 211.

245 Ibid. 211.

246 Carsten Bäcker, *Begründen und Entscheiden: Kritik und Rekonstruktion der Alexyschen Diskurstheorie des Rechts* (n. 24), 143–145.

247 Ibid. 131.

248 Robert Alexy, 'Discourse Theory and Human Rights' (n. 10), 209–233, at 211.

249 I should like to turn to Taylor's definition according to which we can say that a set of conditions is sufficient for the occurrence of an event, if every change of this set will affect its occurrence. Taylor wrote: "[W]e can simply assert that the cause, A, of an event, B, is that totality of conditions, from among all those, but only those, that occurred, each of which was necessary for the occurrence of B. Now if this set of conditions, A, is thus understood, as it should be, to include every condition, out of that totality that occurred, that was necessary for the occurrence of B, then we can say that the set of conditions, A, is also sufficient for B, since no other condition was necessary. We can, accordingly, understand the relationship between any set of conditions A, and any set B, expressed in the statement that A was the cause of B, to be simply described in this fashion: That A was the set, from among all those conditions that occurred, each of which was necessary, and the totality of which was sufficient, for the occurrence of B." (Richard Taylor, 'Causation', *The Monist. An International Quarterly of General Philosophical Inquiry*, vol. 47, no. 2, 1963, 287–313, at 298.)

accordance with Alexy's explicit recognition of the categorical validity of rationality principles. From the objective practical point of view this principle has a hypothetical validity – due to the hypothetical validity of rationality principles which underlies Alexy's justification. However, if the hypothetical nature of the principle of universalization is assumed, then this principle will no longer be necessary for achieving the good, but just for achieving the utility, and hence, the principle of universality will no longer be a moral norm in Kantian sense.[250] In this way, the rational discourse theory will lose its distinctiveness.[251]

Concluding Remarks

As we have seen, based on a Kantian distinction,[252] Alexy has defined the participating subjects in a discursive practice according to their cognitive abilities related to the possibility of making judgments and action. With regard to the first one, Alexy's theory assumes that the subjects are generally capable of distinguishing between good and bad reasons for substantive propositions.[253] This ability involves general requirements of rationality prior to the discursive practice. These requirements "include freedom from contradictions, universalisability in the sense of a consistent use of the predicates employed, linguistic-conceptual clearness, empirical truth,

250 In this vein, Kant wrote that: "[m]eine Absicht hier eigentlich auf die sittliche Weltweisheit gerichtet ist, so schränke ich die vorgelegte Frage nur darauf ein: ob man nicht meine, daß es von der äußersten Notwendigkeit sei, einmal eine reine Moralphilosophie zu bearbeiten, die von allem, was nur empirisch sein mag und zur Anthropologie gehört, völlig gesäubert wäre; denn daß es eine solche geben müsse, leuchtet von selbst aus der gemeinen Idee der Pflicht und der sittlichen Gesetze ein. Jedermann muß eingestehen, daß ein Gesetz, wenn es moralisch, d.i. als Grund einer Verbindlichkeit, gelten soll, absolute Notwendigkeit bei sich führen müsse; daß das Gebot: du sollst nicht lügen, nicht etwa bloß für Menschen gelte, andere vernünftige Wesen sich aber daran nicht zu kehren hätten; und so alle übrigen eigentlichen Sittengesetze; daß mithin der Grund der Verbindlichkeit hier nicht in der Natur des Menschen oder den Umständen in der Welt, darin er gesetzt ist, gesucht werden müsse, sondern *a priori* lediglich in Begriffen der reinen Vernunft, und daß jede andere Vorschrift, die sich auf Prinzipien der bloßen Erfahrung gründet, und sogar eine in gewissem Betracht allgemeine Vorschrift, sofern sie sich dem mindesten Teile, vielleicht nur einem Bewegungsgrunde nach, auf empirische Gründe stützt, zwar eine praktische Regel, niemals aber ein moralisches Gesetz heißen kann." (Immanuel Kant, *Grundlegung zur Metaphysik der Sitten* (Hamburg: Felix Meiner Verlag, 1999), 5.

251 This loss is due to adding hobbesian ideas to the rational discourse theory (this aim is explicitly pursued by Alexy in his *Nachwort*, see Robert Robert Alexy, 'Nachwort (1991): Antwort auf einige Kritiker' (n. 8), 399–435, at 425.) In this way, as stated by Hilgendorf: "Interessenerwägungen, insbesondere solche Hobberscher Provenienz, sind mit transzendentalphilosophischen Überlegungen in der Nachfolge Kants nicht vereinbar; sie bilden sogar deren geistesgeschichtlichen Gegenpol. Kant verstand seine transzendentalphilosophisch begründete Morallehre ausdrücklich als Gegenentwurf zu Hobbes und den Utilitaristen und lehnte jede 'bloß empirische' Beimischung zur Begründung einer Moral strikt ab. Man könnte deshalb meinen, Alexy habe sich mit seiner Erweiterung des transzendentalpragmatischen Letztbegründungsargumentes eines schweren ekklektischen Fehlgriffs schuldig gemacht." (Eric Hilgendorf, 'Zur traszendentalpragmatischen Begründung von Diskursregeln' (n. 12), 183–200, 197.)

252 Robert Alexy, 'Nachwort (1991): Antwort auf einige Kritiker' (n. 8), 399–435, at 407.

253 Robert Alexy, 'Problems of Discourse Theory' (n. 21), 43–65, at 56.

consideration of consequences, and weighing."[254] With regard to the second one, it is fair to argue that Alexyan theory assumes that the participating subjects in a discursive practice must be able to follow rules. This competence allows them, on the one hand, to apply the discourse norms, and on the other hand, to communicate with each other.

In response to the possibility of a monological justification of the practical statements proposed by Tugendhat,[255] Alexy has held that communication is a necessary condition for correctness.[256]

In turn, against Habermas,[257] Alexy has noted that the construction of practical statements does not aim at finding shared interests, but on the contrary, what should be the central focus of this construction is interpreting and balancing the discourse participants' interests. Nevertheless, by basing the construction of practical statements on interpreting and balancing the discourse participants' interests, Alexy has thrown out the universal task of our communicative practices.[258] In consequence, he has left the subjects free to perform behaviors directed towards mutual understanding.[259]

That is why the distinction between motivation and moral obligation takes on an essential meaning in Alexy's proposal. Furthermore, Alexy's justification strategy of constitutive discourse norms has been supported on this distinction. On the one hand, due to the fact that a communication structure is a necessary condition for the claim to rationality of the practical statements, the universal validity of discourse norms must be justified at the pragmatic level. On the other hand, due to the fact that the subjects are free to perform behaviors directed towards mutual understanding, the universal validity of discourse norms must be justified at the practical level.

Due to the need for a communication structure for practical statements correctness, and due to the restrictions of the justification method chosen by Alexy,[260] he undertakes the justification of the constitutive norms of the rational practical discourse by focusing on a privileged subset of these norms.[261] This privileged subset is composed of norms which, firstly, do not play any role in monological discourses, and secondly, are targeted to ensure the impartiality of the discourse by means of guarantee of freedom and equality of its participants.[262] These norms have the structure of principles.[263] Therefore, they require the optimal achievement of the ideal discourse, i. e. the optimal achievement of these norms is a sufficient condition for

254 Robert Alexy, 'Discourse Theory and Human Rights' (n. 10), 209–233, at 211.

255 See above n. 62.

256 See above n. 63.

257 See *i. a.* Jürgen Habermas, 'Diskursethik-Notizen zu einem Begründungsprogramm' (n. 4), 52–125, at 83 (at n. 27).

258 See above n. 15.

259 Peter Gril, *Die Möglichkeit praktischer Erkenntnis aus Sicht der Diskurstheorie* (n. 18), 140.

260 Robert Alexy, *Theorie der juristischen Argumentation. Die Theorie des rationalen Diskurses als Theorie der juristischen Begründung* (n. 3), 232.

261 Robert Alexy, 'Nachwort (1991): Antwort auf einige Kritiker' (n. 8), 399–435, at 418.

262 Robert Alexy, 'Discourse Theory and Human Rights' (n. 10), 209–233, at 211; Robert Alexy, 'Nachwort (1991): Antwort auf einige Kritiker' (n. 8), 399–435, at 418.

263 Carsten Bäcker, *Begründen und Entscheiden: Kritik und Rekonstruktion der Alexyschen Diskurstheorie des Rechts* (n. 24), 143–145.

reaching the aim of the ideal discursive practice which is defined by the principle of universalization.[264]

In order to justify rationality principles at the pragmatic level, Alexy uses a variant of the transcendental argument.[265]

A transcendental argument can be defined by virtue of its aim rather than by virtue of its form. Nevertheless, a transcendental argument so defined, when used in order to justify practical discourse, raises it at the level of a theory of rationality. In consequence, based on a transcendental argument so defined are imposed practical requirements on the pragmatic level, by interpreting the weak coercion in which this level lies in a strong moral sense.[266]

Another possibility arises, when the most ambitious ontological claim of transcendental arguments is abandoned. This possibility leads one to define transcendental arguments by emphasizing their form.[267] However, this emphasis should not lead to the removal of all ontological claims, in a way that could be possible to define transcendental arguments only by virtue of their structure. Such a way of defining trivializes this kind of argument.[268] However, claiming that transcendental arguments maintain a certain ontological claim implies the assertion that transcendental arguments are targeted to make explicit the conditions of what is assumed as true.

The transcendental argument used by Alexy for the justification of the discourse constitutive norms at the pragmatic level assumes the claim to contest that postmodern or communitarian skeptic who not only raises doubts about the possibility of rationality principles, but instead is willing to accept that assertion[269] is necessary in an existential sense from the participant's point of view.[270] Nevertheless, as a result of the empirical foundations of this argument in the Alexyan justification, the skeptic should accept it solely on the grounds of its plausibility. An argument so described does not seem strong enough to sustain the ontological claim required for making explicit the constitutive norms of our discursive practices.

Nevertheless, this statement about the weakness of the starting point of the Alexyan justification strategy would be demonstrable, only if it could be possible to replace it for a stronger argument that meets at least two kinds of requirements. First, from a general point of view – i. e. concerning the task of any transcendental argument – this new starting point would be acceptable, if the skeptic must accept it as true rather than as merely plausible. Second, from the particular point of view – i. e. referring to Alexy's theory – this argument would be acceptable, if it were compatible with an institutional theory of assertion given that such a theory is assumed by Alexy's attempt.

Such an argument is offered by Brandom's normative inferentialist theory of meaning. From the normative inferentialist point of view, assertion is necessary for

264 Robert Alexy, 'Discourse Theory and Human Rights' (n. 10), 209–233, at 211–212.

265 Robert Alexy, 'Nachwort (1991): Antwort auf einige Kritiker' (n. 8), 399–435, at 418.

266 See above n. 120.

267 Barry Stroud, 'Kantian Argument, Conceptual Capacities, and Invulnerability' (n. 122), 231–251, at 241.

268 Barry Stroud, 'The Goal of Transcendental Arguments' (n. 115), 155–172, at 158.

269 Robert Alexy, 'Discourse Theory and Human Rights' (n. 10), 209–233, at 214.

270 Ibid. 217.

determining the meaning, and therefore, for communication. In this vein, abandoning this practice means waiving a behavior we consider characteristically human.[271]

However, while a certain deontic dynamic system is shown by Alexy in order to justify the underlying static deontic system – or better said, a system of immunities – expressed by the rationality principles, and while Alexy has somehow highlighted the relation between the ideal discursive practice described by him and the game of giving and asking for reasons described by Brandom,[272] Alexy's theory does not seem willing to accept the consequences that draw from an inferentialist normative interpretation of the institutional feature of assertion. This fact has led Alexy to overlook the epistemic privileged feature that assertion shows according to a general theory of meaning. By overlooking this privileged feature of assertion, Alexy has turned to an empirical argument for the justification of the transcendental-pragmatic argument's starting point.

In order to complement the universal validity justification of rationality principles at the practical level, Alexy has introduced a Kantian distinction in the field of speech between subjective and objective validity.[273] Regarding the first one, Alexy has held the categorical validity of rationality principles.[274] Regarding the second one, since Alexy's account attempts to demonstrate the universal validity of these priniciples based on their motivational power, Alexy's account has assumed by implication that rationality principles are hypothetical in nature. Given that the validity of rationality principles is a sufficient condition for validity of the principle of universalization, the hypothetical validity of rationality principles turns the principle of universalization into a matter of interest, i. e. into a non-moral rule in Kantian sense.

271 John R. Searle, *Speech Acts. An Essay in the Philosophy of Language* (n. 42), 186 (at n. 1).
272 See Robert Alexy, 'Menschenrechte ohne Metaphysik?' (n. 23), 20.
273 Robert Alexy, 'Discourse Theory and Human Rights' (n. 10), 209–233, at 220.
274 Ibid. 218.

Alexandre Travessoni Gomes Trivisonno*

Discretion and the "Problem of Practical Knowledge" in Ideal and Real Discourses

Introduction

In the essay "Law, Discourse and Time", published in 1995, Alexy poses the question of whether it is possible to find a single solution to every practical, and therefore to every legal question, and he terms this question as "the problem of practical knowledge".[1] This question is especially relevant when one handles legal application, for if the law does not determine one single answer to every legal question, the one who applies it has discretion to create a new legal obligation, that is to say, an obligation that did not exist before his decision.[2]

In this paper I will inquire into Alexy's theory on the problem of practical knowledge, and try to present further developments of this theory. To set the stage I should first place Alexy's Discursive Theory among other modern theories that have taken up legal application. This is done in part one, where I identify and explain four different models of legal application. This classification will provide a first glance into the features of Alexy's theory that are important for my reasoning.

After that, in part two, I will handle the problem of practical knowledge and its relation to the application of law in the early works of Alexy. Alexy has always connected the concept of correction with the concept of discourse, and although he suggests that correction would have different features in the ideal and in real discourses, he has never analytically explored this division of the connection between correction and discourse. I want to distinguish analytically the relation that correction has with the ideal discourse and the relation it has with real discourses or, in other words, I want to radicalize the distinction between these two kinds of connection. This methodological radicalization, which, as shall be seen, has didactic purposes, will be suggested in part two, but executed in part three, where, on the basis of Principles Theory, I investigate whether, in the ideal discourse, there would be one single solution to every legal question. The main argument in this section will be that while in the ideal discourse there would be one single solution to every question in which a single solution is possible, on real discourses that is not the case. On the basis of Alexy's Weight Formula, which I consider the "Real Weight Formula", I will develop a Weight Formula for the ideal discourse, which I will term "The Ideal Weight Formula". I will also develop, still in section three, an investiga-

* Special thanks to Robert Alexy, for his hospitality in Kiel as well as for his very valuable comments and critics, to Stanley L. Paulson and to the Alexander von Humboldt Foundation, for funding a research stay in Kiel, whose results are partially published here.

1 Robert Alexy, 'Law, Discourse and Time', *Archiv für Rechts- und Sozialphilosophie*, 64 (1995), 101–110, at 108 f. See also R. Alexy, 'Problems of discourse theory', *Crítica*, 20 (1988), 43–65, at 49. For a critical analysis of Alexy's Discourse Theory see Carsten Bäcker, 'Recht als institutionalisierte Vernunft?', *Archiv für Rechts und Sozialphilosophie* 97 (3) (2011), 346–359.

2 Ronald Dworkin, 'The Model of Rules I', in R. Dworkin, *Taking Rights Seriously* (Cambridge/Ma.: Harvard University Press, 1977), 14–45, at 31 ff.

tion about the possibility and the role of infinitesimal scales in both the ideal and real discourses.

Alexy has been working, in the recent past, on a revision of his Principles Theory, especially because of the problems related to the role of formal principles. Recently he has revised his Weight Formula by presenting a new version, which he termed the "Refined Complete Weight Formula". In section four I will analyse the (possible) reflections of Alexy's new position and new formula on my argument.

In section five I reach the core of my argument: I connect the conclusions that I have developed up to and including section four with Kelsen's quantitative distinction between legislation and jurisdiction. My thesis is that, on the one hand, Alexy's distinction between legislation and adjudication comprehends, as in Kelsen, a quantitative distinction, but also that, on the other hand, it comprehends a qualitative distinction, which is not present in Kelsen's writings. In other words, my thesis says that while, in Kelsen's work, the distinction between legislation and adjudication and therefore between legislative discretion and judicial discretion is only quantitative, in Alexy it is both quantitative and qualitative.

In the end I attempt, as a conclusion, briefly to formulate the results of the previous analysis.

Part One: Four Models of Legal Application

The problem of practical knowledge has been at the centre of legal theory, at least since Kant. Since the way one handles it turns on one's conception of legal application, it is worth identifying the main models of legal application that were developed in modern legal theory. Carsten Bäcker has identified three models of legal application: Kelsen's discretion model, Dworkin's cognition model and Alexy's argumentation model.[3] I will develop Bäcker's classification by adding one more model to it so that, in the end, there are four models, and by adding one more author (Hart) to his discretion model.

The first model, which is not present in Bäcker's classification, is the Kantian model, according to which duties of right are strict, provide "mathematic precision",[4] and thus leave no room for discretion in their application. Following the classification of perfect and imperfect duties, which, according to Kant himself, was typical in his day,[5] he considers duties of right as perfect duties.[6] Because of that I will term the kantian model the "perfection model".

The second model is the positivist model of Kelsen and Hart. Kelsen and Hart diagnosed the same characteristic of legal application: legal norms (Kelsen) or legal

3 Carsten. Bäcker, *Begründen und Entscheiden: Kritik und Rekonstruktion der Alexyschen Diskurstheorie des Rechts*, (Baden-Baden: Nomos, 2007), 25–40.

4 I. Kant, 'The Metaphysics of Morals', in I. Kant, *The Cambridge edition of the works of Immanuel Kant – Practical Philosophy*, trans. and ed. by Mary J. Gregor (Cambridge: Cambridge University Press, 1996), 353–604, at 411.

5 I. Kant, 'Groundwork of the Metaphysics of Morals', in I. Kant, *The Cambridge edition of the works of Immanuel Kant – Practical Philosophy*, trans. and ed. by Mary J. Gregor (Cambridge: Cambridge University Press, 1996), 37–108, at 421.

6 I. Kant, 'Groundwork of the Metaphysics of Morals' (n. 6), 390 ff.

rules (Hart), due to their generality, provide not only one but rather a number of different solutions to every legal question. Kelsen handled this topic in his early works,[7] as well as in the eighth chapter of the second edition of his "Pure Theory of Law": due to generality, there is a relative indetermination when a legal norm is produced from a superior norm.[8] This means that the superior norm partially determines the content of the inferior norm, but also that the content is partially undetermined. In his "Concept of Law", Hart diagnoses the same phenomenon, but uses the term "open texture of law" to describe it.[9] The essential feature, common to Kelsen and Hart, is that the law provides different solutions to legal questions, and the one who applies the law has discretion. In opposition to Kant's model I will term this model the "imperfection model".

The third model is Dworkin's: there is only one single solution to every legal question.[10] Yet the single solution is not provided, as in Kant, by the mere application of legislation, which is already mathematically perfect. The *prima facie* indetermination of law is recognized, but the single solution would stem from the application procedure. Since perfection here comes from legal application, I will term this model the "model of the perfect application".

The fourth model is Alexy's. It shares with Dworkin's model the rejection of both the kantian and the positivist models. It has another point in common with Dworkin's model: the solution of a legal question should not stem from legislation alone, but from legal reasoning, which, of course, includes authoritative material, but is not limited to it.[11] In short, in Alexy's terms, the solution of a legal question comes from legal argumentation. But, unlike Dworkin's model, Alexy's does not claim that only one solution to every legal question exists. As we are going to see, it asserts that even in the ideal discourse, it is questionable whether there is only one solution to every legal question, and it considers the idea of one right answer a regulative idea, that is to say, something that should be pursued, but that cannot, at least not in all cases, be achieved.[12] I will term this model the "model of the relatively perfect application".

Part Two: The Problem of Practical Knowledge and its Relation to Judicial Discretion in the Early Works of Alexy

In order to understand Alexy's thesis on the problem of practical knowledge it is essential to recall that in his "Theory of Legal Argumentation", first published in German in 1978, he adopts Habermas's ideal speech situation,[13] which is a metho-

7 See, for instance, Kelsen, 'Zur Theorie der Rechtsfiktionen', *Annalen der Philosophie*, 1 (1919), 630–558.

8 H. Kelsen, *Reine Rechtslehre*, 2. Auflage (Wien: Verlag Österreich, 1960), 346 ff.

9 H. L. A. Hart, *The concept of law*, 2nd ed. (Oxford: Clarendon Press, 1992), 123 ff.

10 See R. Dworkin, *Taking rights seriously* (n. 2); R. Dworkin, *Law's empire* (Cambridge/Ma.: Harvard University Press, 1986).

11 R. Alexy, *Theorie der juristischen Argumentation* (Frankfurt a. M.: Suhrkamp, 1978 [Neudruck 1983; 3. Auflage 1996]), 259 ff. See also R. Alexy, *Begriff und Geltung des Rechts*, (Freiburg/München: Alber, 1992), 201 ff.

12 R. Alexy, *Theorie der juristischen Argumentation* (n. 11), Nachwort, 413–414.

13 R. Alexy, *Theorie der juristischen Argumentation* (n. 11), 19–197.

dologically constructed speech situation characterized by five idealizations: unlimited time, unlimited participation, unlimited conceptual-linguistic clarity, unlimited knowledge and absolute absence of prejudices.[14] Under these ideal conditions that, as contra-factual features, can never be fully obtained in real discourses, would it be possible to find a single solution to every legal question? In 1987, in the essay "Diskurstheorie und Rechtssystem",[15] Alexy expressly handled the problem of practical knowledge, saying that "it can remain open, whether under a complete idealization, there is exactly one right answer to every question. (...) It is important the fact that it is possible to construct, near an ideal concept of practical correction, a real and relative concept".[16] According to Alexy, defending the idea that there is a single answer to every practical question means connecting the concept of procedure with the concept of an absolute correction. Alexy then adopts a model which also connects correction and procedure, but in which the concept of correction is relative, because it depends on the real discourse, and in which the concept of absolute correction is a regulative idea.[17]

These ideas about the problem of practical knowledge, which appeared between 1978 and 1995, were consolidated in the "Postscript" of the second German edition of the "Theory of Legal Argumentation", published in 1991, where Alexy asserts that from the fulfilment of the requirements of the ideal discourse it does not logically follow that in the ideal discourse there is only one answer to every legal question. He also asserts that the right answer thesis is a strong assumption that has more disadvantages than advantages. Yet, he accepts its role as a regulative idea, that is to say, as something that in fact does not exist but has the character of something that should be pursued.[18]

After that, in the already mentioned essay "Law, Discourse and Time" (1995), Alexy reaffirms that even under the conditions of the ideal discourse, one cannot be sure that one single answer for every practical question could be found.[19]

It is time for a synthesis of what Alexy's early works say about the problem of practical knowledge. It is clear that, for Alexy, it is not possible to find, in real discourses, one single solution for every legal question. This is due to the fact that in real discourses, because of limitations of time and participation, it is not possible to determine whether every solution is discursively necessary or discursively impossible. There are cases in which both solutions S and $\neg S$ are discursively possible, for the concept of correction is relative. Adopting the right answer thesis would mean, as we have seen, disconnecting correction and procedure, at least partially, because it would assume that there is only one right answer to every legal question without, however, providing a procedure to obtain it.

What about the ideal discourse? What is Alexy's position on the possibility of one single answer for every practical question in it? In my view, it is not clear

14 R. Alexy, *Theorie der juristischen Argumentation* (n. 11), 19–197.

15 First published in Croatian, 'Teorija diskursa i pravni sistem', *Filozofska istrazivanja* 20 (1987), 185–194 (translation by Maja Uzelac), and then in German, 'Diskurstheorie und Rechtssystem', *Synthesis philosophica* 5 (1988), 299–310.

16 R. Alexy, 'Diskurstheorie und Rechtssystem' (n. 15), 304–305.

17 R. Alexy, 'Diskurstheorie und Rechtssystem' (n. 15), 304–305.

18 R. Alexy, *Theorie der juristischen Argumentation* (n. 11), Nachwort, 413–414.

19 R. Alexy, 'Law, Discourse and Time' (n. 1), 108.

whether in Alexy's early works there is, in the ideal discourse, a single solution to every legal question. As we have seen, on the one hand Alexy affirms that a complete idealization does not logically guarantee a single solution. This might suggest that he believes it to be impossible, in ideal discourses, to find a single solution to every legal question. But, as we have also seen, on the other hand, he also says that it can remain open whether there is, in the ideal discourse, a single solution to every legal question. Thus, we can conclude that the position Alexy presented in his early works is the following: he leaves open the question of whether there would be, in the ideal discourse, a single solution to every legal question, and affirms that the idea of a single answer should remain a regulative idea. Before I move to the following section, in which the problem of practical knowledge will be connected to Principles Theory, I should emphasize that although Alexy is concerned, in his early works, with the question of whether there is a single solution to every legal question when the law is applied. In other words, he is concerned with the question of whether judicial discretion exists or not. And this is so because Alexy's first book, "A Theory of Legal Argumentation", is dedicated to legal application and has in its centre the figure of the judge.[20]

Part Three: The Problem of Practical Knowledge, The Principle's Theory, The Real and The "Ideal Weight Formula"

I want to use the Principle's Theory,[21] particularly in the form in which it is presented in the Weight Formula, to inquire into how the problem of practical knowledge can be solved.

Although Alexy has taken up the structure of balancing in many of his previous works,[22] it was only in 2003 that he developed, in the essay "Die Gewichtsformel"[23] (The Weight Formula), a formula to represent this structure. The abstract weights of the colliding principles, the degree of interference in one principle and the impor-

20 R. Alexy, *Theorie der juristischen Argumentation* (n. 11).

21 The first sketch of Alexy's Principles Theory appeared in the essay "Zum Begriff des Rechtsprinzips" (On The Concept of Legal Principles) (see R. Alexy, 'Zum Begriff des Rechtsprinzips', *Rechtstheorie* 1 [1979], 59–87), and was later developed in his "Theory of Constitutional Rights" (see. R. Alexy, *Theorie der Grundrecht* [Baden-Baden: Nomos, 1985; Neudr. Frankfurt a.M.: Suhrkamp, 1986]). After that, Alexy's Principles Theory has become internationally renowned, received many critics in Germany and worldwide, been subject to various developments and exerted a great influence in legal theory as well as in legal practice worldwide.

22 Besides the works just mentioned in the previous note, it is worth also mentioning the following ones: Robert Alexy, 'Die logische Analyse juristischer Entscheidungen', *Archiv für Rechts- und Sozialphilosophie* 14 (1980), 181–212; Robert Alexy, 'Rechtsregeln und Rechtsprinzipien', *Archiv für Rechts und Sozialphilosophie* 25 (1985), 13–29; Robert Alexy, 'Grundrechte im demokratischen Verfassungsstaat', in *Justice, Morality and Society. Festschrift für Aleksander Peczenik*, ed. by A. Aarnio, R. Alexy and G. Bergholtz, (Lund: Juristförlaget i Lund, 1997), 27–42; R. Alexy, 'Zur Struktur der Rechtsprinzipien', in *Regeln, Prinzipien und Elemente im System des Rechts*, ed. by B. Schilcher, P. Koller and B.-C. Funk (Wien: Verlag Österreich, 2000), 31–52; R. Alexy, Postscript, *A Theory of Constitutional Rights*, trans. By Julian Rivers (Oxford: Oxford University Press, 2002), 388–425.

23 Robert Alexy, 'Die Gewichtsformel', in *Gedächtnisschrift für Jürgen Sonnenschein*, ed. by J. Jickeli, P. Kreutz and D. Reuter (Berlin: De Gruyter, 2003), 771–792.

tance of the fulfilment of the other principle, as well as the reliability of the empirical assumptions related to both principles should be weighted through this formula, which says:[24]

$$W_{i,j} = \frac{W_i \cdot I_i \cdot R_i}{W_j \cdot I_j \cdot R_j}$$

$W_{i,j}$ stands for the concrete weight of P_i, that is to say, the concrete weight of the principle P_i when it collides, in a concrete case, with P_j. W_i stands for the abstract weight of the principle P_i, I_i stand for the intensity of the interference in the principle P_i, and R_i stands for the reliability of the empirical assumptions related to P_i. W_j stands for the abstract weight of the principle P_j, I_j stands for the importance of the fulfilment of the principle P_j, and R_j stands for the reliability of the empirical assumptions related to P_j.[25]

The formula, which is formal, demands content, that is to say, values for the abstract weights of both principles, for the degrees of both the interference in one principle and the importance of the fulfilment of the other principle, as well as for the reliability of the empirical assumptions related to both principles. Alexy developed a triadic scale (which can be developed into a double triadic scale) to fulfil the variables of the Weight Formula: light, medium and serious,[26] which are represented by 2^0, 2^1 and 2^2, that is to say, 1, 2 and 4,[27] and, in the case of the reliability of the empirical assumptions, by 2^0, 2^{-1} e 2^{-2}, that is to say, 1, $\frac{1}{2}$, and $\frac{1}{4}$.[28] In a concrete case, after applying these values, if the result is greater than 1, then P_i should prevail, if the result is lesser than 1, then P_j should prevail, and if the result is equal to 1, the result would be a stalemate.[29]

According to Alexy, the possibility of an infinitesimal scale is excluded, for an infinitesimal scale cannot be understood.[30]

What is the impact of the Weight Formula in the problem of practical knowledge? The answer to this question is related to the role of scales in practical reasoning, and therefore in law.

24 R. Alexy, 'Die Gewichtsformel' (n. 23), 790.

25 R. Alexy, 'Die Gewichtsformel' (n. 23), 788 f. In the original German formulation, *G* (*Gewicht*) stands for the weight of the principles, *I* (*Intensität*) stands for the intensity of both the violation of one principle and the importance of the fulfilment of the other principle, and *S* (*Sicherheit*) stands for the reliability of the empirical premises. Thus, in the original German text the formula says:

$$G_{i,j} = \frac{G_i \cdot I_i \cdot S_i}{G_j \cdot I_j \cdot S_j}$$

26 R. Alexy, 'Die Gewichtsformel' (n. 23), 15.

27 R. Alexy, 'Die Gewichtsformel' (n. 23), 21.

28 R. Alexy, 'Die Gewichtsformel' (n. 23), 25. Although the triadic scale can be, according to Alexy, developed to a double triadic scale, for the sake of simplification it will be used here the triadic scale.

29 R. Alexy, 'Die Gewichtsformel' (n. 23), 25–26.

30 R. Alexy, 'Die Gewichtsformel' (n. 23), p. 25.

In order to investigate whether Alexy is correct in sustaining that an infinitesimal scale is not possible, I want to suggest analysing the possibility of its existence in connection with the duality ideal-real discourses.

I want to defend the idea that an infinitesimal scale is not possible in real discourses, but that it is possible in the ideal discourse. The reason why an infinitesimal scale is not possible in real discourses is that it would not be intelligible. In my view, those who defend a single solution to every legal question would have to defend the possibility of an infinitesimal scale in real discourses. It is hard to accept such a possibility. Yet, in my view, in the ideal discourse, because of the complete fulfilment of the five idealizations adumbrated by Alexy in his early works, the development of an infinitesimal scale for measuring the degree of interference in one principle and the importance of the fulfilment of the other principle, as well as the abstract weights of both principles, would not only be possible, but would also be a fact. The possibility of an infinitesimal scale in the ideal discourse will be, from now on, assumed. Its justification will be presented below.

If an infinitesimal scale is possible in the ideal discourse, the variable that stands for the empirical assumptions can be excluded from the Weight Formula. This is so because, in the ideal discourse, due to complete knowledge, this reliability would be maximal on both sides of the colliding principles. Thus, I can present the Weight Formula of the ideal discourse or, in other words, the "Ideal Weight Formula", which says:

$$W_{i,j} = \frac{W_i \cdot I_i}{W_j \cdot I_j}$$

Now, since an infinitesimal scale would be possible in the ideal discourse, in the ideal discourse one would also be able to measure precisely the interference in one principle and the importance of the fulfilment of the other principle, as well as the abstract weights of both principles. I want to defend that, because of this precision, a single solution to every legal question would be possible in the ideal discourse. This thesis has to be explained.

If, in the ideal discourse, it is possible for an infinitesimal scale to measure precisely the abstract weights of legal principles, as well as the degree of interference in one principle and the importance of the fulfilment of the other principle, then many cases in which in real discourses the result is a stalemate, that is to say, the result is not only one single answer, would have, in the ideal discourse, one single answer. Imagine that, in a real discourse, two principles, P_1 and P_2, have the same weight, and that both the interference in one principle and the importance of the fulfilment of the other principle are medium. Leaving aside the reliability of the empirical assumptions, the multiplication of the abstract weight of P_1 by the degree of interference in P_1 divided by the multiplication of the abstract weight of P_2 by the degree of importance of the fulfilment of P_2 would be 1, that is to say, there would a stalemate:[31]

31 The fact that I am not using the Complete Weight Formula, which has, besides the variables that I am applying, a variable for the reliability of the empiric assumptions, does not mean that I am suggesting that the Weight Formula of the real discourse, that is to say, the "Real Weight

$$W_{i,j} = \frac{W_i \cdot I_i}{W_j \cdot I_j} \qquad W_{i,j} = \frac{2 \cdot 2}{2 \cdot 2} = 1$$

Imagine now that this situation is analysed in the ideal discourse, and due to complete knowledge, which expresses itself through the infinitesimal scale, it is discovered that although both principles have the same weight, the result is not one, for the interference in P_1, say 2,1, is not as great as the importance of the fulfilment of P_2 say 2,2. The result, which in the real discourse would be a stalemate, providing two discursively possible answers, yields in the ideal discourse only one, namely, that of giving priority to P_2:

$$W_{i,j} = \frac{W_i \cdot I_i}{W_j \cdot I_j} \qquad W_{i,j} = \frac{2 \cdot 2{,}1}{2 \cdot 2{,}2} \qquad W_{i,j} = 0{,}954\ldots$$

One could say that, even in the ideal discourse, the possibility of a stalemate is not excluded. Indeed, even in the ideal discourse a stalemate seems to be possible. Two situations should be distinguished. The first one is the case in which the abstract weights of the colliding principles are equal and the degree of interference in one principle is equal to the importance of the fulfilment of the other principle. There would be, in such case, a stalemate:

$$W_{i,j} = \frac{W_i \cdot I_i}{W_j \cdot I_j} \quad W_{i,j} = \frac{2{,}1 \cdot 3{,}1}{2{,}1 \cdot 3{,}1} = \quad W_{i,j} = \frac{6{,}51}{6{,}51} \qquad W_{i,j} = 1$$

The second case is the one in which the abstract weights of the colliding principles are different, the degree of interference in one principle is also different from the importance of the fulfilment of the other principle, but the result of the multiplication of the abstract weight of one principle by the degree of interference in this principle is equal to the result of the multiplication of the abstract weight of the other principle by the importance of the fulfilment of this other principle, that is to say, the numerator and the denominator of the Weight Formula are equal:

$$W_{i,j} = \frac{W_i \cdot I_i}{W_j \cdot I_j} \quad W_{i,j} = \frac{1{,}1 \cdot 2{,}8}{2{,}0 \cdot 1{,}54} = \quad W_{i,j} = \frac{3{,}08}{3{,}08} \qquad W_{i,j} = 1$$

If, on the one hand, the Weight Formula and an infinitesimal scale show that the ideal discourse does not exclude a stalemate, they show, on the other hand, that this stalemate would not be the result of a "problem of knowledge", that is to say, would not be a stalemate due to lack of knowledge, but rather an ontological or a deontological stalemate. Because of that, it can be said that, in the ideal discourse, a solution would be found for every question to which there is a solution. How the cases

Formula", has only two variables. I am dismissing the variable R also in the real discourse, that is to say, I am considering the reliability of the empirical assumptions regarding both principles equal in the real discourse, only for the sake of simplification.

in which there is a stalemate in the ideal discourse should be resolved would then be a logical or a deontological problem, not a "problem of knowledge".[32]

Therefore, when I say that in the ideal discourse one right answer for every question could be found, I mean that one right answer could be found for every question to which there is one single answer. As we have seen, this thesis depends on the possibility, in the ideal discourse, of an infinitesimal scale, which was assumed, but not justified. Now it is time to provide such a justification.

The definition of the ideal discourse itself means that the scale in the ideal discourse is more precise or refined than the scale in real discourses. As we have seen, Alexy defines the ideal discourse through five idealizations: unlimited time; unlimited participation; unlimited conceptual-linguistic clarity; unlimited knowledge and absolute absence of prejudices.[33] In real discourses, on the other hand, time, participation, conceptual and linguistic clarity and knowledge are limited, and prejudices are evident. This is sufficient to prove that, in the ideal discourse, one knows more than in real discourses. And if that is true, in the ideal discourse one can perceive things that are not perceived in real discourses. The form by which this greater possibility of perceiving things is represented in the Weight Formula is a more refined scale. Two things that are considered equal in a real discourse must be represented in the Weight Formula by equal values, for example, 2. But it may well be the case that these two things that are considered equal in a real discourse are different in the ideal discourse, exactly because in the ideal discourse one can perceive things that in the real discourse cannot be perceived. Thus, two things that are considered equal in a real discourse, being represented by the same values in the Real Weight Formula, (for example 2), can be considered different in the ideal discourse, being therefore represented in the Ideal Weight Formula by different values, such as, for example, 1,9 and 2,1.

One could agree with the fact that, in the ideal discourse, one can know more than in real discourses, but nevertheless challenge that this guarantees that, in the ideal discourse, one can know everything that is possible to know. One could defend, for instance, the idea that in the ideal discourse a more refined scale is possible than the triadic scale or the double-triadic scale of real discourses, but it is not possible to arrive at an infinitesimal scale. The reason for this would be that the ideal discourse is a discourse developed by human beings, and human beings, even under the conditions of the ideal discourse, that is to say, even under the five idealizations mentioned by Alexy, do not possess the capacity to understand very small differences between two violations of constitutional rights, such as, for example, violations whose values were 2,801123456 and 2,801123457. If this reasoning were correct, in fact an infinitesimal scale would not necessarily exist in the ideal discourse. But, I should argue, this objection cannot stand.

Not only a more refined scale than the triadic or double-triadic scale is possible in the ideal discourse. Rather, an infinitesimal scale is possible in it. The unlimited time, participation, conceptual-linguistic clarity and knowledge, together with the absolute absence of prejudices, which are the characteristics of the ideal discourse, guarantee the possibility of an infinitesimal scale. And this is so because the ideal

32 I will refer to these cases below.

33 R. Alexy, *Theorie der juristischen Argumentation* (n. 11), 19–197.

discourse is, by definition, the one in which knowledge is *unlimited*. Now, if knowledge is *unlimited*, every difference that exists between two things can be perceived. If every difference can be perceived, is must be possible to express this difference somehow in the scale. It seems to me that the only scale that is capable of expressing the possibility of an unlimited knowledge is the infinitesimal scale. To which extent this feature of the ideal discourse is coherent with the properties of human intelligence or supposes an abstract intelligence is a question that can remain open here. What is important here is that the idea of an infinitesimal scale is *not only* coherent with the assumption of unlimited knowledge, which is an essential feature of the definition of the ideal discourse, but *rather* it is, in my view, by definition, the kind of scale of the ideal discourse, in the way it is conceived here. Thus, if I am right, in the ideal discourse one would be able to perceive a *very small*, *tiny* difference between the violation of one principle and the importance of the fulfilment of the other principle, whose values could be, for instance, the already mentioned values of 2,80112345**6** and 2,80112345**7**.

Part Four: Alexy's New "Refined Complete Weight Formula" and The Problem of Practical Knowledge

In his recent essay "Princípios Formais"[34] (Formal Principles), first published in Portuguese, Alexy has reformulated his Weight Formula. The reason he did so, he reports, is that in the original formula, presented in the already mentioned essay "Die Gewichtsformel", the variable *R* (in German *S*) had to do with the reliability only of the empirical assumptions. On the one hand, Alexy emphasizes that he had already noticed, in some of his previous works, such as, for example, the "Postscript" of the English edition of "A Theory of Constitutional Rights", "the systematic importance of the distinction between empirical epistemic discretion and normative epistemic discretion."[35] Yet, on the other hand, he recognizes that the Weight Formula did not make this distinction clearly. According to Alexy, the variable *R* must be understood as referring to both normative and empirical premises, and this can be expressed through the following equation, which he terms the reliability equation:[36]

$$R = R^e \cdot R^n$$

34 This article was originally presented as a conference at the "Congresso-Brasil Alemanha de Teoria do Direito e Direito Constitucional: Conceito e Aplicação do Direito em Robert Alexy", which took place at the Law Scholl of the *Universidade Federal de Minas Gerais-UFMG*, in Belo Horizonte-Brazil, on February 12th 2014. The first publication of *Princípios Formais* appeared, in Portuguese, in the book containing the conferences that were held at the Congress, under the title *Princípios Formais* (see Robert. Alexy, 'Princípios Formais', *Princípios Formais e Outros Aspectos da Teoria Discursiva do Direito*, trans. By A. T. G. Trivisonno, ed. by A. T. G. Trivisonno, A. T. Saliba and M. S. Lopes [Rio de Janeiro: Forense Universitária, 2014]). The publication of the English version is already foreseen, but was not yet released at the time this essay was finished.

35 R. Alexy, 'Princípios Formais' (n. 34), 19; see also R. Alexy, *Theorie der Grundrechte* (n. 21), 414–425.

36 R. Alexy, 'Princípios Formais' (n. 34), 10.

Thus, the new Weight Formula, which Alexy terms the "Refined Complete Weight Formula", says:[37]

$$W_{i,j} = \frac{I_i \cdot W_i \cdot R_i^e \cdot R_i^n}{I_j \cdot W_j \cdot R_j^e \cdot R_j^n}$$

After introducing the new formula, Alexy investigates the repercussions of its refinement for the question of legislative discretion, as well as for the role that formal principles, especially the principle of democracy – democratically legitimated legislature, play when constitutional rights are balanced. In short, Alexy's argument says that the unreliability both of empirical as of normative premises must be taken into consideration. The more reliable the empirical and normative assumptions regarding the violation of a constitutional right are, the greater the justification of intervention by a constitutional court. The less reliable they are, the greater the justification of leaving the decision in the hands of the legislator, providing him with discretion to decide the question. According to Alexy, this does not mean that the variable R is a formal principle, but only that it can generate discretion. And when this occurs, formal principles, such as the principle of the democracy, come into consideration.[38]

What are the repercussions of the "Refined Complete Weight Formula" on the question that I handle here, that is to say, on the "problem of the practical knowledge" ?

In order to answer this question I will begin approaching the repercussions of the "Refined Complete Weight Formula" for the relation between the "problem of the practical knowledge" and the duality ideal-real discourses. Then I will investigate the repercussions of the new formula for the relation between the "problem of practical knowledge" and the duality legislative discretion-judicial discretion.

As we have seen in the previous section, my argument for the exclusion of the R variable from the Weight Formula in the ideal discourse is, in short:

1. The (Real) Weight Formula says:

$$W_{i,j} = \frac{W_i \cdot I_i \cdot R_i}{W_j \cdot I_j \cdot R_j}$$

2. In the ideal discourse, due to the complete realization of the five idealizations adumbrated by Alexy in his initial writings, the development of an infinitesimal scale to measure the degrees of interference in the colliding principles and their abstract weights would not only be possible, but would also be a fact;[39]
3. therefore, the reliability of the empirical assumptions can be excluded from the weight formula, for in the ideal discourse, due to complete knowledge, this reliability would be maximal regarding both colliding principles;

37 R. Alexy, 'Princípios Formais' (n. 34), 11.

38 R. Alexy, 'Princípios Formais' (n. 34), 13 f.

39 Since it would be an ideal fact, that is to say, a fact of the ideal discourse, one could talk here, using Kant's terminology, of a "fact of reason".

4. thus, in the ideal discourse, the weight formula would say:

$$W_{i,j} = \frac{W_i \cdot I_i}{W_j \cdot I_j}$$

In order to know whether this argument is still valid, that is to say, in order to know whether it is valid after the development of the new Refined Complete Weight Formula, it is enough to ask whether what was said about the reliability of the empirical assumptions is valid for the reliability of the normative assumptions. Now, it should be clear at this point that the ideal discourse – if one takes the conception adopted here – is a discourse in which everything can be known. As we have seen, this does not exclude "stalemates", but stalemates are not, in the ideal discourse, the result of a "problem of knowledge". They are rather ontological or deontological stalemates. If, in the ideal discourse, one can know everything, then the reliability of the normative assumptions will also always be maximal (on both sides of the colliding principles). Thus, in the new version of the Weight Formula,

$$W_{i,j} = \frac{I_i \cdot W_i \cdot R_i^e \cdot R_i^n}{I_j \cdot W_j \cdot R_j^e \cdot R_j^n},$$

not only the values of R_i^e and of R_j^e will *always* be maximal and equal, that is to say, will *always* be 1, but also the values of R_i^n and of R_j^n will *always* be maximal and equal, ant thus would also *always* be 1. Since the values for both pairs will *always* be equal, both pairs can be withdrawn of the formula. Thus, the refinement recently presented by Alexy, namely, the fact that *R* speaks not only to the empirical assumptions (R^e), but also to the normative assumptions (R^n), does not affect the argument presented in this essay.

Therefore, one can say that, even when one departs from the new refined version of the Weight Formula, the Weight Formula of the ideal discourse or the Ideal Weight Formula still says:

$$W_{i,j} = \frac{W_i \cdot I_i}{W_j \cdot I_j}$$

In short, what was said about the reliability of the empirical assumptions is valid also for the reliability of the normative assumptions. The repercussion of the new Weight Formula on the relation between the "problem of practical knowledge" and the duality legislative discretion-judicial discretion should be analysed now.

Part Five: The Problem of Practical Knowledge and the Distinction between Legislative and Judicial Discretion

The problem of practical knowledge consists in the possibility of knowing whether, for a practical (and therefore legal) question, a single solution exists, or whether the one who produces a norm (a general or an individual one) has discretion. The question I want to take up now is whether the problem of practical knowledge shows itself in different ways in the production of general norms (legislation) and of individual norms (adjudication). An analysis of Kelsen's distinction between legislation and adjudication is an interesting starting point.

In Kelsen, the distinction between legislation and adjudication is not a qualitative distinction, but rather a matter of degree. Kelsen rejects the traditional notion that the legislator creates norms, while the judge applies them. According to Kelsen, both legislation and adjudication represent, at the same time, the production and application of norms: when the legislator produces a statute, he applies the constitution, and when the judge applies a law, he produces an individual norm. The only acts that do not present this double character are the production of the first historic constitution (or of a revolutionary constitution), which does not consist in the application of a superior norm and is therefore an act of mere creation, and the act of enforcing a legal decision, which is an act of mere application.[40]

The production of a norm is relatively determined by the superior norm, and thus relatively undetermined. The legislator's leeway is, according to Kelsen, greater than the judge's, but in both cases one *cannot* deduce, from a superior norm, *only one* inferior norm.[41] In short, since out of the constitution one cannot deduce only one general norm about a matter, and since out of statutes one cannot deduce only one decision for a case, both the legislator and the judge have discretion. Since the legislator's discretion is greater than the judge's, the distinction between legislation and adjudication is a matter of degree.

As we have seen above, in Alexy's "model of the relatively perfect application", the solution for legal questions does not come from the authoritative material alone, but the authoritative material is considered as a(n) (essential) partial source for the solution of a legal question. According to Alexy, all arguments that are admitted in the production and application of law are part of the concept of law.[42]

Alexy developed his "Theory of Legal Argumentation"[43] to handle the problem of the correction of legal decisions. In fact, this theory can be seen as an attempt to reduce the scope of judicial discretion. Later, when Principles Theory was developed, the problem of legislative discretion came into play, for some critics have argued that Principles Theory would threaten legislative law-making. Alexy answered this objection in the "Postscript" of the English edition of "A Theory of Constitutional Rights", where, he says, in short, that Principles Theory means neither *too much* by way of constitutional rights, that is to say, it does not mean too much power for the constitutional courts and therefore a diminishing legislative power, nor *too little* by way of constitutional rights, that is to say, it does not mean too much power for the legislator and therefore a diminishing of the role of constitutional courts.

In the recent essay "Princípios Formais" (Formal Principles), Alexy reaffirms that the legislator possesses two kinds of discretion: structural and epistemic.[44] In the

40 H. Kelsen, *Reine Rechtslehre* (n. 8), 346 ff.

41 H. Kelsen, *Reine Rechtslehre* (n. 8), 347–349.

42 R. Alexy, *Begriff und Geltung des Rechts* (n. 11), 201. He had already affirmed that in the Postscript of *Constitutional Rights* (n. 22).

43 R. Alexy, *Theorie der juristischen Argumentation* (n. 11).

44 R. Alexy, 'Princípios Formais' (n. 34), 13.

field of constitutional law, structural discretion comprehends everything that the constitution does not govern; in this case, the legislator is free to decide how to legislate. Epistemic discretion is related to the problem of practical knowledge: when it is not possible, due to the unreliability of the empirical and normative assumptions, to determine whether a certain measure constitutes a violation of a constitutional right, the legislator possesses epistemic discretion.[45] And since epistemic discretion is related not only to the empirical assumptions, but also to the normative assumptions, the new Weight Formula, or, using Alexy's denomination, the "Refined Complete Weight Formula", includes a variable for the reliability of the normative assumptions. Does it affect judicial discretion in Alexy's theory? The answer to this question is yes and no. Naturally, the insertion of a variable that is related to the reliability of the normative assumptions affects the character of judicial discretion, for, from now on, judicial discretion (as well as legislative discretion) depends not only on the reliability of the empirical assumptions but also on the reliability of the normative assumptions. In this sense, the new Weight Formula reverberates on judicial discretion. But, on the other hand, the insertion of a variable for the reliability of the normative assumptions does not change the features of the distinction between legislative and judicial discretion in Alexy.

My thesis is that, in Alexy, the difference between legislation and adjudication, and therefore, between legislative discretion and judicial discretion, is *quantitative* as it was in Kelsen, but *also qualitative*. The reason why legislation and jurisdiction are, in Alexy, quantitatively different, is that in Alexy as in Kelsen, the legislator and the judge possess, in principle, discretion, and, in Alexy as in Kelsen, legislative discretion is greater than judicial discretion, for the judge is bound not only to the constitution but also to the authoritative material produced by the legislator.[46]

The difference between Alexy's and Kelsen's respective models, which by the way is not small, is generated by the insertion, in Alexy's model, of legal argumentation, which is a special case of general practical argumentation, as well as of Principle's Theory. These two instruments have a double effect.

The first effect diminishes considerably judicial discretion, for, in Alexy's model, the one who applies the law has at his disposal the possibility of rationally controlling the many interpretations that the authoritative material admits *in principle*. These tools, that are not present in Kelsen's Theory, make discretion considerably less in Alexy than in Kelsen. But greater and lesser mean a quantitative distinction. If a diminished judicial discretion, as I have just described it, were the only difference between Alexy's and Kelsen's respective models, the difference between legislation and adjudication and therefore between legislative discretion and judicial discretion would remain, in Alexy's model, merely quantitative, as in Kelsen. The difference between Kelsen and Alexy would then only be the fact that judicial dis-

45 R. Alexy, 'Princípios Formais' (n. 34), 13 ff.

46 This is affirmed when Alexy, in "A Theory of Legal Argumentation", defends the special case thesis, that is to say, the thesis that legal argumentation is a special case of general practical argumentation, for the difference between general practical argumentation and legal argumentation turns on three features of legal argumentation that are not features of general practical argumentation: the connection to valid law (that is to say, to the authoritative material [statutes]), to legal dogmatics (legal science) and to precedents. See R. Alexy, *Theorie der juristischen Argumentation* (n. 11), 261–272; R. Alexy, 'The Special Case Thesis', *Ratio Juris* 12 (1999), 374–384.

cretion in Alexy is narrower than in Kelsen. But this is not the only difference, for there is another aspect to consider, namely, that in Alexy, in the case of judicial application, the regulative idea of a single answer is assumed. This has to be explained.

The difference between legislative and judicial discretion in Alexy is not merely quantitative, for *only* adjudication admits the regulative idea of a single answer to every legal question. With some exceptions, that are not significant here,[47] when a judge handles and decides a case he is looking for the best juridical solution for the case. Even if he is aware that a single solution is something unrealizable in this world, when he handles and decides the case he does not believe he possesses discretion. Now, the regulative idea of a single answer means exactly searching for the *one very best* solution to a case even when one can never be sure that the solution he finds is *the* best solution. When the legislator creates a statute, he does not assume the idea that there is only one legally valid statute to be produced from the constitution. He assumes he is bound to the constitution, but this does not mean that there is "one single statute" to be produced from it. This is the place of politics. Legislative discretion guarantees, as Alexy states, the possibility of democracy.

Concluding Remark

The Weight Formula is a tool to identify precisely whether there would be one single solution to every legal case, in both the ideal and real discourses. Indeed, it shows that, in the ideal discourse, there would be one single answer for every legal question to which there is an answer at all. Does it affect the situation regarding real discourses? In my view the answer to this question is yes and no.

On the one hand, if there are cases even in the ideal discourse for which there are no single answers, the single answer, as a regulative idea, does not exist, at least in some cases. Because of that, it would make no sense to search for a single answer in real discourses, at least in some cases, namely the ones in which there is, in ideal discourses, no single answer. On the other hand, there may be a solution to this problem. I want to sketch this solution.

The ideal discourse does not exist: it is a methodological construction for optimizing the rationality of real discourses. Two situations can be distinguished. (i) The first situation is the one where, in the ideal discourse, there is a single answer. In this case the single answer remains as a regulative idea for real discourses. (ii) The second situation is the one when, in the ideal discourse, there is no single answer. These are the cases of stalemates in the ideal discourse. In such cases there would be, as we have seen, legislative discretion. The legislator can command something that is permitted in the ideal discourse. And as we have also seen, the judge does not have such discretion. If a situation for which there is no single solution in the ideal discourse is not positively regulated by the constitution and by the ordinary legislator, the judge has only one option, namely to consider the action in question as permitted.

How can this ideal solution be accomplished in real discourses? We do not live in the ideal world and, therefore, when we face a stalemate in the real discourse we

47 These exceptions include cases in which a court acts as a legislator.

cannot know whether it is also a stalemate in the ideal discourse. The solution provided by Alexy's theory is the combination of the democratic principle and constitutional rights, in the cases of both legislation and adjudication.

When one faces a stalemate during the legislative process, the question whether the matter is really a matter of legislative discretion or the legislature is bound should be solved, at the first moment, in parliament (democratic principle). Although one must seek in real discourses the optimization of the five idealizations that are typical of the ideal discourse, one should not talk here about the regulative idea of one single statute. Yet, the ideal discourse keeps its function as a procedural model when a statute is being enacted, for the legislative procedure is a real discourse, and in every real discourse the ideal discourse must be fulfilled to the greatest degree possible. But because of constitutional rights, at a second moment the constitutional court can check whether the legislator stayed in the frame of legislative discretion. Therefore, by constitutional courts the matter turns on legislative discretion.

When one faces a stalemate during the process of coming to a legal decision, the democratic principle demands that the judge not change the range of what is legally commanded and permitted by the legislator. The criterion the judge should use to decide such cases is the regulative idea of one single solution. These are, in my view, the conclusions we can draw from Alexy's model of legal application.

Part II – Human Rights

Jean-Christophe Merle

Robert Alexy's Conception of Human Rights

Part One: The problems with the thesis "All individuals possessing property φ have human rights"

Robert Alexy presents a twofold approach to human rights in several of his essays on human rights. On the one hand, he analyzes the concept of human rights, finding five properties that characterize all human rights:

> The general idea [of human rights] can be expressed by means of a definition according to which human rights are, first, moral, second, universal, third, fundamental, and, fourth, abstract rights that, fifth, take priority over all other norms[1].[2]

On the other hand, he looks for a justification of human rights. Unlike his previous essays, such as "Menschenrechte ohne Metaphysik", his essay "The Existence of Human Rights" entails a general formula for all foundations that have ever been offered for human rights:

> "All individuals possessing property φ have human rights".[3]

Yet, unlike his prior conceptual analysis of human rights, the remaining part of the latter essay does not present characteristics common to all attempts to provide a foundation of human rights, nor does it present characteristics common to all particular foundations of particular human rights. Rather, Alexy presents several foundations, each claiming to be valid for all human rights, and he rejects all of these foundations but the "explicative argument", which is part of his foundation of human rights, but not his whole foundation. Indeed, it has to be complemented by an existential argument; ultimately, Alexy offers an "explicative-existential justification"[4] of human rights.

Alexy's definition of human rights, as well as his justification of human rights, raises a major problem. However, as I will suggest, modifying his theory at two decisive points can solve the problem while fulfilling the intention that he might have had in mind while formulating this definition.

The formula "All individuals possessing property φ have human rights" assumes that all human rights have the same foundation, because it does not say "All individuals possessing property φ have the human right(s) x [or x, y, z…]". Thus, possessing the property φ is the foundation of *all* human rights. Referring to Alexy's "explicative existential justification", property φ consists of a combination of two

1 See Robert Alexy, "Die Institutionalisierung der Menschenrechte im demokratischen Verfassungsstaat," in *Philosophie der Menschenrechte*, eds. Stefan Gosepath and Georg Lohmann, (Frankfurt: Suhrkamp, 1998), 244–264, at 246–54.

2 Robert Alexy, "Law, Morality, and the Existence of Human Rights," *Ratio Juris*, 25 n. 1 (March 2012), 2–14, at 10; see also Robert Alexy, "Menschenrechte ohne Metaphysik?" *Deutsche Zeitschrift für Philosophie*, 52 n. 1 (2004): 15–24, at 16.

3 Robert Alexy, "The Existence of Human Rights," *Archiv für Rechts- und Sozialphilosophie*, supplement 136 (2013), 9–18, at 13.

4 Alexy, "The Existence of Human Rights" (n. 3), at 17.

properties. Alexy formulates the first property, on which the "explicative justification of human rights" relies, in two different ways. At first, this property consists of "what is necessarily implicit in human practice".[5] Then, Alexy specifies the explicative justification that he defends, i.e., a "discourse-theoretic" explicative justification. In fact, unlike Kant's "transcendental philosophy", and Alan Gewirth's foundation of human rights,[6] Alexy does not refer to action in general, but to a specific kind of action, that is, "the practice of asserting, asking, and arguing".[7] Alexy does not seem to distinguish, as philosophy of action does, between the ability to do x and the capability to do x, which makes it possible to acquire an ability that one does not currently possess. I am not able to sing, but I am capable of singing; a worm is not capable of singing because it does not have the organ for that. Here, I leave the question open whether the property ϕ is a capability or an ability. Thus, according to Alexy, part of the property ϕ is to have either the capacity or the ability to "assert, ask and argue". The remaining part of property ϕ is provided by the "existential justification":

> The interest in making use of discursive capabilities solely in the sphere of discourse might be called a 'weak interest in correctness'. By contrast, the interest in making use of discursive capabilities not only in the sphere of arguments, but also in the realm of action can be characterized as a 'strong interest in correctness'. [...] This again includes the interest in solving social conflicts by means of discursively generated and discursively controlled rules.[8]

Thus, the complete formulation of property ϕ is the following bundle of properties:

(i) Property ϕ_1: Either the discursive ability or the discursive capability to "assert, ask and argue"
(ii) Property ϕ_2: The interest to make use of property ϕ_1 while arguing and acting
(iii) Property ϕ_3: The interest in solving social conflicts by means of "rules generated" under the control of property ϕ_1.

Thus, we can modify the foundation of human rights in the following way: All individuals possessing the bundle of properties ϕ_{1-3} have human rights.

Now, since this is the formulation of the foundation of human rights, it means that all human rights are justified by the possession of the bundle of properties ϕ_{1-3}. It implies that, if we formulate the following proposition, we have the following implication:

p: there are human beings who do not possess the bundle $\phi_{1-3)}$
q: they don't have human rights
r: some human rights are not justified.
$p \Rightarrow q \vee r$

Now, the only valid conclusion is that the proposition (r) is true, for the following reasons.

5 Alexy, "The Existence of Human Rights" (n. 3), at 15.
6 See Alan Gewirth, *Human Rights. Essays on Justification and Applications* (Chicago: Chicago University Press, 1982).
7 Alexy, "The Existence of Human Rights" (n. 3), at 15.
8 Alexy, "The Existence of Human Rights" (n. 3), at 17.

Let us assume that (r) were false. Alexy states that "Human rights are rights that belong to all human beings"[9], so that (q) is false. Thus, if (r) were false, the proposition (q v r) would be false. Since a true proposition cannot imply a false proposition, (p) would be false. Now, there are human beings who do not possess the bundle ϕ_{1-3}, so that (p) is true. One may be tempted to see a reply to this objection in Alexy's following assertion:

> [...] human rights are admittedly rights that belong to all, but some human rights cannot always be claimed by all. Thus, only those who are needy can claim assistance, only kids can claim education, and only those who are endangered can claim protection. This makes clear that the difference between human rights and other rights does not consist in the fact that they are categorical rights, by virtue of their logical structure, but rather in the fact that they belong to everybody without having to be acquired.[10]

Now, this distinction between being the bearer of a right and being able to use the same right is relevant for the definition of human rights, but it does not concern their justification, while the bundle ϕ_{1-3} is referred to for the sake of justifying human rights. Among those human beings not possessing the bundle ϕ_{1-3} belong, for instance, some seriously mentally disabled persons who are not, never were and never will be able to assert, ask and argue, because they are not capable of doing so, that is, during their entire existence they can never develop this ability. Yet, there is no controversy about the fact that those persons enjoy at least some human rights, for instance, the right not to "be subjected to torture or to cruel, inhuman or degrading treatment or punishment"[11] or "the right to a standard of living adequate for the health and well-being of himself and of his family, including food, clothing, housing and medical care and necessary social services"[12]. The logical conclusion of this is that (r) is true: some human rights are not justified.

Now, the problem with Alexy's formula is even worse. Since, as we observed, the formula "All individuals possessing property ϕ have human rights" assumes that all human rights have the same foundation, that is the bundle ϕ_{1-3}, not a single human right is justified, although part – or probably even a huge majority of human beings – possess the bundle ϕ_{1-3} that would justify human rights if everybody possessed it.

9 "Menschenrechte Rechte sind, die allen Menschen zustehen". Alexy, "Die Institutionalisierung der Menschenrechte..." (n. 1), at 247.

10 "[...] daß Menschenrechte zwar Rechte sind, die allen zustehen, einige Menschenrechte aber nicht stets von allen geltend gemacht werden können. So kann nur der Hilfsbedürftige für sich Hilfe, nur das Kind für sich eine Erziehung und nur der Bedrohte für sich Schutz fordern. Dies macht deutlich, daß Menschenrechte sich von anderen Rechten nicht dadurch unterscheiden, daß sie ihrer logischen Struktur nach kategorische Rechte sind, sondern vielmehr dadurch, daß sie jedem zustehen, ohne daß sie erworben werden müssen." Alexy, "Die Institutionalisierung der Menschenrechte..." (n. 1), at 248.

11 UN General Assembly, *Universal Declaration of Human Rights*, 10 December 1948, 217 A (III), art. 5.

12 UN General Assembly, *Universal Declaration of Human Rights* (n. 11), see art. 25.

Part Two: How to solve these problems, modifying this thesis

Now, why does Alexy choose a bundle such as ϕ_{1-3} for the justification of human rights? This bundle cannot provide a justification for human rights, but it is quite capable of determining the conditions for being able to respect human rights (in the case of ϕ_1) and for actually respecting them (in the case of ϕ_{1-2}). Instead of justifying or grounding the validity of human rights, the bundle ϕ_{1-3} instead shows the source of the obligation of those who bear the correlative duties of human rights. As is well known, whereas all human beings are bearers of human rights, the groups constituted by human beings and the group constituted by bearers of correlative duties to human rights are neither the same nor is the one included in the other. Some human beings – for instance, some seriously mentally disabled human beings – do not have any duty correlative to human rights. Conversely, some bearers of correlative duties to human rights do not have themselves human rights. Institutions, such as governments and their agencies – the police, the courts, the health system and the educational system, etc. –, international organizations, companies, etc. do have duties correlative to human rights. Now, all of these bearers of correlative duties to human rights, whether human beings or institutions, possess the property ϕ_1 and can develop properties ϕ_{2-3} under appropriate circumstances, although they must not develop them. In fact, as Alexy notices, developing properties ϕ_{2-3} is an "existential decision"[13].

Referring the bundle ϕ_{1-3} to the grounding of the obligation to fulfil the duties correlative to human rights rather than referring it to the justification of the validity of human rights would also explain why Alexy provides a single bundle of properties for all cases of human rights instead of different bundles of properties or different single properties depending on which human rights are referred to. Here is the *first decisive modification* that I suggest. In fact, if one refers to the *justification of the validity* of human rights, the right not to be tortured might be justified by the normative requirement to protect from suffering, whereas the right to life might be justified by transcendental arguments, freedom of expression by the requirement of procedural means to guarantee other human rights, freedom of religion and freedom of education by the requirement to provide for the possibility to develop one's own character, the right to health care by a requirement of minimal well-being as well as by the right to life, etc. Yet, if one does not refer to the justification of the validity of human rights but to the *source of obligation* to fulfill the correlative duties, one sees that possessing the bundle ϕ_{1-3} *may imply recognizing* all the different justifications of the validity of the different human rights. In fact, the use of the ability to ask and argue, and the universal criteria that this use entails, may lead to recognizing those different foundations, and they are a condition for this recognition. Here, I shall not inquire into the issue whether possessing the bundle ϕ_{1-3} *really implies* this recognition.

Now, no longer referring the bundle ϕ_{1-3} to the justification of the validity of human rights but to the *source of obligation* to fulfill the correlative duties is only one of the two decisive modifications that I announced at the beginning. However, the *second decisive modification* is connected to the first one. I suggest that, handling the

13 Alexy, "The Existence of Human Rights" (n. 3), at 17.

normative dimension of human rights, after having defined their concept, one should not first think of the correlative duties to human rights. Admittedly, rights are correlative of duties and vice-versa, and the order between both does not matter for their *functioning*. Though, this order matters for their justification. Justifying correlative duties to human rights y of bearer B by human rights x of bearer A is not the same as justifying human rights x of bearer A by the correlative duties x of bearer B. What comes first in our consistent moral intuitions – and what did come first in the declarations of human rights – is the justification of the validity of human rights x of the bearer A. Only afterwards do our moral intuitions – and did the declarations of human rights taking into account Jeremy Bentham's[14] critique of them – draw the conclusions that there are correlative duties to human rights that must be first defined and then grounded in the source of the obligation.

In my view, these two decisive modifications should be accepted by Alexy, since they not only solve a major problem, but they also fail to collide with any other element of his theory of human rights.

Part Three: Data's alleged human rights

However, Alexy presented in a lecture at the University of Kiel called "Data und die Menschenrechte" (*Data and Human Rights*)[15] a solution for the problem aforementioned, and, whereas this solution identifies a danger resulting from that problem, it does not identify this problem itself, and it underlies, in my view, the same fatal problem.

Let me first review the problem as presented by Alexy, which, in my view, is merely the consequence of a more radical problem. Referring to Episode 35 of "Star Trek: The Next Generation" series, Alexy examines the case *Data vs. Maddox*, in which the machine Data claims the right not to be submitted to a research experimentation designed by Professor Maddox which would endanger Data's existence. The argument of Data's attorney Picard relies on the claim that Data is a bearer of human rights. The sentence decided by Judge Louvois is that Data enjoys an inviolable right to make decisions concerning its[16] own person and that Data is the bearer of rights, so that Data has the right to refuse to be submitted to Maddox's experimentation. Alexy introduces the debate about this claim in the following way:

> In the dispute about whom human rights belong to, one can distinguish two main positions. According to one of these positions, human rights belong to all human beings, though only to human beings. Thereby the concept of a human being is defined biologically. [...] The thesis that human rights belong only to human beings, though to all human beings, should be called "human-beings-thesis". The opposite thesis is the "person-thesis". The person-thesis does not rely on the concept of a human being, but on the concept of a person.[17]

14 See Jeremy Bentham, "A Critical Examination of the Declaration of Rights," in *Bentham's Political Thought*, ed. Bhikhu Parekh (London: Croom Helm,1973), 257–290.

15 Robert Alexy, "Data und die Menschenrechte. Positronisches Gehirn und doppeltriadischer Personenbegriff," (2000). Accessed at www.alexy.jura.uni-kiel.de/data/DatasMenschenrechte.pdf

16 I employ the pronoun "it", because to my knowledge, Data's gender – if this category applies to Data – is not specified, having no better grammatical solution for this case.

17 Im Streit um die Frage, wem Menschenrechte zustehen, lassen sich zwei Hauptpositionen unterscheiden. Nach der einen stehen Menschenrechte allen Menschen, aber auch nur Menschen

Yet, Alexy sees the danger of the person-thesis, and offers a solution to prevent this danger:

> Consciousness belongs to personhood. Now, there are diseases that definitively suppress consciousness in the human beings. Should these human beings lose their human rights when there are affected by such a disease? [Here Alexy implicitly assumes that the answer is no.] The solution consists in reformulating in a first step the human-being-thesis in such a way that it is compatible with the person-thesis, in order to then in the second step link it to the person-thesis. […] The compatibility of the human-being-thesis and of the person-thesis is obtained by keeping the part of the human-being-thesis that asserts that all human beings are bearers of human rights, whereas suppressing the part that asserts that only human beings are bearers of these rights. […] This construction escapes the reproach of *speciesism* and simultaneously keeps the human rights protection for everything that has human appearance [*Menschenantlitz*]. Its justification is that the deepest and most important reason for human rights is the quality of being a person.[18]

Alexy's compatibility thesis between the human-being-thesis and the person-thesis does consist in a *set of two theses*:

(i) All human beings have human rights;
(ii) All persons have human rights.

A hidden, yet obvious third thesis also belongs to the set of Alexy's compatibility thesis:

(iii) What is neither a human being nor a person does not have any human right.

Part Four: The difference between Data's "human rights" and the human beings' human rights

In fact, there is no contradiction between thesis (i) and thesis (ii) (nor is there between any of them and thesis (iii)). However, one observes that thesis (i) and thesis (ii) do not share the same foundation.

zu. Der Begriff des Menschen wird dabei biologisch definiert. […] Die Position, daß Menschenrechte nur, aber auch allen Menschen zustehen, soll als "Menschenthese" bezeichnet werden. Die Gegenposition ist die "Personenthese". Die Personenthese stellt nicht auf den Begriff des Menschen, sondern auf den der Person ab. Alexy, "Data und die Menschenrechte. Positronisches Gehirn…" (n. 15), at 8 f.

18 Zum Personsein gehört Bewußtsein. Nun gibt es Krankheiten, die Menschen auf Dauer das Bewußtsein nehmen. Sollen diese Menschen mit ihrer Krankheit auch ihre Menschenrechte verlieren? Die Lösung besteht darin, daß die Menschenthese in einem ersten Schritt so umformuliert wird, daß sie mit der Personenthese vereinbar ist, um dann in einem zweiten Schritt mit der Personenthese verbunden zu werden. […] Die Vereinbarkeit der Menschen- mit der Personenthese wird dadurch hergestellt, daß der Teil der Menschenthese, der sagt, daß alle Menschen Träger der Menschenrechte sind, beibehalten wird, während der Teil, der sagt, daß nur Menschen Träger dieser Rechte sind, gestrichen wird. […] Diese Konstruktion entgeht dem Vorwurf des Speziezismus und beharrt doch gleichzeitig auf dem menschenrechtlichen Schutz all dessen, was Menschenantlitz hat. Ihre Begründung findet sie darin, daß der tiefste und wichtigste Grund für die Menschenrechte die Personenqualität ist. Alexy, "Data und die Menschenrechte. Positronisches Gehirn…" (n. 15), at 9 f.

Thesis (ii) relies on the concept of a person, which Alexy defines as having a "*double triadic*" (*doppeltriadisch*) structure.[19] According to him, the concept of personhood includes the following *three capacities*: "intelligence" (*Intelligenz*), "sentiments" (*Gefühle*) and "consciousness" (*Bewußtsein*).[20] He further defines the kind of consciousness contained in the concept of a person that forms the basis of human rights. This consciousness consists in a *triple reflexivity*, which is the reason why he speaks of a *double triadic structure*: "three kinds of reflexivity [...]: the cognitive one, the volitional one, and the normative one."[21]

Thesis (i) relies on the concept of a species ("the concept of a human being is defined biologically.",)[22]. Now, *fully developed* members of a species may have a certain set of capacities in common, and, in the case of the human species, this set may include personhood. However, belonging to the species is not defined by any set of individual capacities of the members, but by the *capacity of interbreeding and producing fertile offspring* that does not necessarily belong to each individual member (some members may be definitively sterile and have always been sterile), but from which each individual member results. For instance, a human being is a being that is the offspring of human beings.[23] Admittedly, one can use for the sake of identifying the members of a species the similarity of DNA, morphology, etc., but this possibility results from the capacity of interbreeding and producing fertile offspring. Nevertheless, a pathology that severely affects the morphology (what one called in the past (physical) "monsters" to whom many people denied any "human appearance") or the DNA does not imply that the individual member does not belong to the species. Thus, being the offspring of some members of humankind does not mean sharing key capacities with all human beings.

Therefore, not only the criterion, but also the *kind of criterion* for being the bearer of human rights, is radically not the same for thesis (i) (being the *offspring* of some other members) as for thesis (ii) (having a double triadic structure of *capacities*). Admittedly, in the current world, the only persons that are known from us as persons are human beings, so that

thesis (i) $\Rightarrow$ thesis (ii), but the reverse is false, so that, unlike what such authors as Alan Gewirth affirm, human rights are not grounded on the personhood or agency *of the bearer* of human rights, although human rights undoubtedly promote agency and personhood of those human beings who are capable of them. On the contrary, thesis (ii) defines the bearers of human rights by the possession of a set of capacities.

If one considers Alexy's double triadic structure of personhood and the capacities belonging to this structure, one observes that some human beings actually have less capacities belonging to that list than some animals do. Critics of *speciesism*, like

19 Alexy, "Data und die Menschenrechte. Positronisches Gehirn..." (n. 15), at 14.

20 Alexy, "Data und die Menschenrechte. Positronisches Gehirn..." (n. 15), at 10.

21 [...] drei Arten der Reflexivität zu unterscheiden: die kognitive, die volitive und die normative. Alexy, "Data und die Menschenrechte. Positronisches Gehirn..." (n. 15), at 13 f.

22 Der Begriff des Menschen wird dabei biologisch definiert. Alexy, "Data und die Menschenrechte. Positronisches Gehirn..." (n. 15), at 8 f.

23 This also applies to test-tube-babies, and it would also apply to human clones with the following modification: "[...] the offspring of a human being".

Peter Singer[24], refer to this point, and would recognize only thesis (ii), while rejecting thesis (i). The complete heterogeneity of the two kinds of criterion, each kind belonging to one of the two theses, does not primarily concern the foundation of human rights, but the *definition* of human rights as well as the *identification* of the bearers of human rights. I try to show this in the following *thought experiment*, relying on assumptions about our shared normative intuitions that I clearly mention.

Imagine that, in a future episode of *Star Trek*, the machines of Data's type, that are persons, are capable of interbreeding, producing machines, that are persons, that, in turn, will be capable to produce machines that are persons and capable of producing machines that etc. The machines will have the capacity of interbreeding and producing fertile offspring, but this will never be the reason why the machines will enjoy human rights. The reason for them enjoying human rights will still remain their personhood. Furthermore, unlike in the case of the pathologies of human beings, the defective machines will not enjoy any human rights. This seems to me to be our shared intuition. In fact, just *imagine* Data being affected by an *irreparable damage* that suddenly suppresses its volitional reflexivity (a capacity belonging to its personhood). Judge Louvois would reverse her decision and allow Maddox's experimentation that endangers the existence of Data itself. Now, imagine a human being losing her volitional reflexivity, or any other capacities, as in the case of those with Alzheimer's or dementia. Any current court would reject any request for doing research on them in a way that may destroy them. One may object that the machine could be repaired. Admittedly, it will be repaired, but only if repairing it is of some use for either human beings or for other machines. It is not a right of the machine to be repaired, whereas, the human right to life applies to all human beings without consideration of their current abilities.

Therefore, we have to *reformulate Alexy's compatibilist thesis or set of theses, in order to take into account our shared moral intuitions*:

(i') All human beings have human rights *during their entire life*, whatever may happen to them;

(ii') All beings that are currently persons have human rights *as long as, and only as long as they remain persons, and not for the entire duration of their existence.*

In other words, what matters here is that humankind is a species, while personhood is not a species. Obviously, making the belonging to a species the criterion for enjoying rights may be seen as *speciesism*, but this criterion really corresponds to our shared *normative intuitions*, which may be speciest on this point.

Part Five: Why should we decide for the human beings' human rights rather than for Data's?

Admittedly, one could reformulate Alexy's compatibilist thesis while defining either *data-machine-rights* or *person-rights*. Data-machine-rights might be, for instance, either *life-time-data-machine-rights* or *current-data-machine-rights*.

24 See Peter Singer, *Animal Liberation* (New York: New York Review – Random House, 1975).

Life-time-data-machine-rights
(j) All data-machines, i. e., all machines that in good functioning have personhood, have data-machine-rights *for the entire duration of their existence, even when they are defect, and cease to have personhood.*
(jj) All human beings that are currently persons have human rights *as long, and only as long, as they remain persons.*

Current-data-machine rights:
(k) All data-machines that are currently in such a good functioning that they have personhood have data-machine-rights, *as long, and only as long, as they have personhood.*
(kk) All human beings that are currently persons have data-machine-rights *as long and only as long as they remain persons.*

Person-rights would be:
(l) All persons have person-rights *for the entire duration of their existence as persons, and only as long as they are persons.*
(ll) All human beings that are currently persons have human rights *as long, and only as long, as they remain persons.*

One could construct such life-time-data-machine-rights, mere current-data-machine-rights and person-rights on the same model as human rights, i. e., giving them the same formal characteristics as Robert Alexy does for human rights.[25] Thus, why should one prefer the following option, related to the belonging to the human species, which I reformulated by modifying Alexy's compatibilist view?

(i') All human beings have human rights during their entire life, whatever may happen to them;

(ii') All beings that are currently persons have human rights as long as, and only as long as they remain persons, and not for the entire duration of their existence.

The reason why "we" – by which I understand a wide consensus in our society – do it is that we rely on our shared normative intuitions. Yet, actually, our normative intuition related to human rights is expressed only by (i'), not by (ii'). (ii') is connected to (i') only through two premises:

(a) The wrong foundation of thesis (i') in the belief that the reason for thesis (i') is that all human beings are persons, i. e., that they all fulfill the criteria for personhood.
(b) A normative requirement resulting from the normative universalization principle: Everything that has the same properties – here the same capacities contained in personhood – should receive equal treatment – here the same human rights.

What is wrong is not premise (b), but premise (a). In fact, this premise necessarily leads to conclusions that contradict our shared moral intuitions. Here I follow John Rawls' method according to which no theory can contradict the entire set of our

25 See the introduction of the present article: "The general idea [of human rights] can be expressed by means of a definition according to which human rights are, first, moral, second, universal, third, fundamental, and, fourth, abstract rights that, fifth, take priority over all other norms." Alexy, "Die Institutionalisierung der Menschenrechte…" (n. 1), at 246–54. See Alexy,"Law, Morality, and the Existence of Human Rights" (n. 2), at 10; see also Alexy, "Menschenrechte ohne Metaphysik?" (n. 2), at 16.

moral intuitions, because there must be a reflective equilibrium between moral theory and moral intuitions. All three aforementioned alternative sets of principles (long-life-data-machine-rights, current-data-machine-rights, person-rights) lead to the exclusion of some human beings. This exclusion contradicts our moral intuitions of what human rights are. Thus, although Alexy's set of theses (i) $\wedge$ (ii) is a non-contradictory set of thesis, this set contradicts the concept of human rights.

In other words, what seems to me to be wrong in Alexy's position, *on the basis of the thought experiment I made about the defect data-machine*, are the following claims related to his compatibilist set of theses:

(1) "Should these human beings lose their human rights when there are affected by such a disease?"[26] Alexy implicitly assumes that the answer is no. This answer is right. Yet, unlike Alexy assumes, it cannot be extended to the data-machine Data, which would lose its human rights, according to our moral intuitions.
(2) "[...] keeping the part of the human-being-thesis that asserts that all human beings are bearers of human rights [...]". Alexy assumes the extension of this thesis to all persons. Unlike Alexy, our moral intuitions lead to the conclusion that not all persons are the bearers of human rights.
(3) "[...] whereas suppressing the part that asserts that only human beings are bearers of these rights. [...]". It is not really suppressed, because unlike human beings, the data-machine would lose its human rights if it became defective.
(4) "This construction escapes the reproach of *speciesism* [...]". It does not, because of point (3).
(5) "[...] simultaneously keeps the human rights protection for everything that has human appearance [*Menschenantlitz*]." It does not, because, although Data has some resemblance with human beings, it would lose its human rights if it became defective.
(6) "Its justification is that the deepest and most important reason for human rights is the quality of being a person." Yet, this quality cannot be the foundation of human rights.

The root of the problem with Alexy's compatibilist set of theses about human rights can be seen as finding its expression in the following assertion: "Its justification is that the deepest and most important reason for human rights is the quality of being a person."[27] Alexy considers the justification and the criterion for being the bearer of human rights to lie in a bundle of properties, which, in this case, is a bundle of capacities. Yet, the criterion for being the bearer of human rights is merely to be a member of the human species, and the foundation of human rights is as diverse as the legally legitimate and fundamental interests of human beings in the full development of their capabilities, which does not imply that the validity of human rights is restricted only to human beings who are actually in possession of all of the abilities that realize these capabilities.

26 Alexy, "Data und die Menschenrechte. Positronisches Gehirn..." (n. 15), at 9f.

27 Ihre Begründung findet sie darin, daß der tiefste und wichtigste Grund für die Menschenrechte die Personenqualität ist. Alexy, "Data und die Menschenrechte. Positronisches Gehirn..." (n. 15), at 9f.

Part III – Principles and Proportionality

Martin Borowski

Robert Alexy's Reconstruction of Formal Principles

Formal principles have been developed in principles theory to reflect the authoritative dimension of certain decisions. The most prominent example of such an authoritative decision in the debate on formal principles is the decision of a democratically legitimated parliament.[1] This is to say that the category of formal principles is a key device in the reconstruction of constitutional review in liberal democracies. Apart from the importance of formal principles in constitutional theory, whether and how formal principles can play a role in the balancing of substantive principles counts as a genuine issue in legal theory.

I. The Context: The "Democratic Objection" to Proportionality in Constitutional Review

Ernst-Wolfgang Böckenförde, who served for twelve years as Judge at the German Federal Constitutional Court in the 1980s and 1990s, warned at the end of his term that proportionality analysis would have a degenerative effect on a liberal democracy with a healthy and lively democratic debate into a state, in which constitutional court judges decide all important matters by means of constitutional review (*verfassungsgerichtlicher Jurisdiktionsstaat*).[2] Metaphorically speaking, this is the admonition that the highest judges would become "juridical kings",[3] for they would be usurping the last word in all matters of legislation. Quite a few academic commentators have found this concern plausible, and it has gained considerable attention in the debate on proportionality in Germany and abroad. It is worth emphasizing, however, that

1 Although this example has been very much in the limelight in the debate on formal principles, it ought to be empasized that every decision that exhibits legal authority in the balancing of substantive principles needs to be reconstructed by means of a formal principle. At the very outset of the development of formal principles, Ronald Dwokin pointed towards a reconstruction of the authority of precedents by means of a "conservative principle" (Ronald Dworkin, *Taking Rights Seriously* (Harvard University Press: Cambridge, Mass., 1977), at pp. 37–38), which would be, in the language of the current debate, a formal principle. This idea was not further developed in modern German principles theory, since the classic doctrine in German jurisprudence understands precedents as merely factually rather than legally binding, see Karl Larenz and Claus-Wilhelm Canaris, *Methodenlehre der Rechtswissenschaft*, 3rd edn (Springer: Berlin *et al.*, 1995), at p. 255; Hans-Joachim Koch and Helmut Rüßmann, *Juristische Begründungslehre* (C.H. Beck: Munich, 1982), at p. 188. There are, however, modern jurisprudential approaches, which question this orthodox view, see, for example, Robert Alexy, *A Theory of Legal Argumentation* (Clarendon: Oxford, 1989), at pp. 274–279; Robert Alexy and Ralf Dreier, "Precedent in the Federal Republic of Germany", in: D. Neil MacCormick and Robert S. Summers, *Interpreting Precedents* (Ashgate: Aldershot *et al.*, 1997), pp. 17–64, at pp. 26–54.

2 Ernst-Wolfgang Böckenförde, "Grundrechte als Grundsatznormen", in: Ernst-Wolfgang Böckenförde, *Staat, Verfassung, Demokratie*, 2nd ed. (Suhrkamp: Frankurt on Main, 1992), pp. 159–199, at p. 190.

3 Ibid.

constitutional review in and of itself faces the "democratic objection".[4] With an eye to the "democratic problem", proportionality, and constitutional review, three aspects deserve to be pointed out.

First, proportionality is exposed to the "democratic objection" only if and when it is employed by courts in constitutional review of decisions taken by democratically legitimated organs of the state. This is certainly a crucial application of proportionality. It is not, however, the only application. For example, if the democratically legitimated parliament itself uses proportionality analysis as a guideline for carving out the provisions of a certain bill in the process of legislation, there is hardly anything undemocratic about this. It is only when parliament has taken its decision and this decision is then reviewed by a court or other organ[5] employing a yardstick characterized by, among other things, proportionality, that the court's or other organ's decision, arrived at by proportionality analysis, may interfere with the result of the democratic process.

Second, constitutional review is not solely about balancing. It extends to assessing claims stemming from constitutional provisions on the whole, and there are elements of the application of provisions of the constitution beyond balancing, namely, subsumption.[6] Thus, the issue of discretion on democratic grounds in subsumption arises. A comprehensive model of discretion in constitutional review has to address this issue, too.[7] In this essay, I shall focus, however, on discretion in balancing.

Third, the democratic problem of constitutional review is an issue in and of itself that has been the subject of a protracted debate.[8] The reconstruction of discretion in balancing by means of formal principles that will be outlined in what follows contributes, I shall argue, to the resolution of the democratic problem in constitutional review. Most importantly, it explains how one can enter the legal authority of a balancing decision (the original decision, eg by the parliament) into another bal-

4 See, on the debate on constitutional review and democracy, for example, Jürgen Habermas, *Between Facts and Norms,* trans W. Rehg (Polity: Cambridge, 1996), at pp. 241 et seq.; Mark Tushnet, *Taking the Constitution away from the Courts* (Princeton University Press: Princeton, N.J., 2000); Jeremy Waldron, "The Core of the Case against Judicial Review", *Yale Law Journal* 115 (2006), pp. 1346–1406.

5 There is, for example, a debate in German constitutional law, as to whether the German President is empowered and obligated to review a parliamentary statute with an eye to its constitutionality from the substantive point of view (Martin Nettesheim, "Die Aufgaben des Bundespräsidenten", in: J. Isensee and P. Kirchhof (eds), *Handbuch des Staatsrechts der Bundesrepublik Deutschland,* vol. 3, 3rd edn (C. F. Müller: Heidelberg, 2005), pp. 1073–1103, at pp. 1091–1094). It is generally the President's task and obligation to issue and promulgate (*ausfertigen und verkünden*) parliamentary statutes, Art. 82, paragraph 1, clause 1, Basic Law. To the extent that the German President is regarded empowered to perform substantive review and to the extent that this substantive review involves proportionality analysis, the "democratic problem" arises in the President's review.

6 See, on the reconstruction of subsumption, Robert Alexy, "On Balancing and Subsumption", *Ratio Juris* 16 (2003), pp. 433–449, at pp. 433–435.

7 Martin Borowski, "Die Bindung an Festsetzungen des Gesetzgebers in der grundrechtlichen Abwägung", in: Laura Clérico and Jan-Reinard Sieckmann (eds), *Grundrechte, Prinzipien und Argumentation* (Nomos: Baden-Baden, 2009), pp. 99–128, at p. 117.

8 See n. 4.

ancing decision (the review decision, eg the decision of a constitutional court in the course of constitutional review).

If one does not insist on extreme positions on both sides of the spectrum – (1) that the decision of the parliament has *no legal authority* whatsoever or (2) that it has *absolute legal authority*, because it may not be questioned by review undertaken by whomever – the issue of legal authority of certain decisions becomes a matter of degree. Democracy, taken on its own, required that no constitutional review of parliamentary statutes be performed. The effective commitment of all organs of the state, among them the parliamentary legislator, to the constitution required *prima facie* that strict constitutional review, review without discretion for the parliament, be performed. There can be little doubt that a reasonable compromise between these two competing requirements is called for.[9] To be sure, the idea that the democratically legitimated parliament has discretion or that its decisions have authority that a court performing constitutional review is required to respect is by no means new. It can be found in the case law of a great many national and international courts. "Respect for authority" is, however, a metaphore rather than a properly reconstructed legal phenomenon. What is needed is a proper model that explains the characteristics of this discretion or authority – how can it be integrated into the assessment of claims stemming from basic rights, and how can we determine the authority of a decision in the review of this very decision?

It would be an interesting exercise in comparative law to analyse and describe how different jurisdictions at the national and international level approach this issue. Owing to differences in legal tradition, legal culture and different institutional frameworks, a broad range of phenomena would very likely emerge. Instead of focussing on differences, I shall undertake to outline a model based on legal theory – a model that serves as a reconstruction of a broad common denominator in liberal democracies. A key device in this model is the idea of legal principles. Formal principles are a special category of legal principles, and these formal principles play a key role in Robert Alexy's principles theory. To analyse the characteristics of formal principles one must have a clear idea of legal principles generally.

II. The Reconstruction of Proportionality by Means of Principles Theory

The foundation of principles theory was developed by *Ronald Dworkin* in the debate on legal positivism in the 1960 s,[10] and this theory has been significantly developed further by *Robert Alexy* from the 1980 s on.[11] In a nutshell, the distinction between principles and rules runs as follows.

9 See Martin Borowski, "Formelle Prinzipien und Gewichtsformel", in: M. Klatt (ed), *Prinzipientheorie und Theorie der Abwägung* (Mohr Siebeck: Tübingen, 2013), pp. 199–250, at pp. 155–158.

10 Dworkin, *Taking Rights Seriously* (n. 1), at pp. 22 et seq.

11 Robert Alexy, "Rechtsregeln und Rechtsprinzipien", in: N. MacCormick, S. Panou, and L.L. Vallauri (eds), *Geltungs- und Erkenntnisbedingungen im modernen Rechtsdenken* (Steiner: Stuttgart, 1985), pp. 13–29; Robert Alexy, *A Theory of Constitutional Rights* (Julian Rivers trans., Oxford University Press 2002), at pp. 44–69 (the original edition of this monograph in German was published by Nomos in 1985).

1. Principles

Principles are norms that lend themselves to balancing. Where principles compete and the conflict cannot be resolved by appeal to other measures, they require balancing. In other words, principles, unlike rules, exhibit the dimension of weight.[12] Principles require that a certain goal be optimised, and they have therefore been characterized as optimization commands.[13] Where principles compete, balancing determines which principle takes precedence in the circumstances of the case at hand. The defeated principle remains, however, valid.[14] Balancing is the characteristic form of application of principles.[15]

2. Rules

Rules, however, do not lend themselves to balancing at all. Conflicts of rules always result in the invalidation of one of the rules or in the introduction of an exemption clause, following one or another of the maxims *lex posterior derogat legi priori*, *lex specialis derogat*, or *legi generali lex superior derogat legi inferiori*.[16] This is to say that principles and rules are differentiated by the dimension of weight. Claims stemming from rules are characteristically assessed by subsumption, the classic form of the application of law, in which the canons of interpretation – wording, the historic intent of the legislator, coherence and the law as a system, and finally the objective purpose of a legal provision, are key.

12 See Dworkin, *Taking Rights Seriously* (n. 1), at p. 26. The second criterion that Dworkin mentions, the alleged "all-or-nothing fashion" (ibid., at p. 24), does not, however, serve as a criterion for the distinction between rules and principles, see Martin Borowski, "The Structure of Formal Principles", in: M. Borowski (ed), *On the Nature of Legal Principles* (Steiner: Stuttgart, 2010), pp. 19–35, at p. 22 with further references.

13 See Alexy, *A Theory of Constitutional Rights* (n. 11), at pp. 47–48 and 67–69; Robert Alexy, "On the Structure of Legal Principles", *Ratio Juris* 13 (2000), pp. 294–304, at p. 300.

14 Dworkin, *Taking Rights Seriously* (n. 1), at p. 25; Alexy, *A Theory of Constitutional Rights* (n. 11), at p. 50.

15 A legal norm that is considered in a legal balancing exercise is necessarily a legal principle. This is not to say, however, that subsumption cannot play a role in the application of a legal principle. For example, Art. 4, paragraph 1 and 2, Basic Law, records religious freedom. There is a definition of "religion" in the legal sense, and if one assesses a claim stemming from religious freedom according to Art. 4, paragraph 1 and 2, Basic Law, one needs to subsume the characteristics of the case at hand under the definition of "religion". Only if the activity for which protection is sought by an individual counts as an instance of "religion", religious freedom will be balanced against competing rights or goods. There may even be no balancing in the application of religious freedom, if no right or good competes with it. At any rate, if the legal conditions of a principle are fulfilled and there are competing principles (rights or goods), balancing decides the outcome of the case.

16 Borowski, "The Structure of Formal Principles" (n. 12), p. 21 with further references.

III. The Development of Robert Alexy's Reconstruction of Formal Principles

In the development of *Robert Alexy's* reconstruction of formal principles, two periods can be distinguished.

1. The Early Reconstruction of formal Principles in *Theorie der Grundrechte* from 1985

With an eye to the reconstruction of discretion on democratic grounds in constitutional review, there can be little doubt that the question of formal principles is a vital question for principles theory in liberal democracies. Thus, it does not come as a surprise that the issue of formal principles is mentioned in *Alexy's* first comprehensive enquiry into principles theory. In his seminal monograph *Theorie der Grundrechte* from 1985 (the German original edition, a translation into English, *A Theory of Constitutional Rights*,[17] was published in 2002), he introduced "a distinction between two fundamental types of principle which is of wide-ranging significance, namely the distinction between substantive or material and formal or procedural principles."[18] One would expect a characterization or definition. In what follows, one encounters, rather, examples: "A formal or procedural principle is, for example, the principle which says that the democratic legislature shall take decisions which are significant for the society as a whole."[19] A number of pages earlier, where *Alexy* employs formal principles in the reconstruction of the *prima facie* character of rules, one reads: "[T]here are other principles which also need trumping, such as the one that rules passed by an authority acting within its jurisdiction are to be followed, and the principle that one should not depart from established practice without good reason. Such principles can be called '*formal* principles'".[20]

It is quite obvious that these passages are inspired by *Dworkin's* distinction between substantive and conservative principles in *Taking Rights Seriously*. After the introduction of his distinction between rules and principles, *Dworkin* takes up the issue of discretion. This is crucial for him, because he undertakes to explain that principles give rise to a specific form of discretion. In the course of his enquiry into discretion, he writes: "[A]ny judge who proposes to change existing doctrine must take account of some important standards that argue against departures from established doctrine, and these standards are also for the most part principles."[21] *Dworkin* mentions as examples "'legislative supremacy', a set of principles that require the courts to pay a qualified deference to the acts of the legislature" and "the doctrine of precedent, another set of principles reflecting the equities and efficiencies of consistency."[22] Both, he argues, "incline toward the status quo."[23] *Dworkin* terms

17 See n. 11.
18 Alexy, *A Theory of Constitutional Rights* (n. 11), at p. 82 (emphasis omitted).
19 Ibid.
20 Alexy, *A Theory of Constitutional Rights* (n. 11), at p. 58 (emphasis in the original).
21 Dworkin, *Taking Rights Seriously* (n. 1), at p. 37.
22 Ibid.
23 Ibid., at p. 37–8.

these principles "conservative principles" and sees them in opposition to "substantive principles."[24]

This backdrop suggests that *Dworkin's* "set of principles reflecting the equities and efficiencies of consistency"[25] prompted *Alexy* to develop his characterization of the "principle that one should not depart from established practice without good reason",[26] although *Alexy* gives no explicit reference.[27] Even though *Dworkin's* emphasis is more on "consistency" rather than "authority",[28] one might say that formal principles in the early period remain somewhat vague in *Alexy's* theory and that *Alexy* did not go significantly beyond *Dworkin's* distinction between substantive and conservative principles in *Taking Rights Seriously*.

2. The Reconstruction of Formal Principles in the Context of the "Weight Formula"

Alexy developed his reconstruction of balancing further in three key publications in 2002 and 2003.[29] A more detailed enquiry into his "Weight Formula" goes well beyond the scope of this essay. In what follows, the implications of his refined approach to balancing for the reconstruction of formal principles shall take centre stage.

a) The Basic Form of the Weight Formula

The basic form[30] of the weight formula runs as follows:[31]

24 Ibid., at p. 38.

25 Ibid., at p. 37.

26 Alexy, *A Theory of Constitutional Rights* (n. 11), at p. 58.

27 This is also suggested by the context. Dworkin develops his distinction of substantive and conservative principles in his book that laid the foundations of principles theory generally, and Alexy developed this very theory further, often with explicit reference to Dworkin's book.

28 See Borowski, "The Structure of Formal Principles" (n. 12). at p. 26; Borowski, "Formelle Prinzipien und Gewichtsformel" (n. 9), at pp. 164–165.

29 Robert Alexy, "Postscript", in: Robert Alexy, *A Theory of Constitutional Rights*, Julian Rivers trans. (Oxford University Press: Oxford, 2002), pp. 388–425; Robert Alexy, "Verfassungsrecht und einfaches Recht – Verfassungsgerichtsbarkeit und Fachgerichtsbarkeit", in: *VVDStRL* 61 (2002), pp. 7–33; Robert Alexy, "Die Gewichtsformel", in: Joachim Jickeli / Peter Kreutz / Dieter Reuter (Hg.), *Gedächtnisschrift für Jürgen Sonnenschein*, Berlin 2003, pp. 771–792 (English translation: Robert Alexy, "The Weight Formula", trans Bartosz Brożek and Stanley L. Paulson, in: J. Stelmach, B. Brożek, and W. Zaluski (eds), *Studies in the Philosophy of Law*, vol. 3 (Jagellonian University Press: Cracow, 2007), pp. 9–27).

30 Alexy actually refers to this formula as the "extended weight formula" (Alexy, "The Weight Formula" (n. 29), at p. 23) with an eye to the simplified version that does not contain variables for the abstract weight of the principles concerned (see ibid., at p. 21). The simplified version of the weight formula is, however, hardly useful in the practical application, since often different abstract weight of the principles concerned is an issue or at least imaginable.

31 This is the notation used in Alexy, "The Weight Formula" (n. 29), at p. 23, with two exceptions. Alexy uses "W" for both the concrete weight of both principles and the abstract weight for individual principles, which may give rise to confusion.

$$CW_{i,j} = \frac{I_i \cdot AW_i}{I_j \cdot AW_j}$$

This formula expresses the concrete weight "CW" of the principles "P_i" and "P_j". "I" represents the intensity of interference with the principle concerned, namely, "I_i" the intensity of interference with the principle "I" and "I_j" the intensity of interference with the principle "j". "AW" stands for the abstract weight of the relevant principle, that is "AW_i" for the abstract weight of the principle "I" and "AW_j" for the abstract weight of the principle "j".

b) The "Complete Form" of the Weight Formula

A crucial innovation in *Alexy's* writings on the weight formula in 2002 and 2003 is the introduction of the variable "R" for the reliability of the relevant premisses. In these publications the reliability of empirical premisses is front and centre, while in later writings he explained that this variable also covers the certainty of normative premisses.[32] The variable is added to both principles in denominator and numerator. The result is the "complete weight formula":[33]

$$CW_{i,j} = \frac{I_i \cdot AW_i \cdot R_i}{I_j \cdot AW_j \cdot R_j}$$

The introduction of a variable for the reliability of premisses for balancing meets with our intuitions. Why should one agree to justify severe interferences with a basic right on the basis of very unreliable premisses? If the empirical and normative premisses on which the justification and its weight are based turn out to be unreliable, this weakens the justification, and if the empirical and normative premisses, on which the interference with the basic right and the judgment on its severity are based, turn out to be unreliable, the interference with the rights weighs less. This is expressed by *Alexy's* "second law of balancing": "The more heavily an interference with a constitutional right weighs, the greater must be the certainty of its underlying premisses."[34] This is a judgment *ceteris paribus*: The higher the product of the severity of the interference with a right ("I_i") and the abstract weight of this right ("AW_i"), the more reliable must be the premisses on which the justification is based ("R_j"). *Nota bene*, this is only a partial relation. Also "I_j", "AW_j" and "R_i" can play a decisive role. This is to say that the comprehensive relation between and among the reliability of the relevant premisses and the other variables for attributing weight to principles is expressed by the "complete weight formula" rather than *Alexy's* second law of balancing.[35]

32 Robert Alexy, "Comments and Responses", in: Matthias Klatt (ed), *Institutionalized Reason* (Oxford University Press: Oxford, 2012), pp. 319–356, at p. 331.

33 Alexy, "The Weight Formula" (n. 29), at p. 25; see also Alexy, "Postscript" (n. 29), at p. 419.

34 Alexy, "The Weight Formula" (n. 29), at p. 25; Alexy, "Postscript" (n. 29), at p. 419; Robert Alexy, "On Balancing and Subsumtion", in: *Ratio Juris* 16 (2003), pp. 433–449, at p. 446.

35 See Borowski, "Formelle Prinzipien und Gewichtsformel" (n. 9), at pp. 170–171.

IV. A Critique of Robert Alexy's Reconstruction of Formal Principles in the Weight Formula

There can be little doubt that the introduction of the variable "R" into the weight formula counts as an important innovation in the reconstruction of balancing and in principles theory. Still, it does not solve the problem of formal principles. The variable "R" is neither a formal principle nor does it give rise to discretion.[36]

To explain this thesis in greater detail, it is well to have a closer look at *Alexy's* "Postscript" from 2002, which is his key publication on formal principles in the context of the weight formula and on the discretion to which they supposedly give rise.[37] In the analysis of proportionality in its narrower sense, he develops the basic version of the weight formula.[38] He then turns, in section "IV. Formal Principles", to epistemic issues. At the beginning of this section, one finds the thesis that "the problem of epistemic or knowledge-related discretion can be resolved by balancing formal and substantive principles".[39] This is basically his position in *Theorie der Grundrechte* from 1985,[40] apart from the clarification that formal principles play a role in epistemic discretion rather than structural discretion. After having characterized and distinguished these two forms of discretion,[41] he explains that the constitutional right as a principle requires *prima facie* that no epistemic discretion be granted to the legislator.[42] The competing principle, *Alexy* continues, is the principle of democracy. It requires *prima facie* that the democratically legitimated legislator have the last say in so far as premisses for balancing are unreliable.[43] A compromise is called for, according to which the required reliability of the premisses relevant for the justification rises with the severity of the interference with the constitutional right – this leads to *Alexy's* "second law of balancing".[44]

In this connection, *Alexy* mentions three different degrees of intensity of review, namely, "intensive review of content", "plausibility review", and "evidential review".[45] With an eye to *Alexy's* idea of tradic scales, the reader is left with the impression that the distinction of three degrees of intensity of review corresponds to values that are attributed to the variable "R" that *Alexy* introduced into the weight formula.[46] Things are, however, more complicated.

36 See, on this thesis, Martin Borowski, "Discourse, Principles, and the Problem of Law and Morality", in: *Jurisprudence* 2 (2011), pp. 575–595, at pp. 585–586; Borowski, "Formelle Prinzipien und Gewichtsformel" (n. 9). at pp. 174–181.

37 In his essay "The Weight Formula" (n. 29) formal principles are not mentioned at all, and in "Verfassungsrecht und einfaches Recht" (n. 29) they are mentioned only in passing.

38 See section III. 2 a).

39 Alexy, "Postscript" (n. 29), at p. 414.

40 See section III. 1.

41 Alexy, "Postscript" (n. 29), at pp. 414–416.

42 Ibid., at p. 416. In this respect, Alexy follows Marius Raabe, see Marius Raabe, *Grundrechte und Erkenntnis* (Mohr Siebeck: Baden-Baden, 1998), at pp. 207–248.

43 Alexy, "Postscript" (n. 29), at pp. 416–417.

44 Ibid., at p. 418. See, on the second law of balancing, section III. 2. b).

45 Alexy, "Postscript" (n. 29), at p. 419; Alexy, "The Weight Formula" (n. 29), at p. 25.

46 See Alexy, "Postscript" (n. 29), at pp. 419–420; see furthermore Alexy, "The Weight Formula" (n. 29), at pp. 25–26.

First of all, if the values for the variable "R" in the weight formula are equal in denominator and numerator of the fraction, the relative weight of the principles "P_i" and "P_j" does not change at all. This applies independently of whether all relevant premisses are perfectly reliable or completely unreliable, or whether they fall somewhere in-between. Considering the epistemic issue, the reliability of the relevant premisses, simply does not change anything at all. If the values for "R" in denominator and numerator are different, then the relative weight of the principles "P_i" and "P_j" does indeed change. *Alexy* claims that the relative weight can change in a manner that a stalemate arises, in which case discretion emerges.[47] This is true. The discretion that arises is, however, structural discretion – a form of discretion that *Alexy* is generally at pains to distinguish from epistemic discretion.[48] The form of structural discretion to which *Alexy* refers is not different from the form of structural discretion that emerges by means of a stalemate between two principles in the basic weight formula, where only the severity of interference ("I_i" and "I_j") and the abstract weight ("AW_i" and ("AW_j") are considered.

This is to say that the introduction of the variable "R" into the weight formula may change the relative weight of two (or more) principles. It does not, however, give rise to a specific form of discretion, namely epistemic discretion beyond structural discretion. A model is needed that can reconstruct two different perspectives on balancing the relevant substantive principles, the perspective of the legislator and the perspective of the court undertaking constitutional review.

Still, more doubt is cast on *Alexy's* reconstruction of formal principles by means of introducing the variable "R" into the weight formula if one asks where the formal principle as a third principle is found. In his early writings on formal principles, *Alexy* treats formal principles as instances of principles in the sense of principles theory: "This procedural principle, together with a substantive principle serving some secondary public interest, can be balanced against a constitutional principle guaranteeing an individual right."[49] This is also in line with *Dworkin's* reconstruction of formal principles, according to which "conservative principles" are instances of principles in the sense of principles theory.[50] Where in the weight formula does this third principle figure? In the basic of the weight formula one finds two substantive principles, namely, "P_i" and "P_j". What is more, one finds factors for attributing weight to these two principles, "I" and "AW", in denominator and numerator. By introducing the variable "R" for both principles, "P_i" and "P_j", another factor for their weight becomes part of the formula. The variable "R" does not represent, however, a principle in the sense of principles theory. What is more, *Alexy's* "Law of Combination" rules out understanding either "P_i" or "P_j" as the formal principle: "Procedural formal principles can override substantive constitutional rights princi-

47 Alexy, "The Weight Formula" (n. 29), at p. 26.

48 See the distinction between the sections "III. Structural Discretion and Balancing" (Alexy, "Postscript" (n. 29), at pp. 394–414) and "IV. Formal Principles" (ibid., at pp. 414–425). See also the distinction between the sections "III. 1. Strukturelle Spielräume" (Alexy, "Verfassungsrecht und einfaches Recht" (n. 29), at pp. 16–27) and "III. 2. Epistemische Spielräume" (ibid., at pp. 27–30).

49 Alexy, *A Theory of Constitutional Rights* (n. 11), at p. 82.

50 Dworkin, *Taking Rights Seriously* (n. 1), at p. 37.

ples only in connection with other substantive principles."[51] This is to say that one needs at least two competing substantive principles, and a formal principle can be only a third (or fourth *etcetera*) principle in the belancing. One would expect the formal principle "P_f" to be added to the denominator or numerator,[52] but there is nothing to this effect in *Alexy's* weight formula.

After all, *Alexy* confuses two separate issues in his reconstruction of formal principles in the "Postscript". The first issue is the reliability of empirical (and normative) premisses that counts as a factor for attributing weight to substantive principles in the balancing. *Alexy's* introduction of the variable "R" into the weight formula serves as a tool for the reconstruction of this first issue, and there can be little doubt that this is an important innovation. To be sure, "R" is neither a formal principle nor does the introduction of this variable into the weight formula solve the problem of formal principles.

The second issue is whether a balancing decision exhibits legal authority, so that the authority of the original decision has to be considered as an issue in and of itself in any review of this decision. This legal authority is represented by a formal principle in the balancing of the court or other organ that carries out the review of the original decision. This formal principle, a principle in the sense of principles theory, needs to be introduced into the weight formula, apart from and in addition to the variable "R" for the reliability of the premisses relevant to the balancing of substantive principles.

V. An Outline of a Formal Principle in Balancing Substantive Principles

1. Three Models

With an eye to the problem of formal principles, three models for considering the legal authority of decisions in balancing can be distinguished.

a) Balancing Substantive and Formal Principles

The first model is the model of balancing substantive and formal principles. An original decision is taken by balancing two or more substantive principles. If there are good reasons to attribute legal authority to this original decision, this legal autority is represented by a formal principle in the balancing that is carried out by the court empowered to undertake review of the original decision. The formal principle is added to the side that is preferred in the original decision, and adds weight to the substantive principle on this side of the balancing. This first model is basically the solution outlined by *Dworkin* in *Taking Rights Seriously* and by *Alexy* in his early writings on formal principles.[53]

51 Alexy, "Postscript" (n. 29), at p. 423.

52 Borowski, "Discourse, Principles, and the Problem of Law and Morality" (Fn. 36), at p. 585.

53 See section III. 1.

b) Balancing Two Formal Principles

A different model is proposed by *Jan-Reinard Sieckmann*. In his view, two different formal principles compete. If a court is empowered to review decisions of the legislator, then, according to *Sieckmann*, one has to distinguish between two prima facie requirements. Because of the authoritative nature of decisions of the legislator, the court is, on the one hand, *prima facie* required to respect the decision taken by the legislator. On the other hand, the court is required to base its decision on its own interpretation of the law, which, *Sieckmann* continues, is also only a *prima facie* requirement. In the case in which the court carrying out the review decides the substantive issue, seen as such, in a way different from the decision of the legislator, two formal principles compete: the formal principle according to which the decision of the legislator ought to be respected, and the formal principle according to which the court ought to follow its own interpretation of the law, seen as such.[54]

c) Rules for Attributing Weight to Substantive Principles in the Balancing

A third model might consist in the strategy to establish certain rules for attributing weight to substantive principles in the balancing. This is to say that only competing substantive principles would be balanced. There were no formal principles as instances of principles in the sense of principles theory. The legal authority of decisions would be considered by rules for attributing weight to substantive principles: The substantive principle that the legislator preferred would receive additional weight.[55]

The third model does not provide for formal principles, since it contains only substantive principles and rules for attributing weight to these substantive principles. It is submitted that this is not convincing, for one can distinguish between different degrees of abstract weight, different degrees on non-realization or severity of interference, and different degrees of reliability of the relevant empirical and normative premisses with an eye to the legal authority of a decision. This is to say that the legal authority shares structural characteristics with principles, which counts as an argument to understand legal authority as a principle in the sense of principles theory – a formal principle.

The second model gives rise to the problem that the balancing in the review of a decision has very little in common with the original decision that is reviewed. Let us assume that the legislator balances freedom to conduct one's business as one wishes with environmental protection, this with an eye to a limit on sulphur dioxide in waste gas stemming from industrial production. This is to say that the legislator balances a constitutional right with a constitutional collective good, and the result is a parliamentary statute. According to *Sieckmann*, a constitutional court perform-

54 See, on this model, Jan-Reinard Sieckmann, *Regelmodelle und Prinzipienmodelle des Rechtssystems* (Nomos: Baden-Baden, 1990), pp. 160–164.; Jan-Reinard Sieckmann, *Recht als normatives System* (Nomos: Baden-Baden, 2009), pp. 200–204; Jan-Reinard Sieckmann, "Probleme der Prinzipientheorie der Grundrechte", in: Laura Clérico and Jan-Reinard Sieckmann (eds), *Grundrechte, Prinzipien und Argumentation* (Nomos: Baden-Baden, 2009), pp. 39–66, at pp. 56–60). Critical on this model Raabe, *Grundrechte und Erkenntnis* (n. 42), at pp. 269–273.

55 See, on such a model, Johannes Badenhop, *Normtheoretische Grundlagen der Europäischen Menschenrechtskonvention* (Nomos: Baden-Baden, 2010), pp. 380–392; see also Alexy, "Comments and Responses" (n. 32), at p. 331.

ing constitutional review of that statute had to balance two formal principles: on the one hand, the formal principle that requires of the court that the decision on balancing the two substantive principles taken by parliament be respected, on the other, the principle that requires *prima facie* that the court bases its decision on its own view with respect to the balancing of the two substantive principles. To be sure, the substantive and the formal level are connected, for there is a widespread intuition to the effect that the extent of discretion for the legislator depends, among other things, on the severity of interference with the basic right in question.[56]

If this widespread intuition is deemed true, it suggests that the first model, the model of balancing substantive and formal principles, be developed further.[57] In what follows, such a model shall be sketched.

2. A Formal Principle in the Balancing of Substantive Principles

A formal principle in the balancing of substantive principles exhibits a couple of characteristics.

a) The Competence to Create a Goal to be Optimized

A formal principle grants competence to create a goal to be optimised in the sense of principles theory.[58] Substantive principles have a fixed, substantive content in the form of a goal to be optimized. By contrast, formal principles stand for a commitment to the results of a procedure. That is, something is to be optimized, for it is the result of a certain procedure or a decision of an authority. Once the procedure has been carried out or once the authority has taken a decision, the substantive content of the goal to be optimized is determined. From this point on, the structure of balancing a formal principle against a substantive principle does not differ from the balancing of two substantive principles.

b) The Authoritative Decision of Balancing Substantive Principles as the Goal to be Optimized by the Formal Principle

In the case of the formal principle that reconstructs the authority of a decision of the democratically legitimated parliament, the authoritative decision that determines the goal to be optimized is the decision on the balancing of the substantive

56 See, for example, Martin Borowski, *Grundrechte als Prinzipien*, 2nd edn (Nomos: Baden-Baden, 2007), at p. 127.

57 This model has received, to date, most support in research on principles theory, see Borowski, *Grundrechte als Prinzipien* (n. 56), at p. 128 with further references in footnote 357. One hastens to add that the second mode, the model proposed by Sieckmann, and even the third model may prove to yield the same results, albeit in a less intuitive and more complicated manner, see Borowski, "Die Bindung an Festsetzungen des Gesetzgebers in der grundrechtlichen Abwägung" (n. 7), at p. 99; Borowski, "Formelle Prinzipien und Gewichtsformel" (n. 9), at p. 159.

58 See, on this characteristic of formal principles and its repercussions, Borowski, *Grundrechte als Prinzipien* (n. 56), at p. 127; Borowski, "The Structure of Formal Principles" (n. 12), at pp. 29–30; Borowski, "Formelle Prinzipien und Gewichtsformel" (n. 9), at pp. 186–188.

principles.[59] This is to say that this formal principle is dependent on at least two substantive principles that need to be balanced.

The consideration of the formal principle has the effect of adding weight to one of the two substantive principles. To which substantive principle weight is added depends on the decision of the parliamentary legislator.[60] Whether the formal principle adds enough weight to the relevant substantive principle to bring about a state of affairs in which both outweigh the competing substantive principle alone depends on the weight of the two substantive principles and the weight of the formal principle in the circumstances at hand. The more weight one attributes to the formal principle, the more the decision of the parliamentary legislator may depart from the result of balancing the substantive principles alone. In short: the greater discretion is accorded to the parliamentary legislator.[61]

c) The Factors for the Weight of the Formal Principle

The question arises as to which factors determine the weight of the formal principle in the balancing of substantive principles. The central idea is that these factors resemble the factors for determining the weight of substantive principles.

aa) Abstract Weight

To begin with, a formal principle boasts of an abstract weight.[62] The greater the abstract weight, the greater the discretion accorded to the democratically legitimated parliament. Those who emphasize the democratic process and a procedural approach will argue on behalf of great abstract weight accorded to the formal principle. By contrast, those who emphasize the substantive commitment of the legislator to the constitution, enforced by a constitutional or supreme court, will argue on behalf of rather low abstract weight accorded to the formal principle.

bb) The Intensity of Interference

One might be tempted to think that respect for an authoritative decision is an all-or-nothing-affair – either you respect a decision or you do not. Respect for an authoritative decision also has, however, a graduated dimension. The farther one departs from an authoritative decision, the higher the degree of non-realization – or, in other words, the more intense the interference with the formal principle.[63] With an eye to the example already mentioned above,[64] supposing that the democratically legitimated parliament decided that 800 ppm sulphur dioxide is the limit and that the constitutional court is convinced that, in balancing environmental protection and freedom to conduct one's business as one wishes, the correct answer must be 900 ppm, the court does not respect the legislator's decision completely. But the court does respect this decision in such a case to a greater degree than in a scenario

59 Borowski, "The Structure of Formal Principles" (n. 12), at p. 33; Borowski, "Formelle Prinzipien und Gewichtsformel" (n. 9), at pp. 190–194.

60 Borowski, "The Structure of Formal Principles" (n. 12), at pp. 34–35; Borowski, "Formelle Prinzipien und Gewichtsformel" (n. 9), at pp. 194–195.

61 Borowski, "The Structure of Formal Principles" (n. 12), at pp. 34–35.

62 Borowski, "Formelle Prinzipien und Gewichtsformel" (n. 9), at pp. 195–196.

63 Borowski, "Formelle Prinzipien und Gewichtsformel" (n. 9), at pp. 196–197.

64 See section V. 1.

in which the court is convinced that the correct result is 3000 ppm. In the case of 900 ppm, the court departs only slightly from the decision of the democratically legitimated parliament, in the case of 3000 ppm, it departs significally. The former case is a minor interference with the formal principle, the latter a more severe interference.

cc) Epistemic Certainty

Just like the weight of substantive principles the weight of formal principles may well depend on the epistemic certainty of relevant premisses. If one draws a parallel to substantive principles, epistemic certainty with an eye to applying the formal principle itself suggests greater weight accorded to this principle, while epistemic uncertainty suggests less weight. In the case of formal principles, however, the aspect at issue is the certainty of the final balancing decision, and "certainty" refers to both empirical-epistemic certainty and normative-epistemic certainty.[65] In a case in which there is no epistemic uncertainty at all, the weight of the formal principle will have been reduced to zero.[66] This will be, however, for cases under practical circumstances, which, with very few exceptions, are characterized by more or less empirical and normative uncertainty.[67]

dd) Generic Factors for the Weight of Formal Principles

Even though there are certain parallels between the factors for determining the weight of substantive and formal principles, there are also differences. For example, according to a well-known paper by *Peter Häberle*, in 1975, a constitutional court ought to take the following stance: the greater the discursive quality of the process of legislation, the greater the discretion accorded to the legislator.[68] If there was a thorough, fair and open democratic debate, in which all relevant arguments were exchanged and evaluated, this counts as an argument for a lesser degree of strict scrutiny by the constitutional court or greater discretion for the legislative process, compared to a process of legislation that was strongly influenced by a group of lobbyists and decided basically behind closed doors without any proper democratic debate.[69] If one applies the idea of discourse theory as developed by *Jürgen Habermas* and *Robert Alexy*, the resulting reconstruction of constitutional review in liberal democracies points in the same direction.[70]

65 Borowski, "Formelle Prinzipien und Gewichtsformel" (n. 9), at p. 197.

66 See Alexy, "Postscript" (n. 29), at p. 424; Alexy, "Comments and Responses" (n. 32), at p. 331; Borowski, "Formelle Prinzipien und Gewichtsformel" (n. 9), at p. 197.

67 Borowski, "Formelle Prinzipien und Gewichtsformel" (n. 9), at p. 197.

68 Peter Häberle, "Die offene Gesellschaft der Verfassungsinterpreten", in: *Juristenzeitung* 1975, pp. 297–305, at pp. 303–304.

69 Martin Borowski, "Subjekte der Verfassungsinterpretation", in: J. Isensee and P. Kirchhof (eds), *Handbuch des Staatsrechts der Bundesrepublik Deutschland*, vol. XII (C. F. Müller: Heidelberg, 2014), pp. 761–782, at p. 779.

70 One hastens to add, however, that Jürgen Habermas, unlike Robert Alexy, is generally quite critical of the idea of constitutional review, see footnote 4.

VI. Conclusion

Even though there are still issues that require our attention before we will have arrived at a comprehensive and detailed model of balancing formal and substantive principles, the parallels in structure between substantive and formal principles – and parallels with an eye to the criteria for their weight – suggest that they can both indeed be considered in one and the same round where balancing is concerned. The critics are correct in pointing out that there are differences between substantive and formal principles. They are mistaken, however, in claiming that these differences preclude a consideration of formal principles in balancing substantive principles.

João Andrade Neto

Should All Arguments Matter?

On the Exclusion of Certain Reasons from the Proportionality Test

Introduction

In *A Theory of Constitutional Rights*, Alexy formulated a method for legal adjudication, the proportionality test, encompassing three sub-tests: suitability, necessity, and proportionality in its narrow sense (also called balancing).[1] Such a method is in the core of the principles theory, for it justifies the central statement that judges must reasonably balance competing principles in order to apply them to concrete cases. Subsequent scripts have given some clarification to the structure of the proportionality test, but the general scheme has not been in dispute.[2] In a work published in 2007, however, Alexy considered a specific change. He conceded that the proportionality test could be correctly described to have four prongs instead of three, with the addition of a sub-test to which he referred as *legitimate aims*.[3]

According to Alexy, the prong of legitimate aims is "identical with the idea of excluded reasons," serving as a barrier against "reasons that are ruled out where any participation in balancing is concerned."[4] Particularly, the new prong would accommodate mechanisms for excluding perfectionist, collectivist, and consequentialist interests. Alexy explained that, "illegitimate ends, like invalid principles, can never justify any limitation of any right," and that "it therefore makes no sense to employ them in the balancing procedure."[5] However convincing this idea is, Alexy showed reluctance to indicate the best placement for the sub-test of legitimate aims within the proportionality scheme.

Alexy suggested that it would be irrelevant to accommodate the filter against illegitimate aims either in a preliminary step specifically designed for that, or within the final sub-test of balancing. He acknowledged that proportionality could be described as a fourfold analysis, but also considered a different solution. He claimed that if reasons such as perfectionist ideals enter the sub-test of balancing, they should be assigned the value of zero in the weight formula: "This would deprive them of

1 Robert Alexy, *A Theory of Constitutional Rights*, trad. Julian Rivers (Oxford: Oxford University Press, 2010, 66–69).

2 See, for example, Robert Alexy, "Constitutional Rights, Balancing, and Rationality," *Ratio Juris* 16, 2 (2003): 135; and more recently, "The Construction of Constitutional Rights," *Law & Ethics of Human Rights* 4, 1 (April 30, 2010): 24.

3 Robert Alexy, "Thirteen replies", in *Law, Rights and Discourse: the Legal Philosophy of Robert Alexy*, org. George Pavlakos (Oxford; Portland, Or: Hart Pub, 2007): 341.

4 Ibid., 341. The text was a reply to Matthias Kumm, who had pointed out that a structural failure of the proportionality test was not stopping anti-liberal ideals from being balanced against constitutional rights. See: Mattias Kumm, "Political Liberalism and the Structure of Rights: On the Place and Limits of the Proportionality Requirement," in *Law, Rights and Discourse: the Legal Philosophy of Robert Alexy*, org. George Pavlakos (Oxford; Portland, Oregon: Hart Publishing, 2007), 131–66.

5 Alexy, "Thirteen Replies" (n. 3), 341.

the capacity to outweigh anything else."[6] His conclusion that, "participating in balancing without any weight is … not really to participate in balancing,"[7] suggests that it is irrelevant where one allocates the firewall against incorrect interests: either in the prong of legitimate aims or in the prong of balancing.[8]

On the contrary, I shall claim here that although Alexy's solution of assigning the value of zero to morally defective ideals within the weight formula is perfectly logical and consistent with the principles theory altogether, it poses two risks. The first risk is that it could trivialise reasoning about obvious and extreme injustice. The second and opposite risk is over-reaction, i. e. to exclude from balancing all morally controversial arguments. As a strategy to avoid the risk of trivialisation, I will defend here that the sub-test of legitimate aims would be better performed before, and not within balancing. And to avoid the opposite risk of over-reaction, I claim that legitimate aims would be better understood as a firewall against obvious and extremely unjust reasons, that is to say it should not accommodate the task of excluding from balancing ideals whose moral status is merely controversial. Furthermore, controversies – discussed below – regarding the best place and the correct function for the sub-test of legitimate aims will raise issues about the exclusion of formally defective measures.

In order to reach these conclusions, I shall answer some questions: first, whether the legitimate aims is part of the proportionality test; secondly, whether it is necessary to exclude certain reasons from the proportionality analysis; and thirdly, what reasons ought to be excluded, how this exclusion can be rationally justified, and how the arguments which justify such exclusion are related to proportionality as conceived by Alexy.

Part One: Is the Test of Legitimate Aims Part of Proportionality Analysis?

Assessing the legitimacy of the goals pursued by a legal measure was not part of the original scheme of proportionality analysis as it appeared in *A Theory of Constitutional Rights*. This is not to say that, according to the principles theory, all reasons should be admitted in the proportionality test. The fact is: if there were conditions other than suitability and necessity for admitting an interest to be balanced against a constitutional right, Alexy had not expressly stated them.[9] Actually, the discussion about introducing a new step to the proportionality test was first conducted by other scholars, particularly due to the different approach to the proportionality analysis as performed by the Supreme Court of Canada.

Admitting that constitutional adjudication demands that the person invested with authority assesses the legitimacy of the goals pursued by a legal measure, there are two ways to accommodate this duty in the general framework of the principles

6 Ibid.

7 Ibid.

8 It is remarkable that in subsequently published texts, Alexy referred to proportionality again as a test with the "three sub-principles of suitability, necessity, and proportionality in the narrower sense," and stated that this scheme "follows logically from the definition of principle, just as the definition of principle follows from the principle of proportionality with its three sub-principles." See, for instance: Alexy, "Construction of Constitutional Rights" (n. 2), 24.

9 Alexy, *A Theory of Constitutional Rights* (n. 1), 66–69.

theory. The first model accommodates the analysis of legitimate aims within the sub-test of balancing. As mentioned in the introduction, Alexy suggested this approach, as he recommended assigning the value of zero to morally defective ideals when performing the weight formula. The second model regards the sub-test of legitimate aims as a proper step within the proportionality test, preceding balancing. In this section, I will explain the development of the second model following an overview of the proportionality test as originally designed.

There was no exclusive prong in the analytical structure imagined by Alexy that was framed to stop suitable and necessary interests from participating in balancing. As initially conceived, the proportionality test encompassed three sub-tests – suitability, necessity, and balancing – which were logically deduced from the conception of constitutional principles as optimization requirements, that is, as norms requiring that "something be realized to the greatest extent possible given the legal and factual possibilities."[10] Within this scheme, an act is considered suitable means to realise a constitutional principle if it promotes the state of affairs to which the principle points. The same act is also necessary if it uses the least intrusive means for doing so. Both suitability and necessity thus constitute the factual possibilities of realising a principle, to which Alexy's definition of constitutional principle alludes.[11]

In its turn, the sub-test of balancing refers to the legal possibilities of realisation, in that every principle is an *optimization requirement*, which indicates an ideal scenario of its full-attainment. However, since every legal system is made up of several principles, each of them pointing to its unconditional fulfilment, the legal possibility of enforcing a principle depends on the limits imposed on it by competing principles and vice-versa. The decision-makers can take these limits into account by balancing the competing principles. An act suitable and necessary to realise a principle is therefore proportional, in the narrow sense, if the restrictions it imposes on competing principles are justified after balancing.[12]

Alexy explained in detail the structural aspects of balancing with the help of the weight formula, which indicates the concrete weight of a principle. The weight formula depends on allocating numbers to elements such as the intensity of interference and importance of competing principles. Either the authority responsible for performing the act or the one reviewing its constitutionality is responsible for qualifying each of these elements as 'light' (weak), 'moderate,' or 'serious' (strong). Furthermore, whereas the weight formula provides for the internal justification of the legal decision, by means of showing what elements are to be considered and how they should be dealt with, it is still the responsibility of the legal authority to justify the values he or she has allocated to the formula. That is a matter of external justification, which requires general practical reasoning,[13] and due to the dual nature of legal principles, includes considerations of political morality.[14]

10 Alexy, *A Theory of Constitutional Rights* (n. 1), 47.

11 Ibid.

12 Ibid., 66–69.

13 Robert Alexy, *A Theory of Legal Argumentation: The Theory of Rational Discourse as Theory of Legal Justification*, trad. Ruth Adler e Neil MacCormic (Oxford; New York: Oxford University Press, 2010), 284–86.

14 Robert Alexy, *The Argument from Injustice: A Reply to Legal Positivism*, trans. Stanley L. Paulson, Bonnie Litschewski Paulson (Oxford University Press, 2010), 68–81.

While the proportionality test as developed by Alexy was based on case law established by the Federal Constitutional Court of Germany, other authors have focussed on alternative versions for the method. In a comparative study of Canada and Germany, Dieter Grimm demonstrated that there are significant dissimilarities between the proportionality test adopted by the Supreme Court of Canada and its German equivalent. Based on the text of the Charter of Rights and Freedoms, which reads that rights and freedoms are "subject only to such reasonable limits prescribed by law as can be demonstrably justified in a free and democratic society,"[15] the Canadian Supreme Court employs the so-called *Oakes test*, with two components: legality and proportionality.[16]

Whereas in Canada, proportionality is a three-step test similar to its German equivalent, the legality test requires the authority to ascertain the purpose of the law considering that it should be of "sufficient importance" or "pressing and substantial."[17] According to Grimm, similar requirements can be found in the German case law, but with two differences. Firstly, "by *legitimate* the [German Constitutional] Court understands a purpose not prohibited by the Constitution. No additional element, such as 'sufficient importance' or 'pressing need,' is required."[18] Secondly, in Canada, ascertaining the purpose of the law is not part of the proportionality test; rather, it serves as a basis and starting point for the test. Contrastingly, in Germany "the question of whether the objective chosen by the legislature is important enough to justify a certain infringement of a fundamental right appears in the third step of the test, where the Court asks whether a fair balance between competing interests has been struck."[19]

Therefore, under the classification explained at the beginning of this section, the case law of the German Constitutional Court falls into the first model, where testing the importance of aims already occurs in the third prong, i. e. balancing, rendering any new steps unnecessary. In contrast, since the Canadian Supreme Court has regarded the analyses of the legitimacy as an external, previous condition to the proportionality test altogether, its case law falls into the second model. Interestingly, other authors who defend the second model, and therefore agree with making room for analysing legitimacy before balancing, tend to allocate this sub-test within the general scheme of proportionality. Julian Rivers, for instance, acknowledges that it is "normal to exclude the 'legitimate aim' from the scope of the doctrine of proportionality," but claims that it would be more convenient and theoretically elegant to include all sub-tests under the rubric of proportionality, for they all justify limitations of rights.[20] Similarly, Stone Sweet and Jud Matthews consider that "in its fully developed form, the [proportionality] analysis involves four steps."[21]

15 Part I of the Constitution Act, 1982, being Schedule B to the Canada Act 1982, C. 11 (U. K.).

16 Dieter Grimm, "Proportionality in Canadian and German Constitutional Jurisprudence", *University of Toronto Law Journal* 57, 2 (2007): 383–397.

17 Grimm, "Proportionality in Canadian and German Constitutional Jurisprudence" (n. 16): 388.

18 Ibid.

19 Ibid.

20 Julian Rivers, "Proportionality and Variable Intensity of Review," *The Cambridge Law Journal* 65, 01 (2006): 181.

21 Alec Stone Sweet and Jud Mathews, "Proportionality Balancing and Global Constitutionalism," *Columbia Journal of Transnational Law* 47 (2008): 76. They acknowledge that "some courts – including those of the EU, the ECHR, and the WTO – normally use a three-part test, leaving out

In conclusion, if we admit that constitutional adjudication demands that the invested authority assesses the legitimacy of the goals pursued by a legal measure, i.e. if we agree that the test of legitimate aims is part of the proportionality analysis, there are two ways to accommodate this duty in the general framework of the principles theory. The first way is to test the legitimacy of the aims before balancing. The case law of the Canadian Supreme Court and the opinions of Rivers, Stone Sweet, and Matthews conform to this model.[22] The other model accommodates the legitimacy test within balancing, rather than in a new prong. In order to demonstrate that the sub-test of legitimate aims would be better performed before balancing, I will examine next whether it is necessary to exclude certain reasons from the proportionality analysis.

Part Two: Is it Necessary to Exclude Some Reasons from the Proportionality Test?

The question of whether it is necessary to exclude certain reasons from the proportionality analysis is connected to the usage that different authors assign to the supposed prong of legitimate aims. In spite of existing divergences among scholars, we can divide the main theses in this respect in three groups. The first thesis claims that the sub-test of legitimate aims shall stop interests without constitutional status. Differently, scholars who support the second thesis argue for the exclusion of unimportant goals. Finally, the third group defends that the legitimate aims should be used as a firewall against ideals that lack minimum moral correctness. I will expose these theses accordingly.

I. Interests Without Constitutional Status

The first thesis, defended by Stone Sweet and Mathews[23] and Klatt and Meister,[24] perceives the legitimate aims as a weak sub-test. According to Klatt and Meister, proportionality is "a four-step test, with the sub-tests of legitimacy [to which they also refer as 'legitimate ends'], suitability, necessity, and proportionality in the narrow sense."[25] The first stage examines whether the act pursues a legitimate aim, and an aim is regarded as legitimate if it has constitutional status. The authors say that "only interests of constitutional value are allowed to play out on the balancing stage," and derive from this idea a rule that they call "the first law of trumping":

the 'legitimate purpose' stage. Nevertheless, they point out that, as a consequence, the analysis performed by these courts is "entirely focused on the relationship between means and ends." (Ibid.)

22 That is also the opinion of Vlad Perju, "Proportionality and freedom: An essay on method in constitutional law", *Global Constitutionalism* 1, 02 (Jun. 6, 2012): 350, 352.

23 Stone Sweet and Mathews, "Proportionality Balancing and Global Constitutionalism" (n. 21).

24 Matthias Klatt and Moritz Meister, *The Constitutional Structure of Proportionality*, 1st ed. (Oxford: Oxford University Press, 2012).

25 Ibid., 7.

"constitutional rights always trump every consideration except for considerations which enjoy constitutional status likewise."[26]

One could address a critique of excessive weakness to this conception of legitimate aim.[27] Reducing the first sub-test to a firewall only stopping interests without constitutional status would be insufficient or lack effectiveness. It is a necessary consequence of a wide conception of rights – as the one presupposed by the principles theory – that prima facie rights with a high degree of abstraction encompass innumerable specific rights and not only those expressly mentioned in written constitutional clauses. The general right of liberty is a remarkable example. Broadly conceived as a right to do or not to do whatever one pleases,[28] its scope includes almost all individual interests, actions, and states of affairs. And for being included in the scope of a constitutional right, these interests, actions, and states of affairs are prima facie under constitutional protection. The problem is: if almost everything is regarded as constitutionally guaranteed, a firewall that only prevents non-constitutional interests from entering the proportionality test excludes too little.

Indeed, one could challenge the necessity of including a sub-test with such weak function within the proportionality test. But since a sub-test so broadly conceived would rather be useless than too restrictive, we can accept for now that its inclusion would cause no problems to legal adjudication. Later (in Part Three), I will suggest a way in which introducing a sub-test against non-constitutional interests other than legitimate aims would contribute to improve the correctness of proportionality analysis.

II. Unimportant Goals

The second thesis is stronger than the first, for it imposes an additional requirement on constitutional aims. In this version, the initial sub-test of legitimate aims should stop not only interests and rights without constitutional pedigree but also – and mainly – measures that are not important from a constitutional perspective. This is in accordance with the practice of the Canadian Supreme Court as described by Grimm,[29] Webber,[30] and Urbina.[31] Webber, for example, affirms that the first query – which he calls the *public interest principle* – examines what is legally possible and

26 Ibid., 23.

27 Grégoire C.N. Webber, *The Negotiable Constitution: On the Limitation of Rights* (Cambridge, UK; New York: Cambridge University Press, 2009), 73.

28 Alexy, *Theory of Constitutional Rights* (n. 1), 225. Kumm observes that: "It has been held by the Constitutional Court [of Germany] to include such mundane things as a right to ride horses through public woods, feed pigeons in public squares, smoke marihuana, and bring a particular breed of dogs into the country." (Mattias Kumm, "What Do You Have in Virtue of Having a Constitutional Right? On the Place and Limits of the Proportionality Requirement," *New York University Public Law and Legal Theory Working Papers* (December 15, 2006): 13\\uc0\\u8221{} \\i New York University Public Law and Legal Theory Working Papers\\i0{} (December 15, 2006).

29 "Proportionality in Canadian and German Constitutional Jurisprudence" (n. 16).

30 *The Negotiable Constitution* (n. 27), 71: "Under European, German, Canadian, British, Israeli, and South African jurisprudence, among others, the principle of proportionality proceeds according to the following four inquires."

31 Francisco J. Urbina, "A Critique of Proportionality," *American Journal of Jurisprudence* 57 (2012).

requires that "the objective of the legislation setting out the limitation must be of sufficient importance to warrant infringing a right."[32]

There are two ways of interpreting the importance of an aim as an additional requirement to its constitutional status. The first would be to consider that only the interests that the constitutional text expressly and exhaustively mentions as limits to a right are important. That is the opinion of Urbina: "the measure that interferes with a right has to have an objective of sufficient importance. What counts as such an objective is commonly established in general terms by the instrument guaranteeing the affected right."[33] This view attaches extra weight to the constitutional language, and there are two arguments against doing so: the risk of artificial interpretation and the absence of theoretical support.

The risk of artificial interpretation arises where the possibility for balancing is hindered or unnaturally narrowed. In cases where proportionality is crucial, but balancing has been artificially eliminated from the process, judges cannot employ the complete test. This may force them to adopt pragmatic solutions to accommodate the outcomes they consider to be correct even where they know that this contradicts the more natural interpretation of the constitution. A judge could, for example, force the inclusion of an interest into the scope of protection of a limit textually admitted. However common the strategy is,[34] it may have adverse consequences. Frequent appeals to readings that do not come naturally from the constitutional text could degenerate into a threat to the binding power of the constitution. Other judges, lawyers, and citizens could end up taking its provisions less seriously. This scenario would weaken the constitutional influence over the legal system instead of reinforcing it.

There also remains a lack of theoretical justification for equating the importance of an aim with the explicit mention of it in constitutional wording, thus regarding unwritten aims as unimportant. In fact, the legislature could hardly succeed in establishing an exhaustive list of limitation clauses by enumerating all the permissible objectives that would limit a right. That is because, as Alexy sees, constitutional rights are optimization requirements, to be realised to the greatest extent possible – i. e., considering the legal and factual possibilities,[35] which include contingencies that were not foreseeable by the framers of the constitution. Hence, although it is possible to "distinguish between articles in which legitimate aims are separately and expressly enumerated and those in which they are not,"[36] the text does not impose a definitive difference in argumentation. To summarize, admitting that the wording of certain constitutional clauses would per se keep them safe from balancing, with-

32 Webber, *The Negotiable Constitution* (n. 27), 71–72.

33 Urbina, "A Critique of Proportionality" (n. 31): 49.

34 Not coincidentally, Webber observes that, while the European Convention on Human Rights provides for a list of limitation clauses that was designed to be exhaustive, the European Court of Human Rights (ECHR) has generally admitted all public interests as falling under the same limit, the open-ended reference of "democratic society," regardless the actual content of the interests at stake. Interestingly, also according to Webber, ECHR's approach is similar to that taken under constitutions that do not "specify the permissible ends of a democratic society," such as "the Canadian Charter, South Africa Bill of Rights, New Zealand Bill of Rights, and the legislative charters of rights in Australia." (*The Negotiable Constitution* (n. 27), 73.)

35 *A Theory of Constitutional Rights* (n. 1).

36 Rivers, "Variable Intensity of Review" (n. 20), 181.

out requiring extra justification, contradicts the very concept of principle underlying the proportionality test.[37]

There are other ways of understanding the assertion that the legitimacy of an aim depends on its "sufficient importance."[38] One could claim that assessing the importance of a right requires a criterion other than a constitutional clause expressly providing for it. It is still disputable, however, what criterion that would be. For instance, the Supreme Court of Canada settled that "the standard must be high to ensure that trivial objectives ... do not gain protection."[39] Nonetheless, such criterion would test positive for circular reasoning, as it simply restates that an interest is important if it is not trivial. Particularly, it treats importance as an intrinsic attribute of certain interests, which contradicts the assumption of relational importance that justified employing the proportionality test from the beginning.[40]

Furthermore, it is also disputable which reasons would support an additional criterion, whatever it might be – for instance, as in the Canadian case law, "to ensure that ... [objectives that are] discordant with the principles of a free and democratic society do not gain protection."[41] It is not too much to call to mind that the third prong of the proportionality test as conceived by Alexy already serves as a sub-test for assessing the importance of a right relative to competing principles. That is the sub-test of balancing. By determining the degree of interference of one right with another, a judge concretely determines the relative importance of each conflicting right. Justification is still needed as to why this analysis should anticipate the sub-tests of suitability and necessity.[42] A risk here is that interpreters use the possibility of anticipation as a strategy to avoid employing the weight formula, thus escaping the duty of exposing in detail the argumentative process that led to the decision.

III. Morally Incorrect Ideals

Finally, the third thesis concerning the sub-test of legitimate aims is that it poses an even stronger claim of minimum moral correctness. That is the opinion of *Möller*, according to whom perfectionist goals (which he calls "paternalist" and "moralist")

37 In fact, it has been generally admitted that "legitimate aims can be expressed in a written general limitation clause, in a written specific limitation clause, or in an unwritten limitation clause." (Klatt and Meister, *Constitutional Structure of Proportionality* (n. 24), 23–4).

38 *R. v. Oakes*, [1986] 1 S.C.R. 103 (Can.).

39 Ibid.

40 Alexy's general understanding on importance is as follows: "The importance which a position must have from the perspective of constitutional law in order for it to be treated as a constitutional right is not an intrinsic importance, but an importance relative to the principles which count for and against characterizing a certain position as a constitutional one." (*Theory of Constitutional Rights* (n. 1), 298). Moreover, assessing the intrinsic importance of a legal act would be questionable. In Grimm's words, "in a democracy the legislature is entitled to pursue any purpose, provided it is not excluded by the constitution. The importance of the purpose is not a condition for legislative action." ("Proportionality in Canadian and German Constitutional Jurisprudence" (n. 16): 388).

41 *R. v. Oakes* (n. 38).

42 "Raising this question [of importance] in connection with the purpose [of the measure under review] would be regarded as a premature anticipation of the final balance." Grimm, "Proportionality in Canadian and German Constitutional Jurisprudence" (n. 16) at 388.

should be excluded from the proportionality analysis.[43] Tsakyrakis adds collectivist reasons (to which he refers as the "protection of the public interest") to those that should be kept out of legal argumentation.[44] Kumm and Waler, in turn, stress that consequentialist arguments should not be balanced.[45] Although the intention of some of these authors is broader than only excluding reasons from the proportionality test – Tsakyrakis, e.g., aims to discredit the test itself[46] –, the core of their criticism can be captured as a claim against submitting certain arguments to the sub-test of balancing.[47] Thus, instead of renouncing the proportionality test altogether, one can ask whether the prong of legitimate ends can accommodate a firewall that would prevent perfectionist, collectivist, and consequentialist reasoning.[48]

A. Perfectionist Ideals

According to Kumm, perfectionist ideals remove from individuals the possibility of answering by themselves questions such as "how they should live their lives, in particular with regard to dominant religious practices" or "what it means to aspire to be the best person you can."[49] He claims that the first prong of the proportionality test, the sub-test of legitimate aims, shall exclude perfectionist purposes because they cannot "justify infringements of individual liberty."[50] Kumm illustrates his assertion by using the example of a legal rule prescribing that "the school day in public schools should begin with a common prayer."[51] For him, the fact that the measure serves the interests of a majority of families that belong to the same religion cannot constitute a legitimate aim to outweigh the freedom of religion for those who do not profess that faith. Because of its perfectionist character, the majority interest would fail to pass the sub-test of legitimacy.[52]

43 Kai Möller, "Proportionality: Challenging the Critics," *International Journal of Constitutional Law* 10, 3 (July 1, 2012) at 712: "At this stage of the proportionality test it is necessary to decide for each goal whether or not it is legitimate, and this will require a moral argument."

44 Stavros Tsakyrakis, "Proportionality: An Assault on Human Rights?," *International Journal of Constitutional Law* 7, 3 (July 1, 2009): 468–93.

45 Mattias Kumm and Alec Walen, "Human Dignity and Proportionality: Deontic Pluralism in Balancing," *Proportionality and the Rule of Law: Rights, Justification, Reasoning* (January 2, 2013); Kumm, "What Do You Have in Virtue of Having a Constitutional Right?" (n. 28).\\uc0\\ u8221{} \\i New York University Public Law and Legal Theory Working Papers\\i0{} (December 15, 2006

46 Stavros Tsakyrakis, "Proportionality: An Assault on Human Rights? A Rejoinder to Madhav Khosla," *International Journal of Constitutional Law* 8, 2 (April 1, 2010): 307–10.

47 This is also the opinion of Madhav Khosla, "Proportionality: An Assault on Human Rights? A Reply," *International Journal of Constitutional Law* 8, 2 (April 1, 2010): 298–306.

48 A statement from Kumm and Walen summarizes the three approaches: "Any plausible structure of rights must be able to accommodate anti-perfectionist, anti-collectivist and anti-consequentialist ideas underlying the liberal democratic rights tradition." ("Human Dignity and Proportionality" (n. 45) at 68. See also Kumm, "What Do You Have in Virtue of Having a Constitutional Right?" (n. 28).

49 Kumm, "What Do You Have in Virtue of Having a Constitutional Right?" (n. 28) at 14.

50 Ibid., 17–8. Möller, "Proportionality" (n. 43): at 712 agrees with this view.

51 "What Do You Have in Virtue of Having a Constitutional Right?" (n. 28) at 15.

52 Ibid., 15–8.

Kumm is correct in affirming that the proportionality test has to provide an answer to the case of prayer in public schools and that the answer must conform to the common thought that it violates the freedom of religion of those who do not affirm that faith. However, it is still disputable, whether the same result could not be reached without adding a moral claim to the sub-test of legitimate aims, or even without employing the respective sub-test. Firstly, it is true that some perfectionist ideals and interests are not constitutionally protected. In this sense, they would fail the sub-test in its weakest version. An example is a law requiring affiliation to a certain church as a condition for admission to the public schools of a state governed by a secular constitution that has established the principle of equal access to public education. Nonetheless, such obvious absence of constitutionally admitted goals – and thus, flagrant arbitrariness – is rare in democratic states, and given the case, the illegitimacy is pronounced due to the indisputable lack of constitutional support, and not due to perfectionism. Secondly, one must acknowledge that several legal systems encompass values that are prima facie perfectionist. These values are regarded as constitutional to the extent that they do not impose a disproportionate burden on the people. Therefore, what makes an interest arbitrary is its lack of proportionality, rather than its perfectionist nature. Thus, there is no reason for stopping it from being balanced against competing rights. An example can be given to support the latter idea.

We could consider a state in which male circumcision on religious grounds is admitted, and forced clitoridectomy is not, even being historically part of the religious traditions of a certain minority. It is not difficult to conceive that people could most probably regard that state of affairs as legitimate, but never the opposite situation in which religious-based male circumcision was prohibited and female genital mutilation not. The difference in treatment that a society gives to both practices is not the result of excluding perfectionist arguments because they are illegitimate. Since both refer to religious practices, if one were excluded because of its perfectionist character, the same should happen to the other. An explanation for religious-based circumcision being accepted in countries where female genital mutilation is not is the sub-test of proportionality in its narrow sense. Only after balancing freedom of religion with body integrity, can one come to the conclusion that in the first case the degree of interference in the child's body might be tolerable, while in the second it cannot.[53]

53 We can also imagine an indigenous tribe that represents a religious minority in a majority catholic society governed by a typically liberal constitution that recognizes human dignity and grants all citizens the right to life and freedom of religion. In this scenario, we would consider legitimate a governmental measure that stopped the sacrifice of twins in that tribe, even if sacrificing twins was part of their religious beliefs. Differently, a governmental policy that forces the natives to dress in accordance with catholic standards by regarding their nudity as indecent exposure under criminal law is mostly regarded as illegitimate. Considering that both measures equally tell people how to live their lives with regard to the religious practices of other people – and thus both are to some extent perfectionist – there must be a reason other than perfectionism for coherently differentiating between them. Such a reason might be the heavier weight that we attach to the right to life when compared to freedom of religion (in the first scenario), and to freedom of religion when compared to local moral or other standards of appropriate behaviour (in the second).

B. Collectivist Ideals

Collectivist ideals are those normally connected to the "general interest" of society.[54] According to Kumm, taking the individual seriously demands giving rights some priority over the "collective good."[55] This idea is based on the liberal conception that the rights of an individual trump collective goals, i. e. they would be legal shields originally framed to protect individuals and minorities from the will of the majority. To correctly understand whether and how this conception can be accommodated within the proportionality test, specifically in the prong of legitimate aims, we shall interpret the priority of rights over collective goals using the language of the principles theory. We shall also consider that the collective goals potentially colliding with individual rights are solely those with a constitutional status – i. e., the collectivistic interests that would pass the sub-test of legitimate aims in its weaker version.[56]

Within this framework, the only way to make room for the image of absolute limits trumping the power of democratically elected authorities would be to conceive individual rights as the result of a proportionality test already performed by the framers of the constitution. From a liberal point of view, yet within the language of proportionality, the individual rights in a constitution are definitive rights, overcoming any opposing interests that might be conceivable. In addition, freedoms such as that of speech, for example, would reflect a concrete case of preference for the general right to liberty over competing principles. Departing from these assumptions, one could conclude that, since submitting definitive rights to balancing would be both pointless – because they are already the outcome of balancing – and dangerous – by opening the chance of an inaccurate, disproportionate outcome –, it would be better to use the prong of legitimate ends to protect them, by stopping collective goals from re-entering the proportionality test.[57]

There are three problems in this construction. The first is that it overestimates the framers' capacity of predicting the future conditions under which constitutional norms will be applied. It is at least counterintuitive to think that a group of men and women gathering together to write and promulgate a constitution could consider all the possible circumstances of social life not only in present, by also for the future, and enact in response an exhaustive list of definitive rights and limitations. Secondly, the idea that bills of rights encompass only definitive rights is not supported

54 Kumm, "What Do You Have in Virtue of Having a Constitutional Right?" (n. 28) at 14.

55 Ibid.

56 See Klatt and Meister, *Constitutional Structure of Proportionality* (n. 24), 49: "Only public interests of constitutional status are considered as legitimate aims."

57 Similar outcome would be produced by systematically excluding constitutional rights from the proportionality test under the general assumption that the constitutional text already expresses their core. One would reach this scenario by taking too seriously the idea that "once an interest has been identified at the core of a right … that interest must not be balanced away." (Perju, "Proportionality and Freedom" (n. 22): 354) Although Perju stated this in a different context – he was not referring to an additional step to the proportionality test –, what he calls "the formalizing technique of distinguishing between the core and periphery of rights" may be regarded as an example of excluded reasons as well. It would be not a previous step to balancing, though. The problem of the core can be solved coherently by attributing more weight to the principle within the weight formula – thus, within balancing.

by the constitutional wording. According to Alexy, the outcome of balancing is necessarily a rule establishing both "the conditions under which one principle takes precedence over another" and "the legal consequences of the principle taking precedence."[58] Consequently, a provision establishing a definitive right – i.e. a right that is the final product of the proportionality test – can only be a rule. Nevertheless, that does not correspond to what we find in actual constitutions and charts. Due to their open texture, which is typical of principles, many constitutional clauses could hardly be (and in fact are not) regarded as rules.[59]

Thirdly, since constitutional rights are principles, and principles are optimization requirements, they require further decision about the extent to which they ought to be applied in a concrete case. A judge in charge of deciding it has to make use of the proportionality test. There is no reason to avoid doing so. The arguments that submitting definitive rights to balancing would be both pointless and dangerous are false. Even if we admit that some constitutional clauses actually provide for definitive rights, to submit them again to balancing should not cause difficulties. Definitive rights should pass the proportionality test without limitations being added to them. The test would then confirm the initial assumption and provide stronger arguments in favour of it.[60] Therefore, as there is no reason to stop collective goals from entering the proportionality test, there is no reason to use the subtest of legitimate aims as an anti-collectivistic firewall.

C. Consequentialist Ideals

Consequentialist ideals treat "persons as a means to achieve some desirable end." Departing from this conception, Kumm criticised the proportionality test because it would be "unable to take into account strong prohibitions on using persons as a means to achieve some desirable end."[61] In a later paper, however, he reconsidered his opinion in accordance with Alexy, who explained that the weight formula works as an anti-consequentialist firewall if an interpreter attributes the value of zero to consequentialist arguments.[62] Based on this, one may wonder why the same interpreter should not anticipate this anti-consequentialist barrier and make it the initial step of proportionality analysis. After all, in some circumstances, the outcome of balancing can be easily foreseen. In such cases, regarding consequentialist ends as

58 Alexy, *A Theory of Constitutional Rights* (n. 1), at 69.

59 To mention three examples, Article 4 (1) of Germany's Basic Law reads: "Freedom of faith and of conscience, and freedom to profess a religious or philosophical creed, shall be inviolable;" Amendment 1 to the U.S. Constitution reads: "Congress shall make no law respecting an establishment of religion, or prohibiting the free exercise thereof; or abridging the freedom of speech, or of the press;" and article 5, VI, of the Brazilian Federal Constitution reads: "Freedom of conscience and of belief is inviolable."

60 Kumm and Walen reached identical conclusion: "By weighing correctly the relevant considerations when conducting the balancing test," the proportionality test would "adequately accommodate anti-collectivist commitments." ("Human Dignity and Proportionality" (n. 45), at 69.

61 Kumm, "What Do You Have in Virtue of Having a Constitutional Right?" (n. 28) at 14.

62 Kumm and Walen, "Human Dignity and Proportionality" (n. 45): 69; Alexy, "Thirteen Replies" (n. 3), at 344.

illegitimate and excluding them from the proportionality test from the beginning would avoid a pointless effort of argumentation.

We cannot conclude from this, however, that the sub-test of legitimate aims should stop all consequentialist interests from entering balancing, or that they will necessarily fail in prevailing over other principles. To illustrate my point, we can think of a state with a constitution that guarantees the right to public health care to the highest possible standard for all its citizens. Imagine an individual living in this state has a very rare disease that demands an extremely costly treatment, which would compromise the financial budget for the assistance of many other citizens. Deciding whether his constitutional right to health encompasses such treatment requires assessing consequentialist arguments. Either his right is granted, which implies treating other people as means, or his fellow citizens' rights are granted, which means treating him as a means.[63] Whether the best solution for the problem remains disputable, excluding consequentialist arguments does not contribute to the debates. In fact, someone who is concerned about the right way to decide such cases would necessarily have to answer to which extent a consequentialist interest passes the proportionality test.

In conclusion, the question whether to accommodate an anti-perfectionist, anti-collectivist, and anti-consequentialist firewall within the proportionality test does not take seriously enough Alexy's claim that balancing is "unavoidable."[64] It departs from the false premise that these ideals exist regardless of the proportionality test. Actually, we can only affirm that these ideals are part of our constitutional life because what we consider to be the correct outcomes of the proportionality test in different cases points in this direction. The outcome – the heavier weight attributed to anti-consequentialist ideals in a judge's opinion or in a court's case law, for example – reflects the moral understanding of an authority or institution. The problem thus does not point to the proportionality test itself, but rather to the philosophical view carried by men and women in charge of operating it. Once this has been made clear, we can answer negatively the question whether a sub-test is required to exclude all perfectionist, collectivist, and consequentialist ideals from the proportionality test. Nonetheless, we cannot conclude from this that no morally defective reasons can be excluded, as I will explain next.

Part Three: What Reasons Ought to be Excluded?

We have provisionally accepted the weaker thesis that the sub-test of legitimate aims might serve to exclude interests without constitutional status from the proportionality analysis. I will now explain in which sense this assertion can be read so that the proportionality test can be improved overall. First, the inclusion of the sub-test of

63 This is a necessary feature of social constitutional rights. As Alexy puts it, "in satisfying social constitutional rights, the state can only distribute what it has taken from others ... But this means that the much discussed limits of the ability of the state to deliver ... [arise] to a large extent on what the state is allowed to take from the owners of these goods for the purposes of redistribution without breaching their constitutional rights." Robert Alexy, *A Theory of Constitutional Rights* (n. 1), at 342.

64 Ibid., at 73.

legitimate aims with the proportionality analysis may have the important purpose of preventing goals above the threshold of extreme injustice from being balanced. Additionally, the general scheme of proportionality is in need of a sub-test to exclude measures performed with nonconformity to procedural principles or by officers not legally invested with power and authority.

I. Extremely and Obviously Unjust Measures

I stated before (in Part One) that there are two ways to accommodate a test on the legitimacy of aims within the proportionality test. The second model suggests testing the legitimacy of aims before balancing. Differently, the first model places the analysis of legitimate aims within the sub-test of balancing. There is a crucial difference between the two models. In the first model, even when a value of zero is attached to a morally incorrect interest, as defended by Alexy,[65] this attachment happens in the last phase of the proportionality test, after the two first sub-tests. The outcome may be the same, for "participating in balancing without any weight is … not really to participate in balancing."[66] And admittedly, Alexy's answer is perfectly logical and consistent with the principles theory. Nevertheless, if we broaden our scope to consider the practical implications of such a scheme, we will see that it poses two risks.

The first risk is that of making trivial the reasoning about obvious and extreme injustice. The risk of trivialisation arises because proportionality encompasses sub-tests that must be performed in succession. Consequently, a judge strictly following Alexy's scheme would have to assess the suitability and necessity (first and second sub-tests, respectively) of reasons that are obviously and extremely unjust. This would be largely regarded as absurd, for instance, if a supreme court had to consider whether an act is suitable and necessary for promoting the right of property of slave owners. Therefore, to reflect what we consider to be the correct way to deal with our moral traditions, we should accommodate the exclusion of morally defective interests such as this, as a previous step within the scheme of the proportionality test.

On the other hand, a judge should not preventively exclude all morally controversial arguments from balancing. That is, in fact, the second risk I mentioned above, that of over-reaction. Alexy showed sympathy for using the sub-test of legitimate aims as a firewall stopping perfectionist, collectivist, and consequentialist ideals.[67] The problem is that from his claim, one could draw the extreme conclusion that any morally controversial interest should be excluded. A judge who adopts this line of argumentation in very difficult cases could be tempted to avoid the burden of justification by excluding a priori reasons that, however morally controversial, are not obviously and extremely unjust. She would, for example, exclude all perfectionist reasons and give perfectionism per se as justification for doing so. As I explained before (in Part Two), this is not a sound solution for the conflicts of principles actual judges have faced in many legal systems.

65 Alexy, "Thirteen Replies" (n. 3), at 344.
66 Ibid., at 341.
67 Ibid.

Departing from the premise that below the threshold of extreme injustice, proportionality analysis is "not in a position to justify which reasons are to be excluded,"[68] we can suggest how to accommodate the exclusion of certain moral interests within the framework of the principles theory. The sub-test of legitimate aims, performed before balancing, should be used to exclude morally defective interests that are clearly beyond the threshold of extreme injustice. It should not, however, impede other morally controversial ideals from entering balancing, where their relative importance can be assessed. Interests are morally controversial if they are clearly above that threshold, or it is disputable whether they are extremely unjust or not. This solution combines the exclusion of certain reasons (similarly to the second model) with correctly balancing others (as suggested by the first model).

Turning the legitimate aims into a firewall only against goals that are extremely immoral brings three systematic advantages. First, it connects Alexy's *argument from principles* with the more general premises that support the principles theory, more specifically with the *argument from injustice*, according to which a norm, act, or policy forfeits legal character if it is unjust above the threshold of extreme injustice.[69] A goal whose injustice is so extreme and evident is deemed an invalid principle of a legal system. For not being valid, it "can never justify any limitation of any right."[70] Secondly, the combined model recognizes that "in many cases, it is not easy to draw a line between norms that are unjust in the extreme and norms that are not."[71] So, it does not admit the exclusion a priori of morally controversial issues from the proportionality analysis. On the contrary, it facilitates the rational analysis and justification of these matters, which can contribute to the debate on the right way to act in those difficult cases. Thirdly, employing the legitimate aims as a permeable barrier – stopping extremely and evidently unjust measures and permitting that morally controversial interests are assessed in the sub-test of balancing – correctly differentiates what is exceptional from what is normal. Thus, it is in accordance with Alexy's thought that "the argument from injustice focuses on an exceptional situation," while "the argument from principles is addressed to the everyday life of the law."[72]

II. Formally Defective Measures

I will now turn my attention to a different problem: there are cases in which the principles supporting a measure are prima facie constitutional, but the measure itself is not. As explained in Part Two, the thesis that the sub-test of legitimate aims should exclude interests without constitutional pedigree from the proportionality analysis is not incorrect; its main problem is excessive weakness or lack of effectiveness. There is, however, a way in which employing a sub-test against non-constitutional interests would contribute to the correctness of proportionality analysis. This could be done by assigning it the task of assessing whether the measure was perfor-

68 Ibid., at 341.
69 Alexy, *The Argument from Injustice* (n. 14), at 40–62.
70 Alexy, "Thirteen Replies" (n. 3), at 341.
71 Alexy, *The Argument from Injustice* (n. 14), at 44.
72 Ibid., at 68.

med in conformity to procedural principles, or if it was by officers entrusted with legal power and authority. In a state governed by the rule of law, the legitimacy of a measure does not depend solely on the aims it pursues, but also on how it pursues them. Measures in clear violation of constitutional rules regarding proceedings and competency would be excluded immediately. In this sense, a more comprehensive sub-test of *legitimacy*, encompassing both legitimate aims and means, would work as a firewall against interests without constitutional support,[73] and the problem of excessive weakness attributed to the sub-test of legitimate aims would be circumvented by an additional formal task.[74]

One could withdraw from the principles theory an objection to this suggestion. In *A Theory of Constitutional Rights,* Alexy expressly refers – more than once – to the possibility of balancing between formal and substantive principles.[75] Consequently, there would be no reason for excluding formal principles from the proportionality test. Nevertheless, not only the premise is questionable, as the objection itself misses the point. First, regarding the premise: despite the existing references to balancing between formal and material principles in Alexy's works, Klatt and Meister showed that formal principles, which "establish how and by whom the substantial content is to be established," differ from material principles, for the former do not have "any substantial content."[76] Formal principles only indicate the authority responsible for either performing or reviewing the legal act, as well as which procedure he or she should follow in each of these instances. It is, therefore, doubtful that they can enter the proportionality test when a material principle is at stake.

Secondly and most importantly, however, is that the objection is addressed to the wrong target. It points to a situation of supposed conflict between a formal and a material principle. But that is not the scenario I described when suggesting an additional formal task in the sub-test of legitimate aims. The officer responsible for

73 A sub-test of legitimacy, requiring that both aims and means are legitimate, has been already suggested by Klatt and Meister. The authors, however, present a different conception of legitimate means. See: Matthias Klatt and Moritz Meister, "*Der Grundsatz der Verhältnismäßigkei: Eine Kernstructur des globalen Konstitutionalismus*", Juristische Schulung (JuS), 54 (2014): 194–195.

74 Whereas some critics may regard the suggestion of introducing a firewall against formally defective measures within the proportionality test as inconvenient or even incorrect, I insist in the pertinence of doing so. The problem here is probably one of context. In Germany and in many other countries, it has long been settled that judicial review starts with the analysis of formal correction, and only after the measure under review passes through a formal checklist, its substantial character is assessed. Under the strength of this long- and well-established legal tradition, it might seem obvious to the authorities responsible for the judicial review that the proportionality test should only apply after the formal exam. Nonetheless, what judges in Germany do almost by inertia might not correspond to the actual practice in other countries, where the test has also been applied. Here, I specifically consider new democracies, such as Brazil, where the constitutional tradition is still being built and the methods for constitutional adjudication are far from ubiquitous.

75 See, for instance, the assertions that: "this procedural principle, together with a substantive principle serving some secondary public interest, can be balanced against a constitutional principle guaranteeing an individual right". Robert Alexy, *A Theory of Constitutional Rights* (n. 1), 82, and "the prognosis problem becomes one of balancing relevant substantive constitutional principles with the formal principle of the democratically legitimated competence of the legislature to take decisions." Ibid., at 313.

76 Klatt and Meister, *Constitutional Structure of Proportionality* (n. 24), at 135–36.

reviewing whether a measure was performed in conformity with constitutional procedure, and by a legally entrusted authority, wants to prevent measures that are formally defective from entering balancing. Thus, before applying the proportionality test as originally designed, he or she should be concerned about formal principles. Only if the measure passes the sub-test of legitimacy (because it is formally perfect), the substantive principles given for or against it will come into play. This is in accordance with Klatt and Meister's conclusion that "we must distribute the issues of competency and the material principles at two different levels" in order to guarantee that "balancing between two material principles … remain possible without any regard to aspects of competency."[77]

Concluding Remark

At the beginning of this paper, I posed some questions that I shall now answer. Concerning the first two questions – whether testing the legitimacy of aims should be part of the proportionality scheme, and whether it is necessary to exclude certain reasons from the proportionality analysis – the answer is affirmative. As regards the third question – what reasons ought to be excluded – a sub-test on the legitimacy of means and aims should be performed before balancing and used to exclude formally defective measures and morally defective interests that are clearly beyond the threshold of extreme injustice. It should not, however, impede morally controversial ideals from entering balancing, where their relative importance can be assessed.

The exclusion of formally defective measures is justified by the assumption underlying the principles theory that only interests with constitutional status should limit constitutional rights. This assumption is excessively weak if read as such that only requires that the content of a legal act conforms to material principles. If almost everything is regarded as constitutionally guaranteed, a firewall that prevents non-constitutional interests from entering the proportionality test actually excludes too few. However, the general scheme of proportionality is in need of a sub-test to exclude measures that do not conform to procedural principles or are enacted by officers not legally entrusted with power and authority. In this sense, a more comprehensive sub-test of *legitimacy*, encompassing both legitimate aims and means, would simultaneously work as a firewall against interests without constitutional support and circumvent the problem of excessive weakness attributed to the sub-test of legitimate aims.

Finally, concerning the requirement of minimum moral correctness attached to the sub-test of legitimate aims, it is necessary to circumvent the risks of trivialisation and over-reaction. I suggest doing so by combining the exclusion a priori of extremely unjust reasons with correctly balancing reasons that are either morally controversial or clearly not unjust. This solution would take Alexy's assertion that balancing is "unavoidable" seriously.[78] Several *values that are morally controversial, such as perfectionist or consequentialist aims, are constitutional to the extent they do not impose a disproportionate burden on people.* These ideals are made arbitrary by their lack of pro-

77 Ibid., at 142.

78 Alexy, *A Theory of Constitutional Rights* (n. 1), at 73.

portionality, rather than any independent moral quality; there is no reason to prevent them from being balanced against competing rights. *Therefore, their exclusion from balancing should be supported by something stronger than perfectionism, collectivism, or consequentialism per se, and that would be their eventual moral defectiveness beyond the threshold of extreme injustice.*

This idea is built on Alexy's assertion that below the threshold of extreme injustice, proportionality is "not in a position to justify which reasons are to be excluded," which is "a question of substantive moral and political theory."[79] Admittedly, the solution can be drawn from the principles theory. Nonetheless, it is not too much to emphasise the increase in clarity that this arrangement brings. There is a positive, practical impact in exposing the risks of trivialisation and over-reaction, as well as the difficulties of balancing formally defective measures. And practical impacts are something with we should be particularly concerned, as the proportionality test has long been more than a theoretical construction, but a method used by courts in several countries for judicial adjudication in deciding on difficult constitutional matters.

79 Alexy, "Thirteen Replies" (n. 3), at 341.

Ralf Poscher

Theory of a Phantom

The Principles Theory's Futile Quest for its Object

Introduction: The Principles Theory's Concept of a Principle

In his theory of fundamental rights, Robert Alexy has taken up Ronald Dworkin's distinction between rules and principles and developed it into an all-encompassing principles theory of fundamental rights. In his circle of students, a little principles theory industry has evolved, within which Alexy's approach has been partly reformulated[1], specified for individual rights[2], extended from fundamental rights to other areas of law[3] and even elevated to the level of a general theory of law[4]. Alexy himself has fostered this development by continually refining, modifying and sophisticating his principles theory. Under his leadership, the principles theory has developed into a general legal theory, which claims to hold insights for diverse areas of the law, as well as for specific legal questions and for the understanding of law in general thanks to the analysis of both the nature and functional structure of principles.[5]

The distinction between rules and principles lies at the heart of the principles theory. For principles theorists, rules and principles are thought to differ in their formal structure. While rules strictly order a certain consequence, principles order a certain consequence only *prima facie*.[6] The differing structure of these two types of norms is thought to be evident from the way in which they collide with other norms. In the case of rule collision, either one of the rules is amended by an exception, or one of them is declared void; in case of a collision of principles, both principles remain valid, because they have only *prima facie* validity and therefore need to be optimized and developed into a precise rule by balancing them in each individ-

1 Martin Borowski, *Grundrechte als Prinzipien*, 2nd ed. (Baden-Baden: Nomos, 2007).

2 Cf. Jan-Reinard Sieckmann, *Modelle des Eigentumsschutzes: Eine Untersuchung zur Eigentumsgarantie des Art. 14 GG* (Baden-Baden: Nomos, 1998); Martin Borowski, *Die Glaubens- und Gewissensfreiheit des Grundgesetzes* (Tübingen: Mohr Siebeck, 2006).

3 Cf. Jeong Hoon Park, *Rechtsfindung im Verwaltungsrecht: Grundlegung einer Prinzipientheorie des Verwaltungsrechts als Methode der Verwaltungsrechtsdogmatik* (Berlin: Duncker & Humblot, 1999); Jörg Pietsch, *Das Schrankenregime der EU-Grundrechtecharta: Dogmatik und Bewertung auf der Grundlage einer Prinzipientheorie der Rechte* (Baden-Baden: Nomos, 2005).

4 Most comprehensivly elaborated by Jan-Reinard Sieckmann, *Regelmodelle und Prinzipienmodelle des Rechtssystems* (Baden-Baden: Nomos, 1990); Sieckmann, *Recht als normatives System: Die Prinzipientheorie des Rechts* (Baden-Baden: Nomos, 2009).

5 As to the different aspects of the principles theory see Ralf Poscher, 'Einsichten, Irrtümer und Selbstmissverständnis der Prinzipientheorie', in *Prinzipientheorie der Grundrechte*, ed. Jan-Reinard Sieckmann (Baden-Baden: Nomos, 2007), 59–79; Poscher, 'Insights, Errors and Self-misconceptions of the Theory of Principles', *Ratio Juris*, 22 (2009), 425–54; Poscher, 'The Principle Theory: How Many Theories and What is Their Merit?', in *Institutionalized Reason. Perspectives on the Legal Philosophy of Robert Alexy*, ed. Matthias Klatt (New York: Oxford University Press, 2012), 218–47.

6 Robert Alexy, *Theorie der Grundrechte* (Frankfurt: Suhrkamp, 1986), 88–90; Sieckmann, *Regelmodelle* (n. 4), 67–71.

ual case of collision.[7] This norm-theoretical difference is supposed to be accompanied by a methodological one: "Rules are applied by subsumption of facts under the conditions of a norm in order to deduce the consequence… The application of principles, on the other hand, requires a specific balancing of the colliding principles."[8] On the level of legal doctrine, the norm-theoretical and methodological theses of the principles theory are combined: Legal norms that can be applied by the method of subsumption are qualified as rules and – due to the norm-ontological dualism stipulated by the principles theory – all other norms are principles. As principles they must be interpreted as optimization requirements for the same norm-theoretical reason. For the principles theory this has a direct impact on the doctrinal understanding of fundamental rights. Since fundamental rights cannot be applied by mere subsumption, they must be qualified as principles in the sense of the principles theory. Accordingly, fundamental rights must be interpreted as optimization requirements. And this is the doctrinal upshot of the principles theory: the doctrinal interpretation of fundamental rights as optimization requirements can be deduced already from the norm-theoretical dualism upheld by the principles theory.

The following critique will not focus on the merits of the principles theory as a doctrinal theory of fundamental rights or on its impact in other areas of the law.[9] Rather, it will challenge the central premise of the principles theory: the very existence of principles in the sense of the principles theory. Of course, their existence is not sufficient for the principles theory, but without it, the theory must collapse and with it the theoretical imposition of a fundamental rights doctrine.

The principles theory presupposes the existence of legal principles. At first sight, this seems a fairly unsuspicious assumption, since legal principles have formed part of the inventory of our legal universe for ages. But when the principles theory refers to legal principles, it does not refer to the rich diversity of traditional legal principles like the standard of the reasonable man, good faith, unjustified enrichment, equality and the like. When the principles theory talks about principles, it refers to the theoretical dualism mentioned above, according to which there are only two kinds of norms: rules, which allow for precise subsumption[10], and principles, which are to be found in the sphere of an "ideal ought", and which express themselves in the form of optimization requirements in the sphere of the real ought. So the concept of a principle in the sense of the principles theory should not be confused with the traditional concept of a legal principle, connected neither to a normative dualism, nor to the idea of an "ideal ought", nor to a monism of optimization. Due to the confusion between "principles" in the sense of the principles theory and "principles" in

7 Alexy, *Grundrechte* (n. 6), 77–87; Sieckmann, *Regelmodelle* (n. 4), 68.

8 Sieckmann, *Regelmodelle* (n. 4), 18; see also Robert Alexy, 'On Balancing and Subsumption', *Ratio Juris*, 16 (2003), 433–49.

9 Criticism of the theory's potential as regards the doctrinal development of fundamental rights was already expressed by Ralf Poscher, *Grundrechte als Abwehrrechte* (Tübingen: Mohr Siebeck, 2003), 82–4; see also Matthias Jestaedt, *Grundrechtsentfaltung im Gesetz* (Tübingen: Mohr Siebeck, 1999), 222–60; Wolfram Cremer, *Freiheitsgrundrechte* (Tübingen: Mohr Siebeck, 2003), 218–27; Jan Henrik Klement, 'Vom Nutzen einer Theorie, die alles erklärt', *Juristenzeitung*, 63 (2008), 756–63, 760; Benjamin Rusteberg, *Der Grundrechtliche Gewährleistungsgehalt* (Tübingen: Mohr Siebeck, 2009), 158–66.

10 As to criticism of the principles theory's notion of a rule see Poscher, 'Einsichten' (n. 5), 70–3; Poscher, 'Insights' (n. 5), 438–41.

the traditional sense, it is rarely noticed how demanding the principles theory's concept of a principle really is: For the principles theory, it is not sufficient to refer to the existence of principles in the traditional sense. Instead, it must prove the existence of principles in its own special understanding, i.e. as a distinct normative entity that differs from other legal norms in terms of its structure and not only due to a more or less abstract content or a greater or lesser importance. Even within the principles theory, there is controversy over what principles are supposed to be, how they should be described and how they need to be theoretically reconstructed. It is a remarkable fact in itself that the central object of the principles theory is so hotly disputed by its own adherents.[11] This dispute is not over the refinement of the theory; adherents too, contest each other's construction of principles in their special sense and thus the object of their own theory.

Initially, Robert Alexy equated principles in the sense of the principles theory with optimization requirements. In his foundational "Theory of Constitutional Rights", the central passage on "principles as optimization requirements" is still written with this equation in mind:

> The decisive point in distinguishing rules from principles is that *principles* are norms which require that something be realized to the greatest extent possible given the legal and factual possibilities. Principles are *optimization requirements*, characterized by the fact that they can be satisfied to varying degrees, and that the appropriate degree of satisfaction depends not only on what is factually possible but also on what is legally possible... By contrast, *rules* are norms which are always either fulfilled or not.[12]

In the beginning, principles were just optimization requirements. And this was the very point of Alexy's conception of principles, namely that it specified Dworkin's idea of a "prima facie ought" as an optimization requirement.[13] Optimization in this sense requires the relativization of the consequence of a norm in accordance with the factual and legal possibilities,[14] which, in turn, specifies Dworkin's dimension of weight. This specifying reconstruction of Dworkin's principles as optimization requirements was the analytical achievement of the early principles theory.

But it did not take long for adherents of the principles theory themselves to see that in fact, optimization requirements present all the features of *rules* in the sense of the principles theory. Like any other requirement, they can be strictly and completely obeyed by performing the required optimization. If a legal norm requires truck drivers to optimize tire pressure for the sake of fuel consumption and safety purposes, truck drivers are strictly obliged to perform the required optimization. Jan Sieckmann, a student of Alexy, thus states "that the problem remains that the optimization requirements ... show just the features that are characteristic for rules, i.e. strict validity and definite satisfiability."[15] The insight that optimization requirements are not structurally distinct from other norms, however, is a problem only for the principles theory. On the basis of a traditional understanding of principles,

11 Cf. the renewed criticism of Alexy's notion of a principle by Sieckmann, *Normatives System* (n. 4), 22–3.

12 Robert Alexy, *A Theory of Constitutional Rights* (Oxford: Oxford UP, 2002, repr. 2010), 47–8 (emphasis in original).

13 Ibid., 57–9.

14 Ibid., 47–8.

15 Sieckmann, *Regelmodelle* (n. 4), 65.

which sees only gradual differences between legal principles and other types of legal norms, the insight would not come as a surprise. It would merely corroborate the traditional view by showing that the traditional understanding of principles also applies to legal principles that can be reconstructed as optimization requirements.

The loss of optimization requirements as candidates for the conception of principles caused the principles theory to slide into a precarious situation: it was threatened with losing its very object. It comes as no surprise that adherents of the principles theory engaged in serious theoretical efforts to provide a concept of principles that could support the theoretical dualism they were claiming. For Robert Alexy, however, the discovery that optimization requirements are not principles was no reason to revise the principles theory, but "only shed an even brighter light on them."[16] Ever since, Alexy has maintained that principles are an "ideal ought".[17]

With regard to rescue attempts like these, it does not seem too far-fetched to object that they only serve the purpose of creating a theoretical artifact to replace the object of the principles theory with the realization of the rule-like character of optimization requirements.[18] In two of his more recent publications, Alexy has responded to this line of critique and defended his conception of principles as an "ideal ought".[19] The critique he faced is twofold: First, that the supposition of an "ideal ought" is superfluous; second, that there is no "ideal ought" in legal systems. And as Alexy has correctly remarked: "The ontological objection is the more radical. If it succeeds, the objection of superfluity would succeed as well".[20]

In what follows, I first want to scrutinize Alexy's reply to the objection of superfluity. This is not for dramaturgical reasons only – superfluity follows from non-existence – but also on strategic grounds. While most adherents of the principles theory agree on why they need their theoretically demanding concept of principles – namely to explain the functioning and normative qualities of optimization requirements – almost every theorist has his own thesis about what principles are supposed to be and how they differ from optimization requirements.[21] Almost half a dozen different conceptions are on offer. The development of the principles theory nourishes the suspicion that critique is confronted with a hydra-like phenomenon. For each candidate of the principles concept rejected by critique, two new ones are advanced.[22] Due not only to the general problem of negative proofs of existence, but also to the promiscuity of the principles theory's conception of principles, the superfluity critique is more suitable for confronting the polyphonic choir of principles theorists. Just as a defender of the laws of mechanics can leave open the existence of angels if he does not need them to explain macro-physical phenomena, a critic of

16 Robert Alexy, 'Zur Struktur der Rechtsprinzipien', in *Regeln, Prinzipien und Elemente im System des Rechts*, eds. Bernd Schilcher and Peter Koller and Bernd-Christian Funk (Wien: Verlag Österreich, 2000), 31–52, 38–9.

17 Ibid.

18 Poscher, 'Einsichten' (n. 5), 10–2; Poscher, 'Insights' (n. 5), 436–8; Poscher, 'Principles' (n. 5), 25–8.

19 Robert Alexy, 'Ideales Sollen', in *Grundrechte, Prinzipien und Argumentation*, eds. Laura Clérico and Jan-Reinard Sieckmann (Baden-Baden: Nomos, 2009), 21–38, 21–2.

20 Ibid.

21 For an overview cf. Borowski, *Prinzipien* (n. 1), 68–105.

22 For a new sprout see Maximilian Reßing, 'Prinzipien als Normen mit zwei Geltungsebenen', *Archiv für Rechts- und Sozialphilosophie*, 95 (2009), 28–48.

the principles theory can leave open the existence of principles as "ideal ought"[23] or "pro tanto ought"[24] or infinitely "reiterated requirements of validity"[25] or "norms with two levels of validity"[26]. If it can be shown that the normative phenomena that the principles theory tries to explain can be perfectly well explained by the idea of optimization requirements, there is no need to worry about a mysterious conception of principles, since even by their own standards optimization requirements are not principles (anymore). If the superfluity thesis can be defended, the existence thesis becomes uninteresting, even offered by the dozen. It would be as if principles theorists insisted that angels have wings or wear white nightgowns: Nothing would follow from it.

In the first section, I will explain the objection that principles in the sense of the principles theory are theoretically superfluous and defend this objection against Alexy's reply (B.). I will discuss the existence objection only with regard to the "ideal ought", which Alexy himself equates with principles (C.). The third section will explain why principles theorists are not satisfied by the discovery that at least some principles can be reconstructed as optimization requirements (D.). In the short final section I will again stress that the critique of the principles theory is not aimed at legal principles in the traditional sense; I will also explain why our traditional – gradualistic – understanding of legal principles is very sensible compared to the theoretically overcharged and misconceived concept of the principles theory.

Part One: The Objection of Superfluity

If optimization requirements are not principles in the sense of the principles theory, then such principles have to be found elsewhere. It would, however, be of no help to the principles theory to completely detach its conception of principles from optimization requirements, since the doctrinal payoff of the principles theory is that all sorts of norms can be interpreted as optimization requirements due to their quality as principles and that all legal conflicts involving principles have to be solved by a balancing with the aim of optimization. The intimate connection between principles and optimization requirements is as vital to the principles theory as the structural distinction between rules and principles itself. Doctrinal suggestions like understanding fundamental rights as optimization requirements could no longer be deduced from the norm-theoretical dichotomy of rules and principles were principles associated with something other than optimization requirements. So it comes as no surprise that Alexy now finds principles inside optimization requirements. Optimization requirements are not principles, but, according to Alexy, principles do the work within optimization requirements. For Alexy, we should "distinguish between

23 Alexy, 'Strukur' (n. 16), 38–9; Alexy, 'Ideales Sollen' (n. 19).

24 Nils Jansen, *Die Struktur der Gerechtigkeit* (Baden-Baden:Nomos, 1998), 101.

25 Jan-Reinard Sieckmann, 'Prinzipien, ideales Sollen und normative Argumente', *Archiv für Rechts- und Sozialphilosophie*, 97 (2011), 178–97, 178, 190–2; Jan-Reinard Sieckmann, 'Zur Analyse von Normkonflikten und Normabwägungen', in *Analyomen 2: Proceedings of the 2nd Conference "Perspectives in Analytical Philosophy"*, ed. Georg Meggle (Berlin and New York: Walter de Gruyter, 1994), vol. 3, 349–56, 349–52.

26 Reßing, *Prinzipien* (n. 22), 46–8.

requirements to be optimized and *optimization requirements*. The requirements to be optimized are the objects of balancing. We can call them 'ideal oughts' or 'ideals'."[27] So now, principles are not optimization requirements as such, but rather the "ideal ought" that forms the object of the optimization. Therefore, optimization requirements are a special kind of rules that incorporate a principle. Although in the sphere of the real ought optimization requirements have the mundane character of a rule only, they are connected to the sphere of the "ideal ought" by their special object, i. e. by principles.

The critique of this reconstruction of principles as the objects of optimization requirements mainly claims that such reconstruction misrepresents the objects of optimization requirements. According to the reconstruction suggested by Alexy, the objects of optimization requirements are themselves normative in character – even of an ideal normative character, namely an "ideal ought". This reconstruction, however, misses the fact that the object of optimization requirements is generally not another norm but rather of an empirical nature. Optimization requirements generally do not demand to optimize norms but rather aim at factual circumstances. Optimization requirements are generally not reflexive in the sense of being norms requiring the optimization of other norms – let alone "ideal oughts". For instance, a requirement to optimize the freedom of speech requires optimizing the empirical possibilities of expression; it does not require optimizing another norm that guarantees the freedom of speech. Optimization requirements generally aim to improve factual circumstances, and not reflexively at the adjustment of other norms. They demand freedom of speech, not an improvement of the norms that refer to the freedom of speech. Accordingly, a repressive state does not follow the requirement to optimize the freedom of speech by signing ever more international conventions on the freedom of speech in order to optimize the guarantee of fundamental rights by international obligations, but only by actually abandoning censorship.

Contrary to some principles theorists, the objects of optimization requirements need not have a normative character if we want to explain the normativity of optimization requirements neither.[28] Such normativity is already established by the requirement to enhance a certain object relative to the given legal and factual possibilities. The normativity of optimization requirements follows from the mere requirement to optimize. There is no need to presuppose a *requirement to be optimized* as the object of optimization. All kinds of objects can be optimized: tire pressure, health, freedom of speech – optimization requirements do not depend on normative objects. The direction of an optimization requirement is usually determined by the context. The context determines whether the object of an optimization requirement is supposed to be maximized or minimized relative to the legal and factual possibilities. If understood as an optimization requirement, the fundamental right to physical integrity demands that infringements on physical integrity are minimized relative to the legal and factual possibilities and not maximized. In public administration, the requirement to optimize the rate of employment must be understood as a requirement to maximize employment relative to the legal and factual possibilities.

27 Alexy, 'Struktur' (n. 16), 38–9; Alexy, 'Ideales Sollen' (n. 19).

28 As claimed by Sieckmann, *Regelmodelle* (n. 4), 66.

The insight that optimization requirements are themselves normative but generally not aimed at a normative object becomes evident in comparison with rare cases in which this is different. Optimization requirements can have any kind of object. They can also have norms as their object. Norms can be optimized as well, i.e. when it comes to closing tax loopholes. But optimization requirements of this sort are a rather rare exception in legal systems. Fundamental rights, which the principles theory takes as a paradigm for optimization requirements, do not aim at the optimization of norms[29] even if they are understood as optimization requirements. They aim at empirical objects or circumstances.

Confronted with this critique, Alexy now concedes: "At first sight the objection seems to be justified, since it is possible to make the object of a requirement directly to the object of an optimization.

(2) *Op*

would then become

(4) *OOpt p*"[30]

In this quote, *Op* in (2) is to be read as a formalization of the proposition *that it is required that p*,[31] which can be expressed in different sentences. In (4) *OOpt p* is supposed to stand for the proposition *that it is required to optimize the object of p*.

Though Alexy's concession of the initial plausibility of the superfluity objection is to be welcomed, it must be stressed that (4) makes use of a misleading notation. In (2) *p* – in accordance with standard notations – stands as a variable for a proposition. In the example that Alexy himself gives, *p* stands for the proposition that people in need should receive aid. With respect to this example, *Op* should be read as: it is required that people in need receive aid. In (4) the expression *Opt* takes the place of an operator, even though *Opt* merely qualifies the content of the proposition *p*.[32] In the example, *Opt p* stands for the requirement that aid for people in need is to be optimized. *Opt* qualifies the object required – in the example, it is not just

29 This might be different for fundamental rights whose object is largely dependent on normative configuration.

30 Alexy, 'Ideales Sollen' (n. 19), 24.

31 This formalization is in line with deontic standard logic as established by Jan Henrik von Wright, who introduced the expression *OA* as an abbreviation for the proposition that the action described by *A* is required. See Georg Henrik von Wright, 'Deontic Logic', *Mind*, 60 (1951), 1–15, 4. Based on von Wright's initial conception of a logic of action, in which the operator *O* was exclusively applied to actions, numerous scholars have developed the deontic standard logic as it is known today. Analogous to predicate logic, deontic standard logic provides for a propositional interpretation of variables and operators, see Arthur Norman Prior, *Formal Logic* (Oxford: Oxford UP, 1962); Alan Ross Anderson, 'The Formal Analysis of Normative Systems', in *The Logic of Decision and Action*, ed. Nicholas Rescher (Pittsburgh: University of Pittsburgh Press, 1967), 147–213. Later, von Wright himself adopted this view. For instance, cf. Georg Henrik von Wright, *A New System of Deontic Logic* (London: Routledge and Keagan Paul Ltd, 1964), 58–75; von Wright, *An Essay in Deontic Logic and the General Theory of Action* (Amsterdam: North Holland Publishing Company, 1968). Accordingly, by applying the conventions of deontic standard logic, the operator *O* has to be read as an abbreviation for the proposition "that it is required" and *p* has to be read as an abbreviation for any proposition "that *p*".

32 Also, *Opt* cannot be read as the predicate of an variable *p* that stands for an individual, since this would violate the rule of consistent notation, because in (2), *p* stands for a proposition.

aid for the people in need that is required, but the optimization of said aid. The qualification clarifies that the proposition *Opt p* is distinct from *p* in having the optimization of the object of *p* as its content. But this would be more precisely expressed by the indexical $p_{opt.}$ Regardless of Alexy's notational idiosyncrasy, it should be noted that *Opt* is a qualification of the content of the proposition *p* and not a modal logical operator – as e.g. the ought operator *O*. The freedom of notational design does not give freedom regarding the substance of the issue.

To refute the plausible objection, Alexy replies to it in two steps: First, he attempts to show that the profane reconstruction of optimization requirements is not the only possible one. He contends that a reconstruction based on an "ideal ought" is also possible. Second, he tries to show that the reconstruction based on an "ideal ought" is not only possible but actually necessary to explain certain features of optimization requirements. Below, both of these theses – the possibility thesis and the necessity thesis – will be refuted. Optimization requirements cannot be adequately reconstructed by relying on normative entities as their objects nor is such a reconstruction necessary to explain their features.

I. The Possibility Thesis

Alongside the profane way of reconstructing optimization requirements as

OOpt p

for Alexy there is "also the possibility to reconstruct the optimization requirement in a way that the object of optimization obtains a normative character... The optimization requirement then takes the form of

(5) *OOpt Op.*"[33]

Alexy's possibility thesis is ambiguous. On the one hand, it can be understood in a reconstructive way. As a reconstructive thesis, it says that any optimization requirement (*OOpt p*) can be reconstructed as a requirement to optimize another requirement. On the other hand, it can be understood as a constructive thesis according to which – irrespective of optimization requirements that have a factual object – we can construct optimization requirements that, in a reflexive sense, have another requirement as their object of optimization. As a reconstructive thesis, however, Alexy's possibility thesis is simply wrong; as a constructive thesis it is trivial and of no interest for the optimization requirements in which the principles theory is interested.

1. Reconstructive Reading

When Alexy talks about the "ideal ought", he consistently refers only to optimization requirements that have factual objects of optimization like aid for people in need. None of his own examples deals with optimization requirements that require the optimization of norms. When he now talks about the possibility of reconstructing optimization requirements he seems to think that a requirement to optimize a

33 Alexy, 'Ideales Sollen' (n. 19), 24.

factual object can be reconstructed as the requirement to optimize a normative object. For him, this interpretation is strongly supported by the fact that the requirement to aid people in need, understood as an "ideal ought", is equivalent to the following optimization requirement:

OOpt Op.[34]

But even if *p* has the same propositional content, the reconstruction proposed by Alexy is not equivalent to the optimization requirement that he intends to reconstruct:

OOpt Op ≠ *OOpt p*.

This can easily be demonstrated by putting a random proposition in the place of *p*. The requirement to optimize health (*OOpt p*) is a different optimization requirement than the requirement to optimize health related norms (*OOpt Op*). Health can be optimized by medical treatments or fitness programs; the requirement to stay or to become healthy might be optimized by a system of sanctions like higher health insurance premiums or less sophisticated medical treatments – but the requirement to live healthily cannot be optimized by massages or workouts. The optimization of a requirement is totally different from the optimization of factual circumstances. Confusing the two will lead to category mistakes.

This is also true of Alexy's own example. Alexy takes the requirement to help people in need as a starting point. Alexy first concedes that it is possible "to make the help for people in need (*p*) the immediate object of optimization.

(2) *Op*

would become

(4) *OOpt p*."[35]

But according to Alexy it would also be possible that "the requirement to aid people in need becomes the object of the optimization. The optimization requirement then takes the following form:

(5) *OOpt Op*."[36]

The simple requirement to optimize aid for people in need (*OOpt p*), though, has a very different content from the reflexive requirement to optimize the requirement to aid people in need (*OOpt Op*). Aid for people in need can be optimized by distributing tents and food supplies. By contrast, the requirement to aid people in need might be optimized by introducing or increasing a penalty for omitting to help people in need or extending the scope of the respective norm. The simple optimization requirement is different from the reflexive requirement.

This difference is further underlined by the different legal and factual possibilities that are of importance for the different objects of optimization. Aid for people in need may find its legal boundaries in the property rights of third parties and its

34 Ibid., 25.
35 Ibid.
36 Ibid.

factual boundaries in the material resources at hand. The legal and factual boundaries for the optimization of the *requirement* to provide aid are of a very different kind: Legally speaking, they might be found in proportionality requirements for sanctions against omissions; factually, they might be found in limited surveillance capacities of the state. As a reconstructive thesis, Alexy's possibility theorem is so obviously wrong that the principle of charity speaks against a reconstructive interpretation of Alexy's defense – despite the many arguments for such a reading in his text.

For the sake of completeness, it should be mentioned that a notational maneuver that Alexy employs in his reply does not change anything in substance. Alexy tries to shift the "ideal ought" to the deontic operator. He attempts to abandon his previous thesis that the normative quality of the object of optimization itself produces principles as well as an "ideal ought". "I thereby retract the... thesis that the ideal and the real ought are a question of the object of the requirement and that they do not touch upon the ontic modality as such."[37] He now contends that the crucial point is the fact, "that not only the object of a requirement can be qualified. Also the modalities of a requirement themselves can be subject to qualification. If the qualification is an idealization, this leads to an ideal ought. The idealization of the modality of the requirement can be expressed by 'O_i'. 'Idealization' thus means that the ought does not relate to conflicting rights and duties."[38]

$O_i p$

shall then be the expression for the "ideal ought". This is supposed to lead to the mutual implication

"$OOpt\ Op \leftrightarrow O_i p$"[39]

O_i, however, is not a normative operator that expresses an ideal ought, nor does $O_i p$ – as defined by Alexy – correspond to *OOpt Op*; nor would an $O_i p$ that corresponds to *OOpt Op* affect the optimization requirements that the principles theory is concerned with.

A norm that requires *p* regardless of the legal or factual possibilities has the form *Op* – there is no need for an index. A requirement of *p* that is independent of contrary legal obligations is not equivalent to *OOpt Op*: first, because *OOpt Op* has a different object, namely *OptOp*; second, because the optimization (*Opt*) just expresses the relativization to the legal and factual possibilities. If *OOpt Op* and O_i were equivalent, then *Opt O* would merely be contracted to the index *i*. But the expression *Opt O* is part of the proposition *Opt Op*. The object of the requirement *OOpt Op* is not *p*, but the optimization of the requirement of *p* (*Opt Op*). The index *i* is only a different way of expressing *Opt Op*. Just as *Opt* is a qualification of the proposition *p*,[40] *Opt O* qualifies the object of the proposition *p*. *Opt Op* stands for the proposition that the requirement of the object of the proposition *p* shall be optimized. Contrary to what Alexy's notation O_i suggests, *Opt O* is not an index of

37 Ibid.
38 Ibid.
39 Ibid.
40 Ibid., 24.

the normative operator *O*. If *i* were to stand for *Opt O*, then the proposition *p* could be qualified by an index p_i. It remains Alexy's secret how this misleading notational suggestion could give birth to an "ideal ought" that is different from *OOpt Op*, which, according to Alexy's newest twist, does not have a principle or an "ideal ought" as its object. And last but not least, it should be remembered that the whole notational maneuver deals with the reflexive requirement *OOpt Op*, which – as shown above – does not affect the optimization requirements of non-normative objects that the principles theory and Alexy are exclusively concerned with in their examples and other writings.

2. Constructive reading

While the reconstructive reading of Alexy's possibility thesis is obviously false, the opposite is true of its constructive reading: It is obviously right, but also so trivial that nothing follows from it for any of the questions that the principles theory is concerned about. If the possibility thesis merely aims to show that, irrespective of the actual requirements that Alexy discusses, like the requirement to give aid to people in need, it is possible to construct requirements that do not aim at aid for people in need, but at the optimization of laws penalizing failure to assist people in danger, there is nothing to object to. As already shown, normative objects can be optimized as well. But these reflexive requirements do not contribute to an understanding or explanation of non-reflexive optimization requirements. They are just requirements with a different object. In our legal order, they are an exception. Accordingly, in Alexy's explanation of principles, we do not find any concrete example of such reflexive optimization requirements, let alone one from an existing legal system. Fundamental rights in particular, which represent the main area of application for the principles theory are not norms that require the optimization of other norms. In their interpretation according to the principles theory, they are norms that demand the state to optimize its non-interference, not norms that demand to optimize the norms of fundamental liberties. They aim at factual, not normative objects.

In its constructive reading, the possibility thesis only explains that the character of a norm as an optimization requirement does not depend on the object of optimization: It is not only empirical objects and factual circumstances that can be optimized, but also norms. Thereby, the possibility thesis only corroborates the idea that optimization requirements do not have to be related to normative objects, let alone "ideal oughts". There is no need to draw on principles of the kind that Alexy equates with an "ideal ought" in order to explain the features of optimization requirements.

II. The Necessity Thesis

Even Alexy's thesis that optimization requirements can be reconstructed by means of an "ideal ought" fails. The reconstruction he proposes does not lead to a reconstruction of the optimization requirements he claims to reconstruct. Rather, it leads to optimization requirements that are hardly relevant to actual legal orders and that do not in any way explain the connection in which an "ideal ought" is supposed to figure in those kinds of optimization requirements that the principles theory is concerned with.

But even though Alexy's explanation of optimization requirements via an "ideal ought" is based on norm-logical errors and only confuses their understanding, there would be some merit in searching for further normative entities were Alexy's second thesis to hold, namely that optimization requirements cannot be fully understood without presupposing some form of principle – whatever its nature. The almost feverish search for new constructions of principles besides, beyond, or within the idea of optimization requirements might then make scientific sense. If there were something about optimization requirements that we did not understand or were not able to explain, this might be due to the fact that we still lack insight into a special kind of normative entity that Alexy might not have fully grasped with his "ideal ought", but for which the concept of principles could serve as a kind of placeholder.

Alexy's argument for why optimization requirements are not sufficient to explain fundamental rights understood as optimization requirements is "that fundamental rights consist of norms and that their collision can thus only be adequately reconstructed as norm collisions… One could think that the problem of normativity could also be solved if one exclusively relied on the idea of optimization requirements."[41] But Alexy thinks that this would be wrong. Alexy believes that optimization requirements as such fail to explain two things: First, the normativity of fundamental rights if they are understood – as the principles theory would have it – as optimization requirements and, second, the way in which the collision of optimization requirements can be dealt with.

1. The Normativity Argument

As concerns Alexy's formulation, it should be clarified that fundamental rights do not "consist of" norms: They *are* norms. Insofar as the formulation is supposed to suggest that fundamental rights have a normative object, since they are described as consisting of norms, it must be rejected. The fundamental right of physical integrity requires the state to abstain from intrusions. It *is* a norm, but does not have a norm as its object. Its objects are actions of the state that intrude upon the physical integrity of the bearers of fundamental rights. Such intrusions of the state are not norms, but factual actions. Norms can only appear as intrusions on fundamental rights insofar as they empower the government to intrude upon the physical integrity of its citizens. So, ultimately, the object of the requirement to abstain from intrusion is not normative but factual in nature.

This also answers the question concerning the normativity of fundamental rights. Fundamental rights are normative because they requirement to abstain from infringements – not because they relate to some other kind of requirement. If fundamental rights are understood as optimization requirements, they simply have – according to Alexy's notation – the form:

$OOpt\,p$.

p represents refraining from infringement on fundamental rights – in the case of the right to personal integrity refraining from physical mistreatment. The normative

41 Ibid., 30.

operator *O* is not only sufficient to explain the normativity of this optimization requirement; it is also the only adequate expression of the requirement. Duplicating the normative operator would not only be redundant, it would also give fundamental rights an object that does not adequately represent them. Article 2 paragraph 2 of the German constitution does not require optimizing the requirement to refrain from intrusions upon the physical integrity, but aims directly against such factual intrusions. There is no need for further normative entities to explain the normativity of optimization requirements.

But those optimization requirements that have a norm as their object also receive their normativity solely from the normative operator relating to the optimization, and not from the normative operator of the requirement that has to be optimized. This can easily be seen when the normative operator is placed by a descriptive one. If *it is required that p* is replaced by *it is a fact that p*, the whole expression becomes descriptive, even though the object (*p*) may be normative. The proposition that the optimization of a requirement *p* is a fact is descriptive. The normativity of the object of optimization has no influence on the normativity of the expression as a whole.

The normativity of optimization requirements is not in any way obscure. As with any other norm, the normativity just follows from the normative operator which relates to the optimization of an object – be it factual or normative.

2. The Collision Argument

The explanation of collisions between optimization requirements does not depend on a redoubling of their normativity either. Collisions of norms are coordinated by collision rules. These collision rules can be integrated into the norms to be coordinated, as is done by the principles theory with regard to optimization requirements by relativizing the requirement to the legal and factual possibilities on the basis of balancing. The content of the collision rule is contingent, though, and leaves the logical structure of the norms untouched. Norms with collision clauses are in no way mysterious. They can be construed and applied like any other norm. There is no need for an "ideal ought" to understand them. This can easily be demonstrated by reference to two norms that Alexy himself presents as examples of principles.[42] A norm N1 empowers the government to take measures to protect its foreign interests. A norm N2 guarantees the freedom of the press.

N1: If an action endangers the foreign relations of the state, this action can be prohibited.
N2: If an action serves to promote the freedom of the press, the state must refrain from prohibiting it.

There is an overlap of scenarios in which both norms apply. For these scenarios, the legal system must introduce a conflict rule that can be incorporated as an exception to both norms. The content of the collision rule is a totally contingent matter. A traditional collision rule would be the *lex posterior* principle (C_a). If norm N1 concerning the protection of state interests stems from a period of military dictatorship and norm N2 from the time after the state became a democracy, the lex posterior principle might even apply to norms like N1 and N2. This would lead to an inter-

42 Alexy, *Grundrechte* (n. 6), 147.

pretation in which N1 is amended by an exception clause, provided that N1 is not diametrically opposed to the new state order and therefore considered invalid. This would give us:

$N1_a$: If an action endangers the foreign relations of the state and if it does not serve to promote the freedom of the press, this action can be prohibited.
$N2_a$: If an action serves to promote the freedom of the press, the state must refrain from prohibiting it.

By inserting the collision element, the normative structure of the colliding norms remains untouched. What is more, the collision rule does not give the norms a reflexive character in the sense that they are not only requirements themselves, but have a requirement as their object. Their structure is still

Op
not
O Op.

Nothing changes when the collision rule incorporates an element of weight. For instance, a teleological reduction might result in the interpretation that N1 is only valid for important foreign relations. According to this collision rule C_b, we would obtain the following norms:

$N1_b$: If an action endangers important foreign relations of the state, this action can be prohibited.
$N2_b$: If an action serves to promote the freedom of the press and does not endanger important foreign relations of the state, the state must refrain from prohibiting it.

Like optimization requirements, $N1_b$ and $N2_b$ require the balancing of interests. The only difference from optimization requirements lies in the fact that in this case the balancing is not relative to another interest. It must only be established that the foreign relation is of importance. As before, the structure of the norms is not changed by the collision rule. There is nothing about norms $N1_b$ and $N2_b$ which requires us to refer to an "ideal ought" or any other phenomenon like infinitely "reiterated requirements of validity" to understand their content.

From a collision rule C_b it is only a short step to a collision rule that relies on the idea of optimization. If a collision rule C_c does not rely on important foreign relations, but on the question of whether the affected relations outweigh the freedom of the press, two norms are created that make it necessary to balance the relative importance of the endangered foreign relations and the freedom of the press. These norms could thus be understood as optimization requirements as defined by Alexy and can be treated in accordance with his rule of balancing.[43]

$N1_c$: If an action endangers foreign relations of the state, this action can be prohibited.
$N2_c$: If an action serves to promote the freedom of the press and if said action does not endanger foreign relations of the state in a way that outweighs the positive impact on the freedom of the press, the state must refrain from prohibiting such action.

43 Ibid., 145–54.

The semantic shift from “important” to “outweighing” leaves the structure of the norms untouched – just like other collision rules. The norms’ object remains factual and does not become normative. Even if the collision rule demands a relative balancing in the form of an optimization process, neither of the norms present any features requiring the presupposition of an “ideal ought” or any other normative entity. The optimization requirements neither have the structure that Alexy thinks they have, nor do they present norm-structural features that could set them apart from norms with integrated collision clauses. For a theory of fundamental rights that suggests solving fundamental rights issues by the process of optimizing, a reconstruction of fundamental rights as optimization requirements should be perfectly sufficient. There is no need for principles that are not identical to optimization requirements.

Part Two: The Existence Objection

So what are principles theorists talking about when they talk about principles? What is meant by the mysterious talk about an “ideal ought”? What Alexy tries to reconstruct as an “ideal ought” in his principles theory are unconditional norm formulations as in N1 and N2 that are not explicitly relativized to their legal and factual possibilities by collision rules. The requirement to aid people in need could also be understood as a rule in the sense of the principles theory. As a consequence, aid would have to be supplied to people in need regardless of the costs and risks to those providing the aid.[44] For principles theorists, such a literal interpretation seems implausible more often than not with good reason. In order to provide a good meaning for such unconditional norm formulations, principles theorists understand the respective norms as an “ideal ought”, as an unconditional ought in the realm of the ideal. In an ideal world, such norms would satisfy their unconditional formulations, because they would not have to be relativized with regard to the legal and factual possibilities. In the realm of the ideal they are principles. In the realm of the real, so the idea goes, principles would become optimization requirements.

The effort of the principles theory to do justice to the wording of a norm formulation is honorable. The distinction and the dialectics between an ideal and a real ought, however, is an unnecessary and unnecessarily complicated interpretation of a norm formulation, which has the further disadvantage of illegitimately limiting interpretative options. Norm formulations like N1 and N2 or the unconditional requirement to provide aid are abbreviated and elliptic expressions of more complex norms, which have to be developed by the classic means of legal interpretation and construction.[45] The legal interpretations of the abridged and elliptic norm formulations will then lead to the collision clauses, which determine the norms’ relations to other legal norms and the legal system as a whole.

44 Alexy, Ideales Sollen (n. 19), 23.

45 Cf. Rusteberg, *Gewährleistungsgehalt* (n. 9), 158–66, who shows that in determining fundamental rights’ scopes of protection, the classic methods of legal interpretation are diluted by the principles theory.

Unlike the interpretation of unconditional norm formulations in the sense of an "ideal ought", which reduces them to principles in the sense of the principles theory and thus always to optimization requirements, collision rules that arise from classic legal interpretations of unconditional norm formulations can take on the most diverse forms and are not restricted – as the little examples with norms N1 and N2 show – to one specific kind of collision clause.

Even where the collision rule amounts to some kind of proportionality test, it is not determined which interpretation of the proportionality principle should be applied – even though the principles theory seems to think that it can take the proportionality principle hostage: "The principles theory implies the principle of proportionality and the latter implies the former."[46] The proportionality principle, though, does not have to be understood in the sense of an optimization requirement. Beyond the pareto-optimum necessity requirement, it can also be understood as a guarantee of a minimum position[47] or as a prohibition against gross disproportionality[48]or in the sense of an equal weight model along the lines of Bruce Chapman's suggestion[49]. Accordingly, most authors generally do not understand constitutional principles as optimization requirements, but rather as minimum guarantees or as a framework guarantee.[50] The interpretation of the abbreviated and elliptic norm formulations, especially as regards constitutional law, is no question for which the purported distinction between rules and principles in the sense of the principles theory can be of any help. It is a contingent matter which collision rule will coordinate N1 and N2. It is even a contingent matter whether an unconditionally formulated norm is modified by a collision rule at all. For the guarantee of human dignity in article 1 paragraph 1 of the German Constitution, the opposite was undisputed for a long time.[51]

The "ideal ought" that Alexy proposes does not relate to norms, but to abbreviated and elliptic norm formulations, which should not be stylized into an "ideal ought", but merely interpreted in the way that laws have always been interpreted. Just as the descriptive formulation "art is free" in article 5 paragraph 3 of the German Constitution must be interpreted, in the first instance, not as a factual statement but as a norm and then as a subjective right against government intrusions, which can only be limited on the basis of colliding constitutional norms. But as little as the interpretation of the descriptive formulation in article 5 section 3 sentence 1 of the German constitution requires the presupposition of some kind of "factual ought", it requires the presupposition of an "ideal ought" for the interpretation of unconditionally formulated norms. In both cases, it only takes the legal interpretation and construction of a concrete norm formulation in its respective con-

46 Alexy, 'Struktur' (n. 16), 35.

47 Bernhard Schlink, *Abwägung im Verfassungsrecht* (Berlin: Duncker & Humblot, 1976), 76–8, 192–5.

48 Bodo Pieroth and Bernhard Schlink, *Grundrechte Staatsrecht II*, 26th edn. (Heidelberg et al.: C. F. Müller, 2010), at marginal no. 304; Poscher, *Abwehrrechte* (n. 9), 224.

49 Bruce Chapman, 'Preference, Pluralism, and Proportionality', *University of Toronto Law Journal*, 60 (2010), 177–96.

50 Karl-Eberhard Hain, *Die Grundsätze des Grundgesetzes* (Baden-Baden: Nomos, 1999), 157; Franz Reimer, *Verfassungsprinzipien: Ein Normtyp im Grundgesetz* (Berlin: Duncker & Humblot, 2001), 329–33, 338–48, each with further references.

51 See Ralf Poscher, 'Die Würde des Menschen ist unantastbar', *Juristenzeitung*, 59 (2004), 756–62 with further references.

text. By presupposing principles in the sense of an "ideal ought", the principles theory hypostatizes abbreviated and elliptic norm formulations.

PART THREE: WHY OPTIMIZATION REQUIREMENTS DO NOT SUFFICE FOR THE PRINCIPLES THEORY

The only object that can reasonably be equated with principles in the sense of the principles theory are the objects that Alexy originally equated them with: optimization requirements. In all practical applications of the principles theory, it tries to support an interpretation of legal norms as optimization requirements and to operationalize the optimization by its law of balancing. Why does it not suffice for the principles theory to be a theory of optimization requirements? Why can it not, as it did originally, equate its principles with optimization requirements and refrain from its strained attempts to postulate principles besides optimization requirements – an issue highly contested even among its own adherents[52]? Why can the principles theory not simply be the theory of optimization requirements?

The answer lies in the strategic function of the dualism postulated between rules and principles within the project of the principles theory.[53] Were the principles theory right in its claim that all norms can be theoretically subdivided into rules on the one hand and principles on the other, and were principles to be understood as optimization requirements which in turn have to be applied by the law of balancing, then the theoretical qualification of a norm as a principle would always be accompanied by a specific doctrinal approach demanded by the underlying theory – namely optimization by balancing. If all other norms are rules and therefore do not pose any serious application problems, then for theoretical reasons all serious issues of adjudication and application of law would have to be solved by optimization via balancing. Norms that are not applicable via simple subsumption are principles, or at least have a principle element, and must therefore be applied by optimization and balancing. Due to the postulated normative dualism, all contested issues of legal interpretation could supposedly be decided via legal theory. For example, the guarantee of human dignity in article 1 section 1 of the German constitution is not a norm that lends itself to mere subsumption; according to the strategy of the principles theory, it must be a principle. Principles necessarily imply an understanding as optimization requirements. Thus article 1 section 1 of the German constitution has to be understood as a requirement to optimize human dignity and can therefore be subject to balancing.[54] Positions of the courts and legal scholars that insist on the

52 With regard to the internal quarrels about the principle concept, Borowski, *Prinzipien* (n. 1), 105, worries: "Although the ongoing specification of the principles theory has to be appreciated from a theoretical point of view, it must not be ignored that a crucial advantage of the principles theory is its intuitive plausibility and this plausibility being endangered by increasing the theory's complexity."

53 See also Kai Möller, 'Balancing and the Structure of Constitutional Rights', *International Journal of Constitutional Law*, 5 (2007), 453–68, 457–8.

54 For an interpretation of human dignity based on the principles theory see Nils Teifke, Flexibilität der Menschenwürde? Zur Struktur des Art. 1 Abs. 1 GG, *Archiv für Rechts- und Sozialphilosophie* Beiheft Nr. H 103 (2005), 142–156.

strictness of the guarantee of human dignity in the German constitution can thus be regarded as refuted by means of legal theory. If, however, principles were just optimization requirements, then principles would be rules in the sense of the principles theory. If principles were rules, the whole normative dualism, on which the principles theory is founded falls apart. Then we would only have norms with different contents and different interpretations and constructions. Their content could no longer be determined by their theoretical qualification as a principle. It would no longer be possible to determine via legal theory whether the guarantee of human dignity in the German constitution is subject to balancing or an absolute guarantee. This would not mean that no argument can be made for an optimization doctrine as such; but this argument would have to draw on traditional legal methods and could not rely on some kind of norm-theoretical dualism. The doctrine of fundamental rights could not be reduced to the idea of optimization and balancing as proposed by the principles theory. Doctrinal arguments would have to be presented in support of the view that an interpretation of fundamental rights as optimization requirements should prevail despite the numerous doctrinal counter-arguments already advanced.

In this text, however, the question is not which interpretation of fundamental rights should prevail. The issue is rather to show the strategic function of normative dualism as proposed by the principles theory. If the principles theory were satisfied with being a theory of optimization requirements, it would have to give up its argumentative strategy, i. e. putting forward a theoretical argument with the aim of supporting a concrete doctrinal approach. The principles theory would become just one doctrinal theory among others and many of the criteria that were (i. a. by Alexy himself)[55] suggested for assessing the quality of doctrinal theories would militate against it.[56] Regarding the argumentative strategy of the principles theory, everything seems to depend on the purported norm-theoretical difference between optimization requirements and principles. This might explain why its supporters come up with ever-new suggestions which are supposed to uphold the difference, and which are increasingly difficult to track for the non-initiate. They try to stabilize the illusion of a difference between principles and optimization requirements – despite all the external and internal arguments against each of these approaches.

Part Four: The traditional Notion of Principle re-established

There are no principles in the sense of the principles theory that are distinct from optimization requirements and that are of any relevance to the explanation of optimization requirements. Measured by its own criteria, the principles theory is a theory without an object, the theory of a phantom. This, however, does not mean that the talk about legal principles in the traditional sense has no object, or that there are no principles in the traditional sense. Quite the opposite, there are far more principles than the principles theory, which reduces principles to optimization require-

55 Robert Alexy, *Theorie der juristischen Argumentation*, 3rd edn. (Frankfurt: Suhrkamp 1996), 326.

56 For more extensive elaborations on this aspect see Poscher, *Abwehrrechte* (n. 9), 81–2, 10–3.

ments, allows.[57] It might be true that some legal principles – e.g. the principle of the protection of legitimate expectations – could be reconstructed in the sense of optimization requirements. But this does not hold true for every legal principle. The principle of good faith does not require optimization, but simply compliance: If something violates the principles of good faith, no balancing is required any more.[58] Equally, the principle of equality with its phenomenologically comparative perspective cannot be forced onto the Procrustes bed of optimization requirements without losing its specificity.[59] And even the principle of proportionality can be interpreted in many other ways than as an optimization requirement – consider pro-rata optimality, minimum guarantee, protection against gross disproportionality, etc.[60] And it might have to be interpreted differently in different legal contexts.

The world of legal principles is much richer and more colorful than the principles theory wishes to make us believe with its narrow understanding of principles as optimization requirements. Contrary to the principles theory, it becomes apparent that the difference between legal principles and other norms is not of a structural, but rather of a gradual nature.[61] Norms can be called legal principles if they are of specific importance[62], especially if their impact is not restricted to a certain area of law. There is no reason not to single out legal norms presenting these features by calling them legal principles. This does not mean, however, that all other norms can

57 This holds also true for the rich variety of meanings and facets of the concept of principle in the philosophical tradition, with one of the origins being the greek idea of "Arché". For information on the impressive history of the concept see Reimer, *Verfassungsprinzipien* (n. 50), 146–71, who rejects the idea of reducing the concept of principle to mere "balancing" on grounds of the conceptual history already, see ibid., 179.

58 On this objection see Ota Weinberger, 'Revision des traditionellen Rechtssatzkonzepts', in *Regeln, Prinzipien und Elemente im System des Rechts*, eds. Bernd Schilcher and Peter Koller and Bernd-Christian Funk (Wien: Verlag Österreich, 2000), 53–68, 64, with more examples.

59 Cf. Alexander Somek, 'Eine egalitäre Alternative zur Güterabwägung', in *Regeln, Prinzipien und Elemente im System des Rechts*, eds. Bernd Schilcher and Peter Koller and Bernd-Christian Funk (Wien: Verlag Österreich, 2000), 193–220.

60 For some of the relevant literature see supra n. 47–50.

61 This conception is in line with most scholars that do not follow Alexy's lead. For instance, cf. Peter Lerche, Übermaß und Verfassungsrecht, 2nd edn. (Köln et al.: Heymann, 1961), XXII: "distinctions between these two categories of quantitative nature only"; Bernd Schilcher, 'Prinzipien und Regeln als Elemente einer Theorie des gebundenen Ermessens', in *Regeln, Prinzipien und Elemente im System des Rechts*, eds. Bernd Schilcher and Peter Koller and Bernd-Christian Funk (Wien: Verlag Österreich, 2000), 153–92, 164, 169; *Franz Reimer, Verfassungsprinzipien* (n. 50), 179–82; in Anglo-American literature, this point of view was expressed by Herbert Lionel Adolphus Hart, The Concept of Law, 2nd edn. (Oxford: Clarendon Press, 1994), 259–60; Andrei Marmor, The Separation Thesis and the Limits of Interpretation, *The Canadian Journal of Law and Jurisprudence*, 12 (1999), 135–50, 145–6; Michael S. Moore, Legal Principle Revisited, in *Educating Oneself in Public*, ed. Michael S. Moore (New York: Oxford UP, 2000), 221–46, 225; Mátyás Bódig, *Rules, Principles, and the Problem of the Limits in Legal Reasoning*, 2008, Archiv für Rechts- und Sozialphilosophie Beiheft 119 (2010), 172–44; for a reconstruction of the gradual difference based on legal logics see Bart Verheij and Jaap Hage and Hendrik Jacob van den Herik, 'An Integrated View on Rules and Principles', *Artificial Intelligence and Law*, 6 (1998), 3–26; For a deconstructive reading of the distinction see Pierre J. Schlag, 'Rules and Standards', *UCLA Law Review*, 33 (1985), 379–430, 405–30.

62 Josef Esser, Grundsatz und Norm in der richterlichen Fortbildung des Privatrechts, 4th edn. (Tübingen: Mohr, 1990), 154.

be applied by mere subsumption and that only legal principles are in need of legal construction. For almost all norms, there are borderline cases in which a need for construction arises and many legal norms employ abstract concepts that are not always applicable by mere subsumption. The difference between legal principles and other norms is a merely gradual one and it can be found in the dimensions of the norm's need for concretization and its relevance to the legal system as a whole.

Concluding Remark

Alexy's renewed attempt to defend the normative dualism of the principles theory by modifying and elaborating upon his specific concept of principles as "ideal oughts" is not convincing. Quite the opposite: his new considerations make it even more apparent how misguided he is to insist on a conception of principles that belong to an "ideal ought" and are not identical with optimization requirements. His argumentation becomes entangled in obvious mistakes, or trivialities at best, which are of no value for the attempt to explain the normative phenomena that the principles theory is concerned with. Instead of losing itself in idiosyncratic debates over phantoms, circling around non-existent normative objects, supporters of the principles theory should rather understand and, for the sake of honesty, call their theory by its correct name: a theory of optimization requirements. Insofar as principles theorists approach doctrinal issues,[63] they provide suggestions that form part of an optimization doctrine, which should be evaluated with respect to the specific fields in which the suggestions are made. But, if duly understood as a contribution to specific doctrinal debates, an optimization doctrine cannot be defended from the high road of a legal theory. Instead, optimization doctrines must convince with doctrinal arguments.

63 For other aspects of the principles theory (e.g. argumentation theory) see Poscher, 'Einsichten' (n. 5), 73–7; Poscher, 'Insights' (n. 5), 441–5; Poscher, 'Principles' (n. 5), 33–9.

Jan Sieckmann*

Alexy's Theory of Principles: The Ideal/Real Dualism

Introduction

An important element of Alexy's theory of law is the dualism between ideal and real "ought" in normative systems.[1] In his theory of principles he suggests that rules include a real "ought", and principles an ideal "ought".[2] Principles are norms that, when in conflict, must be balanced against each other. Rules are definitive norms, or norms with a special *prima facie*-character, that result from the balancing of principles.[3]

As soon as normative justification proceeds by means of balancing it becomes necessary to make this distinction. Norms that result from balancing have a different character to those that figure as arguments in the balancing. The resulting definitive norms apply only one at a time, or at least claim to exclude incompatible norms. Principles, i. e. norms that must be balanced against each other apply concurrently even though they are incompatible. Whilst one might regard the former as stating normative facts, one cannot understand in the same manner norms that are incompatible but that are, nonetheless, valid and applicable.

The need for such a distinction seems to be obvious. The arguments balancing starts with follow different logical rules than the judgments, statements, and norms that result from the balancing, and the structure of norms reflects this difference. This issue has been widely discussed under the heading of the distinction between rules and principles.[4] The dualism of ideal and real "ought" seems to be a convenient way to highlight the difference between them. Principles include an ideal "ought" because they define which norms one ought to recognize as definitively valid in a balancing. There may be limitations, however, based on competing principles. They therefore cannot command immediate compliance and do not state what actually ought to be done. Nevertheless, they present an ideal "ought" in the sense of what should be done if there were no obstacles or objections. By contrast definitively valid norms, i. e. those that result from balancing, demand actual compliance. Since at the end of the balancing all conflicts have been resolved, no objection can remain that one might advance against the claim of the resulting norm. As

* I would like to thank Anthea Connolly for corrections and improvements in the English of my text.

1 Robert Alexy, The Dual Nature of Law, in: Ratio Juris 23 (2010), 167–82.

2 Robert Alexy, Zum Begriff des Rechtsprinzips, in: Rechtstheorie Beih. 1 (1979), 59–87.

3 Robert Alexy A Theory of Constitutional Rights, Oxford, Oxford University Press, 2002, 57.

4 Dworkin has pointed out the difference between rules and principles and its connection with the structure of balancing (Ronald Dworkin, Taking Rights Seriously, 2. ed., Cambridge (Mass.), Harvard University Press, 1978, 24pp.), although he never presented a precise account of it and did not use it as a foundation for his theory of law. His proposal has faced, however, many criticisms, and proponents of such a distinction do not agree as to what should be the criterion to distinguish rules and principles. On the discussion of rules and principles see Jan Sieckmann, Prinzipien, ideales Sollen und normative Argumente, in: ARSP 97 (2011), 178–197.

a consequence, one ought to apply and follow this norm.[5] In this sense definitively valid norms include a real "ought".

However, plausible as it is, the distinction between ideal and real "ought" faces some problems which are surfaced, in particular, in Alexy's account of this distinction. As we will see, Alexy does not give an adequate explication of the notion of ideal and real "ought". The distinction between normative arguments and normative statements, despite a number of objections does, however. In addition, Alexy's own analysis of an ideal "ought" supports the notion of normative arguments underlying this distinction.

Part One: The Notion of Ideal "Ought"

A crucial problem of the notion of ideal "ought" is how to explain that norms can be valid in a normative sense[6] without actually commanding compliance.

1. Alexy's Notion of Ideal "Ought"

Alexy interprets ideal "ought" as a requirement of optimization which demands that some particular norm ought to be realized to as high a degree as possible.[7] The notion of optimization requirements is ambiguous, however. One could regard them as obligations to realize competing requirements to an optimal degree but such obligations would present a real "ought" of second order and not an ideal "ought" that figures as an argument in the balancing itself.[8]

Alternatively, one might call "principles" the norms that form the objects of the second-order requirement of optimization.[9] As I have suggested on a previous occasion, one might call such norms 'principles' in a wider sense.[10] Alexy indeed tries to save his theory of principles as requirements of optimization by assigning "ideal ought" to the norms that are the objects of requirements of optimization.[11] This, however, is doomed to failure right from the start. Since norms that form the objects of optimization requirements do not have any particular logical structure, they cannot form a logically distinct type of norm and, as a consequence, one must

5 This does not exclude the possibility to re-open the argument.

6 That is, they demand that one ought to apply and follow them, though not strictly. By contrast, one might call mere membership in a system of norms 'validity', but this type of validity does not imply a demand of application. Therefore it is not normative in a genuine sense.

7 See Alexy's definition of principles as requirements of optimization, Alexy, A Theory of Constitutional Rights (n. 3), 47.

8 For a critique of Alexy's conception of principles which suggests that he defines them as definitively valid norms and does not present arguments that could figure as reasons within a balancing, see Jan Sieckmann, Regelmodelle und Prinzipienmodelle des Rechtssystems, Baden-Baden, Nomos, 1990, 52pp.

9 See Robert Alexy, On the Structure of Legal Principles, in: Ratio Juris 13 (2000), 294pp.

10 See Jan Sieckmann, Regelmodelle und Prinzipienmodelle des Rechtssystems (n. 8), 1990, 75.

11 See Alexy's defence of his conception of principles in Alexy, On the Structure of Legal Principles (n. 9), 300; id., Ideales Sollen, in: L. Clérico / J. Sieckmann (Hg.), Grundrechte, Prinzipien und Argumentation, Baden-Baden, Nomos, 2009, 22.

abandon the "strict separation"-thesis which forms the core of the theory of principles.[12]

Alexy, however, does not seem to understand the problem. He defends his view by pointing out that the term "ought" may be used in a wider sense, including obligation, prohibition and permission.[13] Such a loose use of the term "ought" is not without precedents although a more precise terminology would be to talk of "optimisation norms". Terminology is not the point, however. The issue is that Alexy's notion of principles does not support the "strict separation"-thesis, which Alexy obviously does not wish to abandon.

In addition, focusing on the objects of requirements of optimization cannot explain the character of the ideal "ought" that is included in the normative arguments that figure as reasons in the balancing process. The objects of the requirements of optimization are norms in a purely semantic sense, that is, pure norm contents with no ascription of validity.[14] Thus, they cannot offer reasons for particular judgments based on balancing. If the relevant norms only were requirements of optimization or the objects of such requirements, the balancing would consist in the application of the requirements of optimization as norms of second order that include requirements actually to be complied with and hence a real "ought".[15] Therefore we conclude that in the framework of the theory of principles based on the "strict separation thesis":

- Principles cannot be defined as requirements of optimization;
- Principles cannot be defined as the norms that are the objects of optimization requirements.

Alexy has suggested another interpretation of the ideal "ought", treating it not as the object of the optimization requirement but placing both on a level footing.[16] Thus, he explicates the meaning of the ideal "ought" by a requirement of optimization. This, again, is possible. The problem remains, however, as to whether the ideal "ought" has any specific content of its own. The indexation of the deontic operator that Alexy introduces does not offer an explication of the notion of ideal "ought". The explication by optimization requirements leads back to the former problem of defining principles as optimization requirements. Alexy seems to believe that the ideal "ought" is indeed a third element beside requirements of optimization and norms in a purely semantic sense, but it remains unclear exactly what this third element consists of. Alexy regards the ideal "ought" as an "ought" that requires, in case of conflict, a certain solution of this conflict, although one must measure it against the possibilities of this world.[17] The issue concerns, however, the way that

12 See Alexy, Zum Begriff des Rechtsprinzips (n. 2), 64p., for the distinction between strong, weak and no-separation thesis.

13 Alexy, Ideales Sollen (n. 11), 25 n. 23.

14 See Alexy, Ideales Sollen (n. 11), 25, where the requirement of optimization is represented as equivalent to an ideal "ought": "OOpt Op $\leftrightarrow$ $O_i P$".

15 For a rejection of this approach as an adequate definition of the notion of principle, see Sieckmann, Regelmodelle und Prinzipienmodelle des Rechtssystems (n. 8), 62pp.

16 In this direction see Alexy, Ideales Sollen (n. 11), 25p., where the ideal "ought" is not regarded as the object of the requirement of optimization, but as being at the same level with it.

17 Alexy, Ideales Sollen (n. 11), 26.

we can understand an "ought" as a reason in the "measurement" against competing reasons. The mere indexation of deontic operators does not give any hint as to how this can be done.

One should note, moreover, that the indexation as such is not the issue. Alexy attributes to the present author the view that the indexation of deontic operators is useless in reconstructing norm conflicts that lead to the balancing of normative arguments.[18] This is not correct, however, since I have myself used indexed deontic modalities in order to distinguish between the "ought" in rules and in principles.[19] By contrast, the passage of my text that Alexy refers to appertains to the approach of Susan Hurley who uses indexes to distinguish norms of different systems of sources of validity. The argument for the inadequacy of this approach in reconstructing the balancing of conflicting arguments is that, in order to balance these arguments against each other, one must consider them as belonging to the same normative system. Alexy overlooks this context and his remarks hence are abrogated. In any case, the objection remains that indexation as such does not offer an explication of what ideal "ought" should mean.

Alexy insists that the indexed "ought" is a genuine "ought" and he distinguishes,moreover, between the concrete and abstract "ought". He writes:

> "Das durch den indexierten Gebotsoperator ausgedrückte ideale Sollen ist ein echtes Sollen, das im Konfliktfall konkretes Sollen impliziert, welches sich freilich noch an den Möglichkeiten dieser Welt, so wie sie ist, messen lassen muß. Das abstrakte ideale Sollen ist ein Grund für dieses konkrete Sollen."

Hence Alexy suggests that the ideal "ought" implies, in the case of conflict, a concrete "ought" which, however, one must still check against the possibilities of our world. In addition, an abstract ideal "ought" presents a reason for this concrete "ought". It is not clear, however, how the distinction between real and ideal "ought" relates to that of concrete and abstract "ought". It seems that both concrete and abstract "ought" present an ideal "ought". The concrete "ought" follows from the application of the abstract "ought" to the facts of a concrete case. In addition, both present a genuine "ought". However, since the ideal "ought" is different from a real "ought", "genuine" cannot mean "real" in this context. The genuine "ought" must, nonetheless, have some normative force: it must exist not only in the sense of a normative meaning content but must also have some form of validity.[20]

I agree with this. Alexy, however, objects that I would deny the normative relevance of an "ought" for the result of the balancing if this "ought" is not backed by an "ought" of higher order. This objection overlooks a fundamental distinction. A norm in a semantic sense presents a normative meaning content and this may or may not include the ascription of validity.[21] Making explicit the attribution of validity is a useful analytical tool that, moreover, has been crucial in developing the

18 See Alexy, Ideales Sollen (n. 11), 26.

19 See Jan Sieckmann, Zur Analyse von Normkonflikten und Normabwägungen, in: G. Meggle (ed.), Analyomen 2, Bd. III, Berlin/Leipzig, de Gruyter, 1997, 355, where "O_p" is used to represent the "ought" of principles and "O_d" the "ought" of definitively valid norms.

20 Alexy, Ideales Sollen (n. 11), 23–4.

21 See Sieckmann, Regelmodelle und Prinzipienmodelle des Rechtssystems (n. 8), 33pp.

conception of normative arguments as reiterated requirements of validity.[22] If one uses this conception, norms as such, that is, norms as mere meaning contents without ascription of validity do not imply a demand of applying them. Such a demand only follows from ascribing normative validity to them. Alexy fails to distinguish between these different conceptions of norms in the semantic sense.

To sum up the issue is not one of indexation, which may be a useful device in order to distinguish between real and ideal "ought". It is evident, however, that the ideal "ought" cannot be defined in terms of optimisation requirements, and nor can it be defined by the status of norms as the object of requirements of optimisation or by the mere indexation of the deontic operator. None of Alexy's attempts serves to provide us with an adequate account of ideal "ought".

2. Ideal "Ought" and Normative Arguments

Since Alexy's account is the most well-known attempt to establish a strict separation of principles and rules as logically distinct classes of norms, his failure to achieve this might cast doubt on the idea that a difference between an ideal and a real "ought" actually exists.[23] These doubts are unjustified, however, since they rest on an unjustified generalization and hence on an elementary methodological mistake. Indeed, one can explain the logical difference between rules and principles as being the difference between, on one hand, normative arguments and, on the other, normative judgments and statements.[24]

What we need to understand is how normative arguments can be both the object of balancing and also figure as reasons for the outcome of a balancing where norms are in conflict with other arguments. The conception that allows one to do this is that of normative arguments as reiterated requirements of validity.[25] In contrast to normative judgments or statements, normative arguments merely claim that one ought to accept a norm as definitively valid. They include *requirements of definitive validity*. This implies the claim that the norm in question is valid in principle.[26]

Normative argumentation in its most elementary form is a procedure whereby individuals make normative claims requiring that a particular norm be definitively valid and, hence, applied and followed. Thus, normative arguments are claims to

22 See Sieckmann, Regelmodelle und Prinzipienmodelle des Rechtssystems (n. 8), 79 n. 93; id., Recht als normatives System, Baden-Baden, Nomos, 2009, 27; id., The Logic of Autonomy, Oxford/Portland (Oregon), Hart Publishing, 2012, 25pp.

23 Some authors believe that by attacking Alexy's conception of principles they can refute the theory of principles (as such). See, in particular, Ralf Poscher, Theorie eines Phantoms. Die erfolglose Suche der Prinzipientheorie nach ihrem Gegenstand, in: Rechtswissenschaft 2010, 349pp.

24 One should note that this does not support Alexy's view that every norm is either a rule or a principle. The thesis advanced here is that a norm cannot be both rule and principle. However, the distinction of rules and principles is not complete. See Sieckmann, Regelmodelle und Prinzipienmodelle (n. 8), 74.

25 See Jan Sieckmann, Principles as Normative Arguments, in: Rechtstheorie Beih. 21 (2005), 197–210; id., Recht als normatives System (n. 22); id., Prinzipien, ideales Sollen und normative Argumente (n. 4); id., The Logic of Autonomy (n. 22).

26 Accordingly, one should read "requirement for validity", if not indicated otherwise, as "requirement for definitive validity".

recognize certain norms as valid, not statements that certain norms exist or are definitively valid. Autonomous agents may make valid normative claims, and thus valid normative arguments, and must take these claims into account in their reasoning processes. Since these arguments can be neither statements nor mere norms in a semantic sense, that is, the meaning of mere norm formulations without any attribution of validity, the only plausible alternative is that their claim to validity rests on higher order requirements for validity. With regard to each requirement for validity of a certain order there must be a higher order requirement that demands its definitive validity. Thus, an infinite set of requirements for validity is necessary to constitute a valid normative argument. Accordingly, a normative argument consists of a set of norms including

(1) A norm N that one argues for,
(2) A second-order norm requiring the definitive validity of the norm N as the result of the balancing,
(3) A third-order norm requiring the definitive validity of the second-order norm, and so on.

One can represent this chain of requirements of validity formally as:

(1) $O\ VAL_{DEF}N$
(2) $O\ VAL_{DEF}\ O\ VAL_{DEF}\ N$
(3) $O\ VAL_{DEF}\ O\ VAL_{DEF}\ O\ VAL_{DEF}\ N$,
etc.

The possibility to saturate this structure is the specific criterion for the validity of normative arguments.

As a result of this construction one can explain the specific character of validity of an ideal "ought". An ideal "ought" is valid if it is backed by an infinite set of requirements of definitive validity, none of them, however, itself being definitively valid. The normative effect of an ideal "ought" is that it constitutes the validity of an argument that one cannot reject as invalid and that one can only attack through counter-arguments. For one can immediately answer any request to give a further argument why one should accept it by a requirement of higher order validity, which forms a new normative argument. Thus it makes no sense to ask why one ought to recognize an argument presenting an ideal "ought" as valid, but the only rational way to proceed is to accept its validity as an argument and, if one is not prepared to accept its conclusion, to offer counter-arguments. In this way it is possible to give an explication of the notion of an ideal "ought".

3. Critique and Comparison

The account of normative arguments as reiterated requirements of validity has encountered some objections.[27] These objections fail, however, in different ways. Either they do not give a correct account of the conception of normative arguments as

27 See the critiques in Thomas Zoglauer, Normenkonflikte – zur Logik und Rationalität ethischen Argumentierens, Stuttgart/Bad Cannstatt, Frommann-holzboog, 1998, 146 ff.; Alexy, On the Structure of Legal Principles (n. 9), 294 ff., and Peng-Hsiang Wang, Principles as Ideal Ought, in: ARSP-Beih. 124 (2010), 29–49.

reiterated requirements of validity, or they disregard crucial elements of it.[28] In particular, Alexy has advanced critiques against the reiteration thesis and the non-propositionality thesis included in this account of normative arguments.

There is no need to discuss Alexy's critique of the reiteration thesis here. As has been pointed out on another occasion,[29] he builds a "straw-man", replacing the infinite structure of reiterated requirements of validity by an "oscillation" between two finites structures, consisting of norms in a purely semantic sense and of definitively valid norms.

Clearly, however, oscillating between these finite structures does not yield the characteristics of the infinite structure that present normative arguments.

More interesting is Alexy's critique of the non-propositionality thesis. This thesis states that normative arguments that figure as reasons for balancing judgements do not have the structure of propositions. An argument in favour of this thesis is that stating norms in the form of propositions amounts to presenting them as normative facts. However, incompatible facts cannot exist at the same time. Normative facts correspond to definitively valid norms which demand actual compliance. Incompatible norms cannot, however, be complied with concurrently and consequently norms that are incompatible with each other cannot be definitively valid simultaneously.

Alexy objects to the non-propositionality thesis that one can represent contradictory norms in the form of normative propositions. He denies my thesis[30] that direct statements of incompatible norms are not admissible in a rational normative system.[31] Now, direct normative statements are, according to my definition,[32] unqualified statements that one ought to do something, that is, they include normative demands without reservation or qualification. By contrast, statements of prima facie-norms, validity in principle or as an ideal, are only indirect normative statements. They qualify the respective normative demand in a certain way so that it does not require immediate compliance. Obviously, I do not deny that indirect statements of incompatible norms may be possible, at least in some cases.

Alexy, however, denies the thesis that direct normative statements of incompatible norms are rationally inadmissible. He claims, accordingly, that direct normative statements of incompatible norms are rationally possible. As an example, he presents the conjunction (&) of an ideal permission P_i and the negation of an ideal permission ($\neg P_i$) of expressing a certain opinion (Ra):[33]

(14) P_i Ra & $\neg P_i$ Ra.

How is one to understand this view? Since the elements of this formula present propositions, one should assume that Alexy presents a scheme of propositional lo-

28 For a defence of this conception against some critiques see Sieckmann, Principles as Normative Arguments (n. 25); id., Prinzipien, ideales Sollen und normative Argumente (n. 4); id., The Logic of Autonomy (n. 22), 58pp.

29 Sieckmann, Principles as Normative Arguments (n. 25); id., Prinzipien, ideales Sollen und normative Argumente (n. 4).

30 See Sieckmann, Recht als normatives System (n. 22), 48.

31 Alexy, Ideales Sollen (n. 11), 28.

32 See Sieckmann, Recht als normatives System (n. 22), 52.

33 Alexy, Ideales Sollen (n. 11), 28.

gic. Accordingly, we have the conjunction of contradictory propositions, that is, of a proposition p and its negation $\neg$p. However, the exclusion of contradictions seems to be the backbone of any rational theory. How could one deny this? One might interpret the scheme in a different way so that the second element does not represent the negation of a proposition. This would be possible if we interpreted the scheme as one of a logic of norms, not of normative propositions.[34] However, this would not support Alexy's claim that one can represent conflicting norms in the form of propositions. Alexy seems indeed committed to admitting logical contradictions. Does Alexy then want to suggest some form of mysticism, claiming that contradictory demands can co-exist even though one cannot comply with all of them?

More plausible than attributing to Alexy an extremely implausible and in fact incomprehensible position is to suggest that his argument arises from a superficial reading of the materials and that he has simply overlooked the distinction between direct and indirect normative statements. On this understanding Alexy merely wants to say that an ideal permission to express an opinion can co-exist with an ideal non-permission to express this opinion. In a certain sense, this seems correct. However, statements of ideal validity are indirect normative statements. Thus, statements of the ideal validity of incompatible norms are possible and do not amount to a logical contradiction.

A problem remains that Alexy presents the normative situation as a contradiction of propositions. The logical functions of negation ($\neg$) and conjunction (&) are defined for propositions. The term "$\neg P_i Ra$" presents the negation of the assertion of "$P_i Ra$", that is, the negation of the assertion that Ra is permitted. It does not present the ideal permission of not-Ra. In addition, the ideal permission of not-Ra does not imply that there is no ideal permission of Ra. It seems that Alexy confuses different types of negation in permissive norms. In any case, he fails to show that one could represent conflicts of normative arguments as conflicts of direct normative statements.

Perhaps, however, the critique of the non-propositionality thesis might have a point. This thesis rests on an interpretation of normative language that makes definitive normative claims the basic form of normative speech. Without further qualification, the use of a normative expression is equivalent to stating a definitively valid norm. Is this interpretation necessary, or might a different interpretation of normative language be possible?

One might suggest that normative statements without qualification state an ideal "ought", and a real "ought" can be expressed only by further qualification. This, however, encounters the problem that the ideal "ought" demands a certain result from the balancing process, and this result consists in the statement of a definitively valid norm. If this norm were an ideal "ought", the statement of definitive validity would refer to an ideal "ought", and we could never get to a statement of a real "ought". Thus, the notion of ideal "ought" presupposes the notion of a real "ought".

34 On the distinction between the logic of norms and the logic of normative propositions see Carlos Alchourrón, Logic of Norms and Logic of Normative Propositions, in: Logique 12 (1969); id., On the Logic of Theory of Change, in: Journal of Symbolic Logic 50 (1993), 510–530.

Alternatively, one might suggest that ideal and real "ought" are independent normative categories so that neither is more basic than the other. Consequently, we cannot interpret direct normative statements as real "ought", but we must always specify which type of "ought" we have in mind. This might follow from the context, without spelling it out, but talking of "ought" as such would be incomplete. Accordingly, one must introduce ideal "ought" and real "ought" as independent normative categories which one might express by the modalities of "iought" and "rought", respectively. This approach, however, encounters the problem that the logical relation between these independent normative categories would remain unclear. We can understand the ideal "ought" as a normative argument just because it refers to a real "ought" that we ought to state as the result of our balancing. If "iought" and "rought" were independent modalities it would not be clear why and how the former would constitute an argument for the latter. Hence, we have to discard also this alternative.[35]

On the other hand it is interesting to note that Alexy, in his own analysis of an ideal 'ought', arrives at premises that provide for the creation of a reiteration of deontic modalities.[36] Alexy introduces the following premises:

He assumes that an optimization requirement regarding a certain object p implies an ideal "ought" regarding p:

(16) $\mathrm{O}\mathit{Opt}\,\mathrm{p} \rightarrow \mathrm{O_i p}$.[37]

In addition, he assumes an equivalence between the optimization requirement regarding a norm Op and an ideal "ought" regarding p:

(7) $\mathrm{O}\mathit{Opt}\,\mathrm{Op} \leftrightarrow \mathrm{O_i p}$.[38]

By substituting Op for p in premise (16) results:

$$\mathrm{O}\mathit{Opt}\,\mathrm{Op} \rightarrow \mathrm{O_i\,Op}.$$

In addition, because of the equivalence (7) follows by substituting Op for p:

$$\mathrm{O}\mathit{Opt}\,\mathrm{OOp} \leftrightarrow \mathrm{O_i\,Op}.$$

Repeating this procedure results in a reiteration of deontic "ought"-operators. In addition, since normative propositions ascribe validity to norms in a semantic sense, one can interpret the reiteration of "ought"-operators as a reiteration of requirements of validity. Thus, Alexy's analysis finally supports the analysis of an ideal "ought" suggested here.

35 In addition, introducing diverse indexed deontic operators as equally elementary does not appear to be plausible, because beside ideal and real "ought", there are other types of "ought", such as various forms of prima facie-ought and pro tanto-ought. Should each of them require a deontic operator of its own?

36 See Alexy, Ideales Sollen (n. 11), 25. On this point, see Sieckmann, Prinzipien, ideales Sollen und normative Argumente (n. 4), n. 65.

37 Alexy, Ideales Sollen (n. 11), 30.

38 Alexy, Ideales Sollen (n. 11), 25.

Part Two: The Notion of Real "Ought"

Balancing starts with normative arguments and ends with the determination of definitively valid norms which are the result of the balancing and command immediate compliance, for after having terminated the balancing no argument remains that could put in doubt the obligation to follow the norms established as definitively valid. Norms that one actually ought to follow present a real "ought". Thus, it seems that the distinction of ideal and real "ought" is well founded in the structure of balancing normative arguments.

However, the notion of real "ought" also presents problems. A standard objection is that it will always be possible to modify a norm recognized as definitively valid by, for example, introducing a new exception to it.[39] However, the fact that any result of a balancing may be questioned and the argument reopened, does not constitute a problem but is a consequence of the openness to critical reflection that any theory of rational argumentation must have. It does not affect the definitive status of norms that present the actual result of a particular procedure of balancing. As long as one does not open a new argument, the definitive result of such a procedure commands immediate compliance.

The problem of the notion of a real "ought" is that balancing requires normative judgments by autonomous agents. Although autonomous agents have the right to form such judgments, however, they cannot establish binding norms for other agents who might hold another normative view.[40] Therefore, what is definitively valid according to the judgment of an individual agent cannot yet be regarded as objectively valid in the sense that it is binding on other agents, and hence cannot command immediate compliance.

A real "ought", i.e. one that one actually ought to comply with, can only result after the reasonable disagreements among autonomous agents have been resolved and, thus, after the relevant group of agents has accepted a single norm as binding. This situation obtains if a reasonable convergence of autonomous agents is achieved as to which norm should be regarded as definitively valid and, in addition, a commonly binding norm is needed. In this situation it is also the case that opponents must accept that the proponents of a norm may claim it to be binding on all its addressees.[41]

39 This is the point of the critique that there are no definitive but only prima facie-norms, often advanced against Dworkin's thesis of the all-or-nothing applicability of rules. See, for example, Alexy, Zum Begriff des Rechtsprinzips (n. 2), 68pp.; id., A Theory of Constitutional Rights (n. 3), 57pp.

40 See Jan Sieckmann, The Concept of Autonomy, in: T. Gizbert-Studnicki/J. Stelmach (eds.), Law and Legal Cultures in the 21st Century. Plenary Lectures of the XXIII. IVR-World Congress of Philosophy of Law and Social Philosophy, Warszawa, Oficina (Kluwer), 2007, 162; id., The Logic of Autonomy (n. 22), 17, 82.

41 See Sieckmann, The Concept of Autonomy (n. 40), 165; id. The Logic of Autonomy (n. 22), 122p.

Concluding Remark

In sum, one finds the dualism of ideal and real "ought" in the structure of autonomous reasoning, that is, in the reasoning of autonomous agents including the balancing of their arguments and a rational discourse including inter-subjective reflection as to which norms should be accepted as definitively valid by all agents, also taking into account a situation of reasonable disagreement amongst them. More precisely, one must distinguish between:

- The normative arguments offered by autonomous agents,
- The normative judgments of these agents based on the balancing of the normative arguments, and
- Normative statements as to the norms that are binding on all their addressees and that are hence objectively valid.

These are elements of any normative argumentation and, since normative validity can be established only by means of such argumentation, of any normative system.

By contrast, Alexy has never managed to provide an account of principles or ideal "ought" that might support the "strict separation thesis" which states that rules and principles are logically distinct types of norms. In addition, he has not been able to offer a valid argument against the notion of ideal "ought" provided by the conception of normative arguments being reiterated requirements of validity. Finally, his own analysis supports this conception. Thus, instead of presenting valid arguments against it, his analysis rather supports the conception of normative arguments as reiterated requirements of validity.

Part IV – Law and Rights

Júlio Aguiar de Oliveira*

Extreme Injustice and the Concept of Law

Introduction

There are two possible approaches to Radbruch's formula namely, (a) as a conceptual claim about the nature of law, and (b) as a prescription for judicial decision-making. Given both approaches as a point of departure, then four different theses are possible: First, Radbruch's formula can be understood both as a conceptual claim about law and as a prescription for judicial decision-making. Second, Radbruch's formula can be rejected as a conceptual claim about law and also as a prescription for judicial decision-making. Third, Radbruch's formula works as a prescription for judicial decision-making but not as conceptual claim about law. Fourth, and now the range of possibilities is rendered complete, Radbruch's formula can be understood as a conceptual claim about law but not as a prescription for judicial decision-making. In this paper, I will try to argue that this last interpretation is not only the best interpretation of Radbruch's formula but, indeed, also makes possible a better interpretation of Radbruch's and Alexy's legal philosophies generally.

What I would like to do here is to think about extreme injustice with an eye on Radbruch and Alexy's theories of law and to argue on behalf of the last of the four theses I have just mentioned, the one that defends the claim that Radbruch's formula can be understood as a conceptual claim about law but not as a prescription for judicial decision-making. It seems to be possible to defend the view that it is an essential element of an adequate concept of law and, at the same time, that the formula is not to be applied by judges as a prescription for judicial decision-making.

In the following sections, I will attempt to develop this investigation on the extreme injustice thesis further by: (1) considering Radbruch Formula within the framework of Radbruch's concept of law; (2) considering Radbruch Formula within the framework of Alexy's concept of law and, finally by (3) considering Brian Bix's arguments on his interpretation of the Radbruch formula as primarily a prescription for judicial decision-making.

* I prepared much of the present paper as a guest of Robert Alexy's in the Faculty of Law at the University of Kiel. I am very grateful to Professor Alexy for stimulating discussion and for his gracious hospitality. I am also grateful to Stanley L. Paulson, my neighbor *im Juristischen Seminar* over the sixteen months of my residence in Kiel. He and I had rich and rewarding conversations, and we became good friends. And I am grateful to Andrea Neisius, stalwart of the Alexy chair, for many kindnesses. Finaly, I thank Svein Eng, Oslo, for a number of useful comments and suggestions on the present paper. My research was supported by Coordenação de Aperfeiçoamento de Pessoal de Nível Superior (CAPES/MEC), Universidade Federal de Ouro Preto (UFOP), and Pontifícia Universidade Católica de Minas Gerais (PUC Minas).

Part One: Radbruch's Formula in Radbruch's Philosophy of Law: the Specificity of the Normativity of the Law

The conceptual nature of the Radbruch formula as an essential element of the specific normative *nucleus* of the law can be more clearly perceived once Radbruch's formula is situated in the context of Radbruch's criticism of legal positivism. According to Radbruch:

> Positivism is, moreover, in and of itself wholly incapable of establishing the validity of statutes. It claims to have proved the validity of a statute simply by showing that the statute had sufficient power behind it to prevail. But while power may indeed serve as a basis for the "must" of compulsion, it never serves as a basis for the "ought" of obligation or for legal validity. Obligation and legal validity must be based, rather, on a value inherent in the statute.[1]

Here it is possible to see clearly the reason why Radbruch cannot accept legal positivism as an adequate theory of law. The decisive reason is not to be found in some alleged of connection between legal positivism and Nazism. As Paulson and others have shown, it is not accurate to infer – from Radbruch's post-War writings – any defence of a causal thesis by means of which some sort of responsibility for the Nazi takeover is attributed to positivism.[2] For Radbruch, legal positivism is not to be accepted as a theory of law – not however on the ground that positivism amounts to a Nazi theory of law (what is simply not true), but because it is not able to explain the "ought" of obligation.[3] This is the point. Radbruch's formula is an attempt to address specifically this problem, a problem that can be expressed by the question: How is the specific normative aspect of positive law to be defined? The answer that Radbruch proposes to this question appears in his post-War writings, but it had already appeared in his pre-War writings. That answer comprises the affirmation of the regulative principle at the *nucleus* of the normativity of the law (its value of justice). At the *nucleus* of the normativity of the law, the regulative principle unfolds into two interconnected elements: (a) a regulative principle (ideal) as the idea of law and, (b) a regulative principle as the limit of extreme injustice, that is, the lowest possible concrete manifestation of the regulative principle in positive law (what came to be known, in the post-War period, as "Radbruch's formula"). These two elements define the horizon of the specific normative aspect of positive law (which in turn is an essential element of the very concept of law). This, I believe, is a good way to understand what is at issue in these writings of Radbruch. In both pre- and post-War writings, Radbruch is proposing a single answer to the problem of the specific normativity of positive law, which comprehends, in its *nucleus*, the regulative principle as unfolded into its two elements (the idea of law and the limit imposed by extreme

1 Gustav Radbruch, "Statutory Lawlessness and Supra-Statutory Law (1946)", *Oxford Journal of Legal Studies*, 26 (2006), 1–11, at p. 6.

2 See Stanley L. Paulson, "Lon L. Fuller, Gustav Radbruch, and the 'Positivist' Theses", *Law and Philosophy*, 13 (1994), 313–359.

3 "In Morals alone may the obligatory force of law be grounded. It has been shown that from legal rules as imperatives, expressions of a will, we may possibly derive a Must but never an Ought. Of legal norms, legal Ought, legal validity, legal duties, we may speak only when the legal imperative is endowed by the individual conscience with moral obligatory force". Gustav Radbruch, *Legal Philosophy*, translated by Kurt Wilk (Cambridge Massachusetts: Harvard University Press, 1950) at 84–5.

injustice, that is, Radbruch's formula). The fact that the limit imposed by extreme injustice is fully explicit only in his post-War writings does not mean that it was not already there in his pre-War writings.[4] What is new in the post-War writings is the search for the substantial aspect of extreme injustice.

This can be seen if one observes that, by affirming the Radbruch formula, one must be ready to face three fundamental questions: (1) Why is extreme injustice not law? (2) Why is only extreme injustice, and not just any instance of injustice, not law? (3) How can one distinguish between a statute with an extremely unjust content and a statute with unjust content that is not extreme? How, as Alexy puts it, does one trace "the boundary line between injustice that is and is not extreme"?[5]

This last question takes us to the problem of defining the material elements of the extremely unjust content of a statute. That is what is new in Radbruch's post-War writings. In three passages of two of his most important post-War writings, "Five Minutes of Legal Philosophy (1945)" and "Statutory Lawlessness and Supra-Statutory Law (1946)", Radbruch deals specifically with the question of what counts as an extremely unjust content of extreme injustice. In "Five Minutes of Legal Philosophy (1945)", he writes:

> There are principles of law, therefore, that are weightier than any legal enactment, so that a law in conflict with them is devoid of validity. These principles are known as natural law or the law of reason. To be sure, their details remain open to question, but the work of centuries has in fact established a solid core of them, and they have come to enjoy such a far-reaching consensus in the so-called declarations of human and civil rights that only the dogmatic sceptic could still entertain doubts about some of them.[6]

In "Statutory Lawlessness and Supra-Statutory Law (1946)", Radbruch gives the following specifications:

> It is impossible to draw a sharper line between cases of statutory lawlessness and statutes that are valid despite their flaws. One line of distinction, however, can be drawn with the utmost clarity: Where there is not even an attempt at justice, where equality, the core of justice, is deliberately betrayed in the issuance of positive law, then the statute is not merely 'flawed law', it lacks completely the very nature of law.[7]

Still in "Statutory Lawlessness and Supra-Statutory Law (1946)", bringing to a close his efforts to define the material content of extreme injustice *stricto sensu*, Radbruch writes:

> Legal character is also lacking in all the statutes that treated human beings as subhuman and denied them human rights, and it is lacking, too, in all the caveats that, governed solely by the momentary necessities of intimidation, disregard the varying gravity of offences and threatened the same punishment, often death, for the slightest as well as the most serious of crimes. All these are examples of statutory lawlessness.[8]

Taking together the substantial elements of the content of extreme injustice as brought together in these two texts, it is possible to affirm that according to Rad-

4 See "scandalous laws" (*Schandgesetze*) in Radbruch, ibid, p. 118.

5 Robert Alexy, *The Argument from Injustice: A Reply to Legal Positivism*, translated by Stanley L. Paulson and Bonnie Litschewski Paulson (Oxford: Oxford University Press, 2002), at 53.

6 Gustav Radbruch, "Five Minutes of Legal Philosophy (1945)", *Oxford Journal of Legal Philosophy*, 26 (2006), 13–15, at 14–5.

7 Gustav Radbruch, "Statutory Lawlessness and Supra-Statutory Law (1946)" (n. 1), at 7.

8 Ibid at 8.

bruch: (a) a statute that disregards the solid core of principles of natural law (or the law of reason), expressed in the declarations of human and civil rights, is not a law; (b) a statute that disregards the *telos* of positive law towards justice, specially by way of a deliberate betrayal of equality, is not law; (c) a statute that denies human beings their human rights, specially by denying human beings the recognition of their status as human beings, is not law; (d) a statute that imposes the same punishment in a class of crimes quite different from one another in gravity, is not law. These contents are not only unjust, they are extremely unjust. Nevertheless, as Radbruch observes, it is not possible to "draw a sharper line between cases of statutory lawlessness and statutes that are valid despite their flaws". This does not mean, however, that such a distinction is impossible. Radbruch's concept of law depends on the possibility of making that distinction.

Still considering Radbruch's search for a better definition of the substance of the extremely unjust content of a statute, as witnessed in his post-War writings, it can be said that that search by no means implies that Radbruch has abandoned the principle of judicial bindingness.

In order to explain this, it is well to observe, in the first place, that legal positivism should not be confused with some kind of proper deference towards positive law, nor should Radbruch's attention to the value of legal certainty (which is expressed through his postulate of judicial bindingness) be taken as a sufficient mark of legal positivism. The due respect for positive law in the process of adjudication (judicial bindingness) is not an achievement, a consequence, or even a distinct exclusive characteristic of legal positivism, and, thus considered, judicial bindingness can be part of a non-positivist theory of law.[9] In fact, by its refusal to accept a necessary connection between law and morality as the expression of the specific normativity of the law, legal positivism makes it impossible properly to understand positive law by making it impossible to understand the specific reasons that we have for observing and applying the positive law as positive law (and not as positive law *with* some extra moral reasons, as is the case in Joseph Raz's theory). As Radbruch shows, the necessary connection between law and morality, necessary to the concept of law, is not simply a matter of importing morality into the realm of law and

9 Paulson: "The doctrine of judicial bindingness can be held, however, without any endorsement of statutory positivism. The point is worth explaining. Given statutory positivism, then it may appear as though the doctrine of judicial bindingness followed: Since, according to statutory positivism, the law is nothing but statutory law, the judge following the law is *eo ipso* following statutory law. But matters are not this simple. Judicial bindingnesss is a normative doctrine, and therefore its following from statutory positivism is not at all obvious. What is more – and more to the point where Radbruch is concerned – there is no logical tie in the other direction: The doctrine of judicial bindingness, taken by itself, does not imply statutory positivism. One can insist that the judge is bound by statutory law, and one can, at the same time, reject the notion that the law is nothing but statutory law. A case in point is Radbruch's own commitment to the doctrine of judicial bindingness, a doctrine not inconsistent with his neo-Kantianism and the basal criterion that he defended in its name. For he regarded the doctrine of judicial bindingness simply as a policy, and his basal criterion prevailed on the question of the nature of law – even if, to be sure, the policy rendered his non-positivistic theory inapplicable in practice. This is obviously an unsatisfactory state of affairs, but – to repeat – no logical inconsistency arises". Stanley L. Paulson, "On the Background and Significance of Gustav Radbruch's Post-War Papers", *Oxford Journal of Legal Studies,* 26 (2006) 17–40, at 36.

still less a submission of positive law to morality.[10] What we find in Radbruch is a recognition of the specific normative character of the law[11], in which – as has been shown – Radbruch's formula plays a fundamental role.

Where Radbruch is concerned, once it is perceived that "the doctrine of judicial bindingness, taken by itself, does not imply statutory positivism"[12], it can also be defended that – by reflecting on the extremely unjust content of extreme injustice – Radbruch need not be necessarily interpreted as if he were abandoning the doctrine of judicial bindingness. On this particular point, my interpretation departs from Paulson's interpretation. According to Paulson: "In his post-war writings, Radbruch puts the basal criterion to work, freeing it of the constraint imposed by the doctrine of judicial bindingness".[13] Paulson understands that a non-positivistic theory of law is not put into practice if the judge is not allowed to apply the Radbruch formula as a prescription for judicial decision-making. In Paulson's words:

> Still, the case on behalf of Radbruch's non-positivistic theory of law remains, for his earlier period, merely a prima-facie case. On the one hand, the import of such a non-positivistic theory of law is clear: It precludes, by appeal to justice qua absolute value, certain ostensibly legal norms – the statue that patently violates equality or the holding that stems from an extraordinary court. On the other hand, a doctrine of Radbruch's found at § 10 of *Legal Philosophy* stands in the way of any application of the theory. In Radbruch's earlier period, then, the non-positivistic theory cannot be put into practice.[14]

The question here is what it means for the non-positivistic theory to be put into practice. If it means it is to be taken as a prescription for judicial decision-making, then I would have to agree with Paulson. But I think it is possible for Radbruch's non-positivistic theory to be put into practice without having been applied as a prescription for judicial decision-making. Considering specifically the role of judges, Radbruch's non-positivistic theory of law has the practical effect of making explicit the possibility of the existence of situations, characterized by the occurrence of extreme injustice, in which a judge's commitment to the law should lead to his or her open renunciation of his or her position as judge. From the perspective of the judge, this can already be seen as a practical effect of an interpretation of Radbruch's non-positivistic theory of law in which judicial bindingness and Radbruch's formula coexist. From the perspective of the ordinary citizen, Radbruch's non-positivistic concept of law makes explicit the need for personal deliberation on the question of whether a certain statutory provision is indeed a law, this with an eye to whether one ought to observe it.

Actually, it seems to be possible to defend the view that Radbruch's formula is an essential element of an adequate concept of law and, at the same time, that it

10 "What must be shown here is that our view does not by any means obliterate the distinction established between the respective contents of law and morals, or incorporate law as a mere province in morals, or turn the legal norm into a moral norm of some particular content. The naturalization of the legal duty in the realm of morals represents an instance of a more general phenomenon, which has as yet been too little examined: the investment of the same material with a twofold value character". Gustav Radbruch, *Legal Philosophy* (n. 3), at 85.

11 "Obligation and legal validity must be based, rather, on a value inherent in the statute". Gustav Radbruch, "Statutory Lawlessness and Supra-Statutory Law (1946)" (n. 1), at 6.

12 Stanley L. Paulson, "On the Background and Significance of Gustav Radbruch's Post-War Papers" (n. 9), at 36.

13 Ibid 38.

14 Ibid 32.

should not be applied by judges as a prescription for judicial decision-making. However, the fact that Radbruch's formula should not be applied by judges as a prescription for judicial decision-making does not mean: (a) that judges are obligated (or empowered) to apply even extremely unjust statutes (in fact, judges are obligated not to apply extremely unjust statutes for the basic reason that extremely unjust statutes are not law), or (b) that judges should not be held judicially accountable for the application of extremely unjust statutes (from the fact that Radbruch's formula is not a prescription for judicial decision-making, it does not follow that it can be used as an argument for exoneration).[15]

In this way, the Radbruch formula does not conceal (or weaken) judicial bindingness to statutes by attributing to them (the judges) the power to decide – as judges – which statute is a law and which statute is not a law based on its extremely unjust content, and it does not work as an argument for exoneration either. Nevertheless, Radbruch's formula has specific implications for judicial adjudication, since it indirectly affirms that a judge should never apply an extremely unjust statute (for the reason that an extremely unjust statute is not law).

The tension considered here between a statute with extremely unjust content and the judicial bindingness to statutes is tragic in nature. Facing this tension, a judge must resist statutory lawlessness. This duty of resistance, as Radbruch understands it, stems from the fact that the "judge's ethos ought to be directed toward justice at any price, even at the price of his own life".[16] This duty of resistance, however, does not imply that the judge can (or should) declare the invalidity of a statute on the ground that it has extremely unjust content. The question here, it must be observed, is not a question on the constitutionality of a statute. It is not a question that falls within the framework of the constitutional interpretation of rules and principles. In confronting extreme injustice, there is as an answer no constitutional interpretation available (if an answer stemming from constitutional interpretation were possible, more specifically, if the allegedly extremely unjust statute could be invalidated due to its unconstitutionality, than this allegedly extremely unjust statute could not be understood as extreme injustice in its specific sense). So, I understand that in that case Radbruch's non-positivistic concept of law leads the judge to the duty of renouncing his office. There is no solution, from the perspective of legal interpretation, to this problem. Facing extreme injustice, the judge is – at the same time – the one who is bound in conscience to consider all properly enacted statutes as law, and the one who is bound by his conscience to regard a properly enacted statute with extremely unjust content (extreme injustice) as no law. It is as if in this situation a person were – at the same time – the judge and the "criminal from conviction". In Radbruch words:

> Yet the judge, who is in conscience bound to consider all enacted law valid, may be faced by a defendant who is bound by his conscience to regard unjust or inexpedient law as invalid although enacted. Against the latter, the law may prove its power but can never demonstrate its validity. That case of the "criminal from conviction" proves a truly tragic case precisely because there is no solution for it.[17]

15 For an analysis of Radbruch on the exoneration thesis see Paulson, "Lon L. Fuller, Gustav Radbruch, and the "Positivist" Theses" (n. 2), at 328–41.

16 Gustav Radbruch, "Statutory Lawlessness and Supra-Statutory Law (1946)" (n. 1), at 10.

17 Radbruch, *Legal Philosophy* (n. 3), at 119.

The judge's confrontation with extreme injustice can also occur in a different mode. A judge can be faced with the allegation that a properly issued and efficacious statute, from a past legal order, was not a law, due to its extremely unjust content, even in that past legal order. That is what was experienced in Germany after the Second World War and after reunification. Once again, I do not think that Radbruch's formula gives the judge the power to declare that a properly issued statute was not a law due to its extremely unjust content. This kind of declaration presupposes a power that cannot be attributed to a judge (or even to a Supreme Court) without jeopardizing not only legal certainty but also the import of the statute, for the law "is of value not only as a precipitation of justice but also as a guarantee of legal certainty, and it is preeminently as the latter that it is entrusted to the judge."[18] This power should reside solely with the legislative body. Considering this specific situation, a judge (judicial power) must recognize that only one who has the power to issue statutes can have the power officially to declare that a past properly issued statute was, due to its extremely unjust content, not law.

Does this mean that my interpretation of the Radbruch formula leads Radbruch to the positivistic side of the bright line drawn by legal theory? Or, considering the widely held thesis of Radbruch's conversion from positivism to natural law during and after the Second World War, does it mean that my interpretation would have Radbruch returning to positivism? I do not think so. In fact, following Paulson, among others, I am convinced that Radbruch never was a legal positivist.[19] So it seems not correct to contend that Radbruch underwent a kind of conversion from an early positivism to a post-War non-positivism. He was not a legal positivist before the War and he was not a legal positivist after the War. A neo-Kantian basal criterion (as Paulson puts it), as a regulative principle, was already at work in Radbruch's concept of law presented in his pre-War writings and remains at work – to an even greater extent – in his post-War writings. The Radbruch formula is, essentially, the result of a further development of Radbruch's Neo-Kantian basal criterion. So it seems to be clear that Radbruch defends a necessary connection between law and morality (*Verbindungsthese*) and that this defence was already present in his pre-War writings.

It can also be asked whether this interpretation lends itself to Radbruch's concept of law as a kind of a super-inclusive non-positivism. Again, I think that that is not the case. The thesis that Radbruch's formula should not be taken as a prescription for judicial decision-making does not imply that there are no classifying consequences for legal validity that stems from extreme injustice. Although I defend the view that a judge (judicial power) is not competent to declare that a statute is not or was not a law owing to its extremely unjust content, extreme injustice (that is, a statute with an extremely unjust content) undergoes no change in its status as being

18 Ibid, at 119.

19 See Stanley L. Paulson, "Radbruch on Unjust Laws: Competing Earlier and Later Views?", *Oxford Journal of Legal Studies*, 15 (1995), 489–500; "On the Background and Significance of Gustav Radbruch's Post-War Papers" (n. 9); Arthur Kaufmann, *Gustav Radbruch – Rechtsdenker, Philosoph, Sozialdemokrat* (München/Zürich: Piper, 1987); Erik Wolf, "Umbruch oder Entwicklung in Gustav Radbruchs Rechtsphilosophie?", *ARSP*, 45 (1972), 481–503; Alexandre Travessoni Gomes Trivisonno, "Gustav Radbruch's (supposed) turn against positivism: a matter of balancing?" (IVR Congress Frankfurt/2011).

non-law, and this means, in practical terms, that it should not be observed or applied. So it also seems to be clear that there are practical consequences from the necessary connection between law and morality.[20]

Considering, then, Radbruch's legal theory in its entirety, the theory, thus understood, seems clearly to deny to the formula any function as a prescription for judicial decision-making, and this in turn can be taken as a well-justified condition for a more coherent interpretation of Radbruch's legal theory.[21] In the next section, I will consider the role of Radbruch's formula in Alexy's concept of law.

Part Two: The Role of Radbruch's Formula in Alexy's Concept of Law

The essence of Radbruch's formula in Alexy's theory, as also in Radbruch's own theory, is to serve as part of the concept of law. Its function, as in Radbruch's theory, is grounding the specific normativity of the law.

In grounding the specific normativity of the law, Alexy identifies two elements: (1) the claim to correctness, and (2) extreme injustice (argument from injustice). These two elements can be seen, analogically, as the two components of Radbruch's regulative principle: (a) the idea of law, and (b) the limits of extreme injustice (Radbruch's formula). Their specificity as elements of the normativity of the law is explained not only by the fact that the claim to correctness is taken together with the argument from injustice, but also by the fact that both – the claim to correctness and the argument from injustice – are connected with the classical law defining elements of authoritative issuance and social efficacy. In Alexy's concept of law, Radbruch's formula is the expression of the specific normativity of the law. It is the proper manifestation of the connection thesis.

The question now is: Are there good reasons for denying to Radbruch's formula the function of serving as a prescription for judicial decision-making in Alexy's concept of law?

I think there are two reasons: (1) democracy and (2) legal certainty.

20 According to Paulson, a non-positivistic theory of law is not put in practice if the judge is not allowed to apply the Radbruch's formula as a prescription for judicial decision-making. See Paulson, "On the Background and Significance of Gustav Radbruch's Post-War Papers" (n. 9), at 32.

21 Much more should be said in order better to defend a coherent and integral non-positivist Radbruch's legal philosophy, especially concerning the difficult point of "Radbruch's relativism". By proposing a distinction between values (*Werte*) and evaluations (*Werturteile*), Marc André Wiegand sustains the notion that the traditional relativistic claim of the irrationality of value in Radbruch should be interpreted as directed not to values, but to evaluations, an interpretation more akin to Radbruch's concept of law and also to Radbruch's Neo-Kantianism. See Marc André Wiegand, *Unrichtiges Recht* (Tübingen: Mohr Siebeck, 2004), at 30–1. Specifically on Radbruch's Neo-Kantianism, see Paulson, On the Background and Significance of Gustav Radbruch's Post-War Papers" (n. 9), at 29–32. Also dealing with "Radbruch's relativism", in a way that makes it compatible with a coherent non-positivist position, Dietmar von der Pfordten writes: "I believe an affirmative and holistic basic attitude towards philosophy can even integrate, to a great extent, a limited and well-defined relativism, as long as this relativism does not produce metastasis and endanger the whole system". Dietmar von der Pfordten, "Radbruch as an Affirmative Holist. On the Question of What Ought to Be Preserved of His Philosophy", *Ratio Juris*, 21 (2008), 387–403, at 399.

The objection to a non-positivistic concept of law based on democracy draws on the idea, as Alexy puts it, that "the non-positivistic concept of law carries with it the risk that the judge, appealing to justice, will oppose decisions of the democratically legitimated legislator".[22] In defence of the use of Radbruch's formula as a prescription for judicial decision-making (which is seen as a necessary consequence of a non-positivistic concept of law), Alexy argues:

> This objection loses its punch if one considers that the non-positivistic concept of law entails the forfeiture of legal character only in cases of extreme injustice. It has an effect only in a core area. The content of the constitutional review of rights violations in democratic constitutional states reaches much further. Whoever appeals to democracy or the separation of powers to argue against the weak connection thesis represented here would have to reject any judicial review whatsoever of the legislator's commitment to fundamental rights.[23]

But in the sequence, Alexy writes:

> The question, though, is what the judge ought to do if the legislator, for whatever reason, fails to act and if the lawless or unjust statute cannot, on the basis of currently prevailing constitutional law, be declared irrelevant for the decision at hand. Should the judge, then, hand down decisions based on, and themselves representing, injustice in the extreme? (…) If the legislator fails to make use of this possibility, and if the lawless or unjust statute cannot, on the basis of currently prevailing constitutional law, be declared irrelevant of the decision at hand, then a non-positivistic concept of law must of necessity be applied in order to protect the fundamental rights of the citizen.[24]

Once a judge (or even the supreme court) – in a democratic constitutional state – declares that some properly issued statute is or was not a law on the ground of its extremely unjust content, democracy is violated. A democratically legitimated legislator could never accept such a decision. The presupposition of this judicial decision must be, as Alexy observes, a judicial statement to the effect that the legislator has failed in a way that lies beyond the limits of what can be characterized as a failure in the constitutional interpretation of the validity of the statute. The possibility of judicial review of the legislator's commitment to fundamental rights must not be denied by means of appeals to democracy in order to criticize the use of Radbruch's formula as a prescription for judicial decision-making. It is a fact that "the content of the constitutional review of rights violations in democratic constitutional states reaches much further" than the threshold of extreme injustice. Then, however, the natural conclusion from this fact would have to be a denial of the possibility of any occurrence of extreme injustice in a democratic constitutional state. Since, however, the possibility of extreme injustice in a democratic constitutional state is accepted, then it must also be accepted that, for whatever reason, the constitutional review of rights is not able completely to avoid extreme injustice. In this way, the criticism stemming from democracy against the use of Radbruch's formula as a prescription for judicial decision-making is not dependent on the rejection of constitutional review, and it seems to be the case that a non-positivistic concept of law in which Radbruch's formula has a function as a prescription for judicial decision-making appears to be at odds with democracy.

22 Alexy, *The Argument from Injustice* (n. 5), at 56.
23 Ibid, at 56.
24 Ibid at 58.

By not endorsing Radbruch's formula as a prescription for judicial decision-making, Alexy's concept of law could be better attuned to the idea of democracy. In a constitutional democratic state, Radbruch's formula – not interpreted as a prescription for judicial decision-making – can be conceived as grounding the specific normativity of the law not only in a person's prudential deliberation in order that a properly issued statute be recognized as law but also as part of a procedural deliberation in a democracy with an eye to creating law. It connects the personal recognized limits of the law with its democratic enactment.

The other argument is legal certainty. According to Alexy, an "argument against the non-positivistic concept of law asserts that this concept jeopardizes legal certainty".[25] Alexy, however, understands that it is not the case that legal certainty is jeopardized by Radbruch's formula. According to him, legal certainty can be preserved in a non-positivistic concept of law by the application of a principle of recognition. Alexy argues:

> Now, the following principle applies: the more extreme the injustice, the more certain the knowledge of it. This principle connects material and epistemological considerations. It provides a justification for the Federal Constitutional Court's views, stated in the decision on citizenship discussed above, not only that the injustice of Ordinance 11 reached an 'intolerable degree', but also that this was 'evident'." So, this non-positivistic connection thesis leads at most, then, to a minimal loss of legal certainty.[26]

I am not entirely clear where the validity of Alexy's principle of recognition is concerned. Although the definition of the extremely unjust content of a statute can be oriented, today, by means of human rights, the recognition of the extremely unjust content of a statute (which means the recognition of extreme injustice) may, however, not be easy (either in personal or in institutional contexts). The extremely unjust content of Ordinance 11, for instance, was not immediately recognized by (probably) the vast majority of the citizens and not by the vast majority of judges and legal authorities either (which can be attested by the fact that there are no records of official resistance). It took time and a radical political transformation in order to gain recognition.

The reason for this difficulty in gaining recognition is due, at least in part, to the fact that extreme injustice is necessarily found in a properly issued statute. Extreme injustice is not simply a terrible act of injustice. It is not simply a violation of human rights. Extreme injustice – considering its specificity as an element of the concept of law – is necessarily found in a properly issued statute with an extremely unjust content. The fact that this extremely unjust content is encapsulated within a properly issued statute is exactly what makes it difficult to recognize it as extreme injustice. But this difficulty, at the same time, is evidence for the adequacy of Radbruch's formula as an element of the concept of law. If the law were merely a morally neutral system of norms, it would be easier to recognize extreme injustice. If there were no specific moral value in the law itself, then the moral values – expressed by the law but existing independently of it – would shine like stars in an unclouded night in the desert, undisturbed by the night lightning of the city. That explains why H. L. A. Hart's proposal seems on first glance so reasonable. It seems to be an excel-

25 Ibid, at 51.
26 Ibid, at 52.

lent way for coming to terms with the possibility of extreme injustice, namely, by removing the specific normative element from the law and reserving it exclusively to the field of morality (outside the law) – thereby, as Hart puts it, refusing "to cloak the true nature of the problems with which we are faced".[27] By stripping from the law its specific normative element (which is necessarily an element of moral character), it should become easier both to identify the cases in which the law is the vehicle for injustice and consequently to resist unjust law. It seems, then, to offer not only an epistemological but also a moral reason to keep morality outside the concept of law, in other words, a moral reason for maintaining the separation thesis (*Trennungsthese*)[28]. The problem with this thesis is comparable to the familiar case of throwing out the baby with the bath water. That is simply impossible to strip law of its specific normative character without casting aside the law itself. What makes law binding is a part of what law is. So although it is a fact that the night lighting of the city does disturb one's observation of the stars, it is not really an option to switch off the lights of the city in order better to contemplate the stars.

Part Three: The Arguments of Brian Bix

Considering the problem of the interpretation of Radbruch's formula, Bix presents two arguments. I will call them respectively: (1) The context argument and (2) the perspective argument. With these two arguments, Bix intends to show that Radbruch's formula is not directed (or not primarily directed) towards questions about the nature of law. First, because it was in fact used as a prescription for judicial decision-making (context argument). Second, because it fails when taken as an element of the concept of law (perspective argument). Consequently, according to Bix, the Radbruch formula cannot work as a criticism of legal positivism. Not being directed towards questions about the nature of law, Bix assumes that Radbruch's formula is better understood as a prescription for judicial decision-making. But this can be no more than an assumption, since Bix does not offer any specific arguments in support of the point.

Bix's first argument is set out in order to show that Radbruch's formula is not directed towards questions about the nature of law. The argument addresses the context where Radbruch and Alexy's writings on the Radbruch formula appear.

27 H. L. A. Hart, "Positivism and the Separation of Law and Morals", *Harvard Law* Review, 71 (1958), 593–621, at 620.

28 As Hart makes it clear: "So long as human beings can gain sufficient co-operation from some to enable them to dominate others, they will use the forms of law as one of their instruments. Wicked men will enact wicked rules which others will enforce. What surely is most needed in order to make men clear-sighted in confronting the official abuse of power, is that they should preserve the sense that the certification of something as legally valid is not conclusive of the question of obedience, and that, however great the aura of majesty or authority which the official system may have, its demands must in the end be submitted to a moral scrutiny. This sense, that there is something outside the official system, by reference to which in the last resort the individual must solve his problems of obedience, is surely more likely to be kept alive among those who are accustomed to think that rules of law may be iniquitous, than among those who think that nothing iniquitous can anywhere have the status of law". H. L. A. Hart, *The Concept of Law*, 2nd edn. (Oxford: Clarendon Press, 1994), at 210.

> At a surface level, there is no doubt that, whatever else it is, the Radbruch Formula(s) *do* work as instructions to judges on how to decide cases. As mentioned earlier, judicial decision-making (by West German courts responding to actions purportedly done under the authorization of Nazi laws) is the context for Radbruch's introduction of his Formula(s) in his post-war articles, and comparable decisions made by the courts in an unified Germany, evaluating actions done purportedly under the authorization of East German law, is the context for some of Alexy's discussion of his version of the Radbruch Formula.[29]

Of course I agree with Bix that Radbruch's formula was applied by West German courts and also by courts in the unified German state, but this does not necessarily mean that Radbruch's formula must be defined as a prescription for judicial decision-making. A crowbar can be used to open a door and, in fact, it is occasionaly used to open doors. Notwithstanding this fact, it does not work as an argument in order to affirm that a crowbar should be primarily understood as a key. The same can be said about the Radbruch formula: from the fact that it was used as a prescription for judicial decision-making, it does not follow that it should therefore be taken primarily as a prescription for judicial decision-making (or even that it should be taken as a prescription for judicial decision-making at all). Bix's context argument simply does not justify such a conclusion.

In addition, dealing with the internal context in which reflections about the Radbruch formula appear both in Radbruch and Alexy's writings, it can be observed that Radbruch's formula was developed in writings centrally devoted to the investigation of the concept of law. In Radbruch's writings, the Radbruch formula is explicit in an article, "Statutory Lawlessness and Supra-Statutory Law", from 1946, which deals essentially with the concept of law. In Alexy's writings, although one can find a deeper reflection on the application of Radbruch's formula as a prescription for judicial decision-making, the more significant discussion occurs in a book focused on the investigation of the concept and validity of the law.

So if one takes the writings themselves where the Radbruch formula is developed – in both Radbruch's and Alexy's writings – one will find that it is developed not in writings directed primarily to questions of adjudication, but in writings directed primarily to the question of the concept of law.

Bix's second argument would have us believe that Radbruch's formula does not work as an element of the concept of law as soon as one interprets it from the perspective of the theorist.

> Additionally, if the Formula(s) *are* to be understood as a conceptual claim about the nature of law, then they are (by definition) claims about all existing and all possible legal systems. That may not be a good description of the Formula(s). Consider Radbruch's argument that significantly unjust norms are not valid norms: one could certainly understand such a claim made internally within a particular legal system, about the criteria of validity of that legal system. It is far less clear what is meant by a theorist, like Radbruch, making this claim about all (and all possible) legal systems.[30]

Bix's second argument is based on the distinction between observer and participant perspectives. According to Bix, a theorist of law must necessarily adopt the observer's perspective, and since Radbruch's formula – also according to Bix – makes no sense

29 Brian Bix, "Radbruch's Formula and Conceptual Analysis", *The American Journal of Jurisprudence*, 56 (2011), 45–57, at 52.

30 Ibid, at 56.

from the observer's perspective, then it should not be taken as directed, or at least not as primarily directed, towards a debate about the nature of law (and so – it goes without saying – it is best interpreted as a prescription for judicial decision-making).

The problem with this argument is that it takes the observer's perspective as an independent perspective. That is not correct. The observer's perspective is dependent on the participant's perspective (this is to why that the observer's perspective cannot make good sense without a participant's perspective). It is dependent on the participant's perspective in two senses: (1) Because a description of the law from the observer's perspective presupposes that there are persons who really do observe or apply the law that is described by the observer, this means that it presupposes persons who adopt a participant's perspective towards that specific law, and (2) because a description of the law from the observer's perspective presupposes that both the observer who describes the law and one who listens to the observer's description are both able to compare that description with their own concepts of law from the perspective of participants (it means that someone who does not already know what a law is from the perspective of a participant will not be able correctly to understand a description of a law-governed activity from the perspective of an observer).

The same confusion on the distinction between participant and observer perspectives appears in claims made by Norbert Hoerster. As Alexy observes, Hoerster makes two claims on this question:

> Norbert Hoerster has claimed, first, that there is a need for a value-neutral designation for authoritatively issued socially efficacious norms like Ordinance 11 discussed above, and, second, that there is no useful alternative to the expression 'law'.[31]

Considering these two claims, first, I do not think that there is a need for a *value-neutral* designation for authoritatively issued socially efficacious norms like Ordinance 11, and, second, the fact that there is no useful alternative expression to name that thing is a very good index for the truth of the claim that that specific thing (an authoritatively issued socially efficacious and *value-neutral* norm) simply does not exist (a very good reason not to be worried at all about trying to invent a name for it, much less to seek agreement to use the expression "law" to name that thing). So, the reason why I think there is no need for a *value-neutral* designation for authoritatively issued socially efficacious norms is the simple fact that no authoritatively issued socially efficacious and *value-neutral* norm exists. Law is not a name that can properly be attributed to something like Ordinance 11. It is possible to use the term "law" from the observer's perspective, but the limits of this possibility are established by Radbruch's formula. The question is not whether Radbruch's formula is possible from the observer's perspective. The question is whether the observer's perspective is possible without Radbruch's formula and – considering that the observer's perspective is dependent on the participant's perspective – the answer here is no.

At the basis of Hoerster's claims lies his faith in moral relativism. Hoerster's claims are based on the presumption that moral relativism is true and, at the same time, these claims are treated as an argument on behalf of moral relativism. This is expressed in the centrality of the observer's perspective in Hoester's (and Bix's) interpretation of the distinction between observer and participant perspectives. But

31 Alexy, *The Argument from Injustice* (n. 5), at 30–1.

since there is no reason to accept the truth of moral relativism, there is also no reason to accept the validity of Hoerster's claims.

Thus, once it is understood that the distinction between participant and observer perspectives can only make sense if the observer's perspective is understood as dependent on the perspective of the participant, the result is that the argument drawn from this distinction does not work as an argument against the interpretation of Radbruch's formula as a part of a conceptual claim about the nature of law.

As far as Bix's arguments are concerned, it seems that neither the context argument nor the perspective argument can be taken as a good argument for grounding the thesis that Radbruch's formula is not primarily directed towards the question about the nature of law (and even less that it should be better understood as a prescription for judicial decision-making).

Concluding Remark

In conclusion, I might reiterate the point that I have taken up in the paper, namely, two approaches to Radbruch's formula, (a) as a conceptual claim about the nature of law, and (b) as a prescription for judicial decision-making. Given both approaches as a point of departure, then four different theses are possible: First, Radbruch's formula is understood both as a conceptual claim about law and as a prescription for judicial decision-making. Second, Radbruch's formula is rejected as a conceptual claim about law and also as a prescription for judicial decision-making. Third, Radbruch's formula works as a prescription for judicial decision-making, but not as conceptual claim about law. Fourth, and now the range of possibilities is rendered complete, Radbruch's formula can be understood as a conceptual claim about law, but not as a prescription for judicial decision-making. In this paper, I have tried to argue that this last interpretation is not only the best interpretation of Radbruch's formula but, indeed, also in making possible a better interpretation of Radbruch's and Alexy's legal philosophies generally.

Appendix: Identifying the Four Theses with an Eye to Those Who Accept and Reject Them

	Radbruch/Alexy	Hart	Bix	My thesis
Radbruch's formula as a conceptual claim about the nature of law	+	–	–	+
Radbruch's formula as a prescription for judicial decision-making	+	–	+	–
	Non-positivism	Positivism	Positivism	Non-positivism

Stanley L. Paulson*

An Issue in Robert Alexy's Theory of the Nature of Law

Introduction

An aspect of Robert Alexy's work on the nature of law, specifically, the "qualifying connection" between the law and morality in his book *The Argument from Injustice* (2002),[1] is the focus of this short paper. I engage in constructive criticism, arguing that Alexy's qualifying connection, as it stands, is underdeveloped and largely programmatic. Still, the issue presented by the qualifying connection, namely, the status of "defective legal norms", lends itself to explication, as, I believe, I am able to show.

The argument proceeds by way of an analogy between defective legal norms and unconstitutional legal norms, calling for a fair bit of stage setting. I turn, first, to an example, drawn from the case law, of an unconstitutional legal norm. Second, I invite attention to the conceptual problem that stems from unconstitutional legal norms. Third, as a means of responding to the conceptual problem, I introduce a doctrine that I dub "presumptive legal validity". The doctrine stands in need of explanation, and I turn, fourth, to an explication of the notion of "content" as it arises in the doctrine, appealing to what I call "working rules of recognition", drawn from H. L. A. Hart's celebrated treatise. Fifth – still in the context of presumptive legal validity – I take up the issue of the strength of the presumption. This is perhaps the key notion in the doctrine of presumptive legal validity, and, in this connection, I introduce holism, known in the philosophical literature from the work of Pierre Duhem and W. V. Quine. Sixth, I touch on the question of ideals, which figure in the matrix whenever presumptive legal validity falls short of the mark. I return, in closing, to the defective legal norms of Alexy's qualifying connection. My interest is in their structure in so far as it can be drawn from the analogy to unconstitutional legal norms. I might add, *en passant*, that my analysis does not contain any great surprises. It is less a matter, here, of discovering something new than of explicating points that may well be intuitively clear but have not been given their due in analytical terms.

So much for the programme. But, asked the White Rabbit: "Where shall I begin?" "The place to begin is at the beginning", said the King.[2] I shall begin there, posing the question: What, exactly, is the qualifying connection? Alexy explains his qualifying connection by contrasting it with the classifying connection. As he writes:

> A *classifying* connection is reflected in the claim that norms…that do not meet a certain moral criterion are, for either conceptual or normative reasons, not legal norms… A *qualifying* connection is reflected in the claim that norms…that do not meet a certain moral criterion can indeed be legal norms…, but, for either conceptual or normative reasons, are legally defective legal

* As always, I am indebted to Bonnie Litschewski Paulson for wellnigh everything, specifically, in the present context, for very helpful discussion and a thorough edit of my draft.

1 Robert Alexy, *The Argument from Injustice* (first publ. 1992), trans. Bonnie Litschewski Paulson and Stanley L. Paulson (Oxford: Clarendon Press, 2002) [hereafter: *AI*].

2 Lewis Carroll, *Alice in Wonderland.*

> norms... What is crucial is that the asserted defect is a legal defect and not simply a moral defect. Arguments addressed to qualifying connections are based on the assumption that necessarily legal ideals are contained within the reality of a legal system.[3]

The classifying connection is familiar from Gustav Radbruch's post-War formula,[4] and I shall not concern myself with it here.[5] Rather, my concern is with the qualifying connection and, in particular, defective legal norms. The problem, quite simply, is that we are given virtually no help on the question of what counts – as expressed in the quotation above – as "a certain moral criterion" or as "legal ideals", and no help either on criteria for identifying legally defective legal norms, let alone criteria for distinguishing the severity of the defect. Alexy speaks in the quotation of "[a]rguments addressed to qualifying connections" but he adduces no such arguments. With a single exception, the entire discussion in the book is devoted to the classifying connection.

The exception has Alexy addressing the case of a theorist – in later work of Alexy's, the "exclusive non-positivist" – who insists that *every* departure from moral correctness implies that the ostensibly legal norm is *not law at all*.[6] Alexy states, and rightly so, that such a thesis is far too strong[7] and cannot be defended. Then he continues:

> [T]he issue here cannot be a classifying connection, it can only be a qualifying connection. Below the threshold of extreme injustice, a violation of morality means not that the norm or decision in question forfeits legal character, in other words, is not law (a classifying connection), but, rather, that the norm or decision in question is legally defective (a qualifying connection). The claim to correctness that is necessarily attached to the law, because it includes a claim to moral correctness, is the reason that, below the threshold of extreme injustice, a violation of correct morality leads not, indeed, to the forfeiture of legal character, but necessarily to legal defectiveness.[8]

One aspect of this passage is especially helpful for my purposes. It hints at the reason for Alexy's concern with the qualifying connection, to wit: He contends that the notion is required by the claim to correctness. As he puts it, individual legal norms "as well as legal systems as a whole necessarily lay claim to correctness".[9]

So far, so good, but the problems adumbrated at the outset remain. No criteria are given for identifying what counts as "moral correctness". And, again, we know very little about the structure of defective legal norms. What distinguishes them

3 Alexy, *AI* (n. 1 above), 26 (emphasis in original).

4 See Gustav Radbruch, "Statutory Lawlessness and Supra-Statutory Law" (first publ. 1946), trans. Bonnie Litschewski Paulson and Stanley L. Paulson, *Oxford Journal of Legal Studies*, 26 (2006), 1–11, esp. §3 (6–8).

5 I have taken up the formula elsewhere. See e.g. Stanley L. Paulson, "Zur Kontinuität der nichtpositivistischen Rechtsphilosophie Gustav Radbruchs", in: *Die Natur des Rechts bei Gustav Radbruch*, ed. Martin Borowski und Stanley L. Paulson (Tübingen: Mohr Siebeck, 2015), 151–182; Stanley L. Paulson, "On the Background and Significance of Gustav Radbruch's Post-War Papers", *Oxford Journal of Legal Studies*, 26 (2006), 17–40, effectively criticized by Júlio Aguiar de Oliveira in his paper "Extreme Injustice and the Concept of Law" (in this volume).

6 See Robert Alexy, "Some Reflections on the Ideal Dimension of Law and on the Legal Philosophy of John Finnis", *American Journal of Jurisprudence*, 58 (2013), 97–110, at 107–108.

7 Indeed, Alexy could go further, pointing out that the thesis of exclusive non-positivism is wrong-headed.

8 Alexy, *AI* (n. 1 above), 79.

9 Ibid. 35–36.

from non-defective legal norms, and what distinguishes severely defective legal norms from those that are less severely defective?

I confine myself to the latter problem, that of the structure of defective legal norms. Specifically, I begin by addressing the issue of unconstitutional legal norms, an issue that runs parallel, for some purposes, to Alexy's issue of defective legal norms.

I. An Example of an Unconstitutional Legal Norm

An example of an unconstitutional legal norm is found in the United States Supreme Court's decision in the case of *Korematsu v. United States*.[10] There is wellnigh universal agreement that the decision is mistaken, yielding an unconstitutional legal norm. A leading scholar of American constitutional history described the result as "the most drastic invasion of the rights of citizens of the United States by their own government that has thus far occurred in the [nation's] history".[11] The United States imposed curfews, issued evacuation orders, and, beginning in the spring of 1942, forcibly moved some 112,000 persons of Japanese ancestry – American citizens as well as resident aliens – from their homes to detention centres, where some were kept for as long as four years.

The petitioner in *Korematsu*, an American citizen of Japanese descent, had been convicted for remaining in a "Military Area" contrary to an evacuation order issued by General John L. DeWitt, the commanding general of the Western Defense Command. The petitioner challenged the validity of the evacuation order, arguing that he had been denied due process of law as guaranteed by the "equal protection" clause of, here, the Fifth Amendment.[12]

Was the evacuation order, or the "exclusion order" as it was known at the time, constitutional? Justice Hugo Black, speaking for the Court, argued that it was, writing that Korematsu was excluded "because we are at war with the Japanese Empire, because the properly constituted military authorities feared an invasion of our West Coast and felt constrained to take proper security measures".[13]

Why, exactly, is the decision mistaken? It is mistaken because Justice Black introduces the "strict scrutiny" standard in this very decision – he calls it "rigid scrutiny" – and then fails to apply the standard in the decision. The standard requires, first, that the measure in question serve a "compelling" state interest, and, second, that this interest cannot be realized in a way that is less onerous, less burdensome, to the disadvantaged group.[14] The first requirement is not at issue.[15] The second

10 Korematsu v. United States, 323 U.S. 214 (1944).

11 Edward S. Corwin, *Total War and the Constitution* (New York: Knopf, 1947), 91.

12 The Fifth Amendment "equal protection" clause triggered here carries over to the federal government the constraints imposed on the member states by the Fourteenth Amendment "equal protection" clause.

13 *Korematsu* (n. 10 above), 223.

14 Ibid. 219.

15 More precisely, the first requirement was not at issue on the official reading of what it came to in the Court's decision, namely, the interest in "tak[ing] proper security measures" in a time of war (see text quoted at note 13 above). Later, however, it was discovered that General DeWitt, commanding general of the Western Defense Command, had been doing the bidding of West

requirement raises the key question: Were there less onerous alternatives at hand? The answer is straightforward: Of course there were. As in England in the summer of 1940, the Americans could have set up special hearing boards to examine the persons in question with an eye to determining their loyalty. And – just to underscore how drastic a departure from the Constitution's promise of "equal protection" this was – no American citizens or resident aliens of German, Austrian, or Italian ancestry were shipped off to detention centres.[16]

Leaving this description of an unconstitutional legal norm, I turn to the underlying conceptual problem.

II. The Conceptual Problem

The standard position is that an unconstitutional legal norm, like other legal norms, is valid[17] unless and until it is overturned – that is to say, unless and until the unconstitutional legal norm is held to be invalid (with, in the common law countries, later courts following the holding of invalidity).[18] In constitutional law, the effects of a judicial holding of unconstitutionality will normally be *ex nunc*, with, of course, the exception that the holding applies, too, to the case at hand (the so-called *Anlaßfall*). To repeat, the unconstitutional legal norm, like other legal norms, is valid. But, Hans Kelsen asks, if the norm is unconstitutional, how can it be valid? Kelsen, as is well known, attempts to resolve the problem by setting out "normative alternatives".

> If a statute enacted by the legislative organ is considered to be valid although it has been created in another way or has [a] content [other than that] prescribed by the constitution, we must assume that the prescriptions of the constitution concerning legislation have an alternative character. The legislator is entitled by the constitution either to apply the norms laid down directly in the constitution or to apply other norms which he himself may decide upon. Otherwise, a statute whose creation or contents did not conform with the prescriptions directly laid down in the constitution could not be regarded as valid.[19]

Coast businessmen, who saw these "military" measures as their chance to be rid of their Japanese competitors.

16 Much later in time, greater attention in governmental and academic circles was drawn to the tragedy. See e.g. *Personal Justice Denied. Report of the Commission on Wartime Relocaton and Internment of Civilians* (Washington, D.C.: U.S. Government Printing Office, 1982); Peter Irons, *Justice at War. The Story of the Japanese American Internment Cases* (New York and Oxford: Oxford University Press, 1983); *Justice Delayed. The Record of the Japanese American Internment Cases*, ed. Peter Irons (Middletown, Conn.: Wesleyan University Press, 1989).

17 For a rich and rewarding discussion of a range of problems found under the rubric of legal validity, see Andrzej Grabowski, *Juristic Concept of the Validity of Statutory Law. A Critique of Contemporary Legal Nonpositivism*, trans. Małgorzata Kiełtyka (Berlin and Heidelberg: Springer, 2013).

18 A departure from this standard is marked by the German doctrine of "*ipso jure* nullity", but this doctrine, whose heyday has passed, was more often than not honoured in the breach. For effective criticism see e.g. Christoph Moench, *Verfassungswidriges Gesetz und Normenkontrolle* (Baden-Baden: Nomos, 1977); Jörn Ipsen, *Rechtsfolgen der Verfassungswidrigkeit von Norm und Einzelakt* (Baden-Baden: Nomos, 1980).

19 Hans Kelsen, *General Theory of Law and State*, trans. Anders Wedberg (Cambridge, Mass.: Harvard University Press, 1945), 156; see also Hans Kelsen, *Reine Rechtslehre*, 2nd edn (Vienna: Deuticke, 1960), §35(j) (at 277–279).

Thus, Kelsen is claiming, the validity of a constitutional legal norm is explained, in an entirely unproblematic way, by following the first alternative. The first alternative represents the prevailing law in the legal system. The validity of an unconstitutional legal norm is explained by following the second alternative. This second alternative represents all the other ostensibly normative possibilities,[20] those not found in the prevailing law. As Kelsen writes, this resolution of the problem has to be the case, lest it not be possible to recognize unconstitutional legal norms as valid.

Not surprisingly, this doctrine of Kelsen's has not fared well; it seems, indeed, to lead straightaway to the collapse of the normative order.[21] A different approach is required.

III. Presumptive Legal Validity

The resolution of the problem of unconstitutional legal norms turns on two doctrines. The first doctrine is straightforward. It is the binary or two-valued character of legal validity – that is to say, a legal norm is either valid or not valid. Just as with the concept of truth, there are no degrees of validity.

Alongside this doctrine, there is a second doctrine, which is a tad less straightforward. It speaks to conformity of content, and the doctrine may be dubbed "presumptive legal validity". The presumption of the validity of a legal norm may well be strong, which is to say, *ceteris paribus*, that the content of the norm comports with the content of the applicable higher-level norms. Contrariwise, in the case of an unconstitutional legal norm, the presumption of validity will, *ceteris paribus*, be weak, for the content of the norm does not comport with the content of the applicable higher-level norms.

Thus, the doctrine of presumptive legal validity offers a resolution of the problem posed by unconstitutional legal norms. The unconstitutional legal norm, as illustrated in *Korematsu*, is valid. The binary character of legal validity is, therefore, respected. At the same time, the status of the norm as unconstitutional is reflected in the very weak presumption of validity. This does not undermine the binary character of legal validity, but it does indicate that something is amiss, that the norm is ripe for invalidation (even if, in the example presented by *Korematsu*, the Supreme Court's judgment represents finality, which is to say that no invalidation will be forthcoming).

To be sure, the notion of "content" is vague. In explicating the notion, two questions arise. First, how is the content of the applicable higher-level norms to be understood? A device drawn from H.L.A. Hart facilitates discussion of this issue. Second, how is the strength of the presumption of legal validity to be understood? Here a scheme drawn from Duhem and Quine is helpful. In the next two sections, I take up these questions in turn, drawing first on Hart.

20 I say "ostensibly normative", for, if the second alternative is in fact in place, the normative order simply collapses. As the Austrian philosopher of science, Paul Feyerabend, put it, albeit in a different context: "anything goes".

21 See the critical rejoinders to Kelsen in *Cognition and Interpretation of Law*, ed. Letizia Gianformaggio and Stanley L. Paulson (Turin: G. Giappichelli, 1995), at section IV.

IV. The "Content" of the Applicable Higher-Level Norms

I appeal, here, to a *plural* construction of Hart's rule of recognition, his "*rules* of recognition".[22] With this device in hand, I construct a "working rule of recognition" for *Korematsu*. This amounts to a criterion that brings together the applicable power-conferring rule along with the constraint on the exercise of the power.[23] Thus, the legal power of the Western Defense Command to issue an evacuation order in time of war stems, in constitutional terms, from the article I war powers of the executive (powers exercised by Roosevelt when he issued the executive order authorizing military commanders to issue specific evacuation orders) and from the article II war powers of the Congress (powers exercised by the Congress when it enacted a statute endorsing the President's executive order). The constraint on the exercise of these powers stems from the due process clause of the Fifth Amendment, which restricts these powers by precluding the exercise of them in a racially discriminatory manner unless such exercise satisfies the conditions imposed by the standard of "strict scrutiny". This "working rule of recognition", constructed *post factum*, facilitates the determination of the strength of the presumption of the validity of the decision in *Korematsu*. The argument, thus far, runs: The norm representing the decision in *Korematsu* is valid, but the presumption of its validity is weak because the decision fails to comport with the constraint found in the criterion or working rule of recognition.

But how, exactly, is the weakness of the presumption to be understood? This, I want to suggest, is an issue that can be resolved, at any rate in some cases, in "holistic" terms.

V. The Strength of the Presumption of Validity

I turn to holism as the notion is understood in the work of Duhem and Quine. In a recent statement, Quine offers a lucid account, for his purposes, of holism:

> Science is indeed an amalgam of linguistic convention and sensory evidence, but there are no clear grounds for separating these two components by distinguishing two classes of sentences. Sensory evidence is not something that can in general be sorted out over the component sentences of science, investing some of the sentences and sparing others. Pierre Duhem stressed already in 1906 that what implies a predicted observation is ordinarily a whole cluster of present observations and theoretical sentences in concert; failure of the prediction falsifies no one sentence of the cluster rather than another. A typical single sentence of a theory has no distinctive

22 See H. L. A. Hart, *The Concept of Law*, 1st edn (Oxford: Clarendon Press, 1961), at 92, 93, *et passim* (emphasis added), 3rd edn (2012), at 95, 96, *et passim*.

23 One might well speculate that complex "justificatory legal propositions" can be constructed that include not only a propositional counterpart of the legal holding (at some suitable level of abstraction) but also the higher-level norms that figured in the justification of the decision. On the conceptual issues that arise in connection with the distinction between norms and normative propositions, see Eugenio Bulygin, "Norms, Normative Propositions, and Legal Statements", in *Contemporary Philosophy. A New Survey*, vol. 3: *Philosophy of Action*, ed. Guttorm Fløistad (The Hague: Nijhoff, 1982), 127–152, repr. Bulygin, *Essays in Legal Philosophy*, ed. Carlos Bernal *et al.* (Oxford: Oxford University Press [forthcoming in 2015]).

> empirical content of its own; it can be singled out for testing, but only by agreeing meanwhile to hold other sentences of the cluster immune.[24]

One can restate the notion of holism by resorting to the metaphor of a sphere. The best-entrenched propositions of the enterprise in question – be it one or another of the natural sciences, be it legal science – are found at the very core of the sphere, the least-entrenched propositions on its periphery. In terms of holism, the doctrine of presumptive legal validity has, at the core of the sphere, an idealized version of the precept in question, which represents, so to speak, the "perfect case". The measure of the strength of the presumption of legal validity is, then, the distance between the perfect case and the decision in question. Since the decision in *Korematsu* counts as an unconstitutional legal norm, the distance is great between the precept at the core – here, "strict scrutiny" – and the decision, severely weakening the presumption of legal validity.

Still, there is a wrinkle that has to be ironed out. Presumptive legal validity, fine as far as it goes, does not go far enough to explicate the nature of the mistake in the *Korematsu* decision. For, at the time of the decision, the "strict scrutiny" standard was not well entrenched. The problem is resolved by appeal to the applicable legal ideal.

VI. Legal Ideals Supplement Presumptive Legal Validity

The "strict scrutiny" standard, introduced in *Korematsu* for the first time, was new to American constitutional law. In the language of the metaphor drawn from holism, it was far from well entrenched and so not to be found at or even near the core of the sphere. The argument above may well be correct, to the effect that the decision in *Korematsu* is mistaken for failing to apply the "strict scrutiny" standard, but this argument cannot be couched in holistic terms. The holistic argument would presuppose that the "strict scrutiny" standard is well entrenched and that this decision is therefore far from the core of the sphere, with the result that the presumption of its validity is weak. If, however, the operative notion here – the "strict scrutiny" standard – is not well entrenched, then presumptive legal validity has to be supplemented.

What is to be done? Happily, an argument can be adduced that makes sense of presumptive legal validity in such a case. One can argue that the "strict scrutiny" standard, as a legally correct doctrine, is properly to be read back into earlier cases. Indeed – so the rhetorical question – might not the outcome in a variety of earlier cases have been more just if judges had been able to avail themselves of the "strict scrutiny" standard?

A major question arises here. Is there a warrant for reading the "strict scrutiny" standard back into earlier cases, thereby creating in retrospect, so to speak, the well-entrenched character of the standard? The answer here is surely grist for Robert

24 W. V. Quine, *Quine in Dialogue*, ed. Dagfinn Føllesdal and Douglas B. Quine (Cambridge, Mass.: Harvard University Press, 2008), 125. Quine, ibid. at 256, has dissociated himself from what he terms, in this volume, the "[e]xcessive holism" of "Two Dogmas", the famous paper of 1953. Duhem's theory is found in Pierre Duhem, *La théorie physique:son objet et sa structure* (Paris: Chevalier & Rivière, 1906), trans. Philip P. Wiener, *The Aim and Structure of Physical Theory* (Princeton: Princeton University Press, 1954); see, in particular, ch. 6 (180–218).

Alexy's mill. The warrant for reading the standard back into earlier cases is the applicable legal ideal. Justice requires that governmental measures compromising the rights of an individual meet two conditions, (i) a showing that there is a compelling state interest at stake, and (ii) a showing that there is no less onerous measure at hand. This is, of course, the "strict scrutiny" standard, now, *ex hypothesi*, at work in earlier cases and therefore well entrenched vis-à-vis the instant case.

This particular use of ideals is, however, a sideshow. For the purposes of my present exposition, their main use is in connection with defective legal norms.

VII. Defective Legal Norms

The structure of the defective legal norm in Alexy's theory is to be understood on the basis of three factors. *First*, there is the ideal in question, which comprises the constitutional precept at issue, along with the underlying moral component. This underlying moral component is an essential part of the matrix that Alexy sets out for defective legal norms.[25] For example, in the case I briefly take up below, the ideal in question is the constitutional safeguard against any application of *ex post facto* law in criminal proceedings, along with the underlying moral component, fairness to the would-be defendant. *Second*, there is the issue, inestimable in its significance, of the standpoint or perspective from which the legal norm in question is judged to be defective. And, *third*, there is the holistic factor, reflecting, now in the context of defective legal norms, an application of presumption legal validity, introduced above in the context of unconstitutional legal norms. The doctrine measures the distance between the legal norm in question and the perfect case found at the core of the holistic sphere.

As an example for discussion of the first factor, the ideal in question, consider the case of an individual with a long history of criminal convictions for having sexually molested children. Shortly before his release from prison, the state enacts the Sexually Violent Predator Law (SVP), providing for the indefinite institutional commitment of those who, owing to a mental abnormality, are predisposed to molesting children. On the authority of the SVP, the state does not release the individual in question, who is instead committed to an institution for an indefinite period. Does the state's action count as a violation of the constitutional *ex post facto* provision, which expressly addresses state law as well as federal law? The state court ruled that the measure did indeed violate the constitutional provision, and it held the offending provision of the SVP to be unconstitutional. The United States Supreme Court, in the case of *Kansas v. Hendricks*, reversed the state court's decision, holding that the SVP did not impose criminal punishment and therefore was not in violation of the constitutional precept.[26]

The second factor, namely, the issue of the standpoint or perspective on the basis of which an assessment is made, would comprise, here, one standpoint reflecting the state court's decision and another reflecting the decision of the Supreme Court. To identify these two standpoints apart from the niceties of adjudication, first in the state court and then in the Supreme Court, we might label them *A* and

25 See the text quoted at note 3 above.
26 Kansas v. Hendricks, 521 U.S. 346 (1997).

B respectively. From standpoint *A*, reflecting the state court's position, the Supreme Court's holding, based on its standpoint, *B*. is a defective legal norm, for, so the argument from standpoint *A*, it violates the constitutional safeguard against *ex post facto* law and is therefore unfair to the individual whose indefinite commitment is now a *fait accompli*.

Or, turning everything around, the assessment based on standpoint *B*, reflecting the Supreme Court's position, is that the state court's holding is a defective legal norm because the state court fails to recognize the role of the "state police power" *qua* constitutional precept, understood here as the state's responsibility for the welfare of its citizens. The moral component is the security and well-being of children.

What, finally, of the holistic factor? Consider a different, albeit hypothetical case, with an eye to comparing it to standpoint *A* in the concrete case discussed above. Suppose, then, that we are confronted with an egregious violation of the constitutional safeguard against the application of *ex post facto* law in a criminal proceeding. The defendant's ostensible violation of the law, negligent homicide in a case of drunken driving, was not proscribed by law at the time the defendant killed the pedestrian with his automobile. The offense of "negligent homicide" had been in the criminal code from the mid-nineteenth century, but the offense specified concrete categories, and there was of course no occasion then to carve out a category for automobiles. Carrying our hypothetical case to the limit, we may assume further that this case became a *cause célèbre*, and, thanks to the public outcry for justice, in addition to incompetent defense counsel, the *ex post facto* issue was overlooked altogether.

The distance here between the perfect case, found at the core of the sphere, and the instant case is far greater than in the concrete case discussed above, reflecting standpoint *A*. There, one interpretation of the provision calling for the indefinite commitment of a child molester would have us reading the provision as an administrative remedy. This interpretation is rejected, of course, from standpoint *A*, but recognition of its possibility underscores the lesser distance between the perfect case and the instant case in our concrete example and the greater distance between them in our hypothetical example.

Finally, it is worth mentioning that competing standpoints or perspectives invite attention to the role of interpretation in the law generally. To pick up on Quine's language, above, this is a whole cluster of issues that goes well beyond the issue I address here.

ARCHIV FÜR RECHTS- UND SOZIALPHILOSOPHIE – BEIHEFTE

Herausgeben von der Internationalen Vereinigung für Rechts- und Sozialphilosophie (IVR).
Die Bände 1–4 sind im Luchterhand-Fachverlag erschienen.

Franz Steiner Verlag ISSN 0341–079X

132. Yasutomo Morigiwa / Hirohide Takikawa (Hg.)
Judicial Minimalism – For and Against
Proceedings of the 9th Kobe Lectures. Tokyo, Nagoya, and Kyoto, June 2008
2012. 99 S., kt.
ISBN 978-3-515-10136-3

133. Thomas Bustamante / Carlos Bernal Pulido (Hg.)
On the Philosophy of Precedent
Proceedings of the 24th World Congress of the International Association for Philosophy of Law and Social Philosophy, Beijing, 2009
Volume 3
2012. 144 S., kt.
ISBN 978-3-515-10150-9

134. Matthias Kaufmann / Joachim Renzikowski (Hg.)
Zurechnung und Verantwortung
Tagung der Deutschen Sektion der Internationalen Vereinigung für Rechts- und Sozialphilosophie vom 22.–24. September 2010 in Halle (Saale)
2012. 184 S., kt.
ISBN 978-3-515-10180-6

135. Carsten Bäcker / Sascha Ziemann (Hg.)
Junge Rechtsphilosophie
2012. 214 S., kt.
ISBN 978-3-515-10268-1

136. Ulfrid Neumann / Klaus Günther / Lorenz Schulz (Hg.)
Law, Science, Technology
Plenary lectures presented at the 25th World Congress of the International Association for Philosophy of Law and Social Philosophy, Frankfurt am Main, 2011
2012. 173 S., kt.
ISBN 978-3-515-10328-2

137. Winfried Brugger / Stephan Kirste (Hg.)
Human Dignity as a Foundation of Law
Proceedings of the Special Workshop held at the 24th World Congress of the International Association for Philosophy of Law and Social Philosophy in Beijing, 2009
2013. 267 S., kt.
ISBN 978-3-515-10440-1

138. Philippe Avramov / Mike Bacher / Paolo Becchi / Bénédict Winiger (Hg.)
Ethik und Recht in der Bioethik / Ethique et Droit en matière de Bioéthique
Kongress der Schweizerischen Vereinigung für Rechts- und Sozialphilosophie, 11.–12. Mai 2012, Universität Luzern / Congrès de l'Association Suisse de Philosophie du Droit et de Philosophie Sociale, 11–12 mai 2012, Université de Lucerne
2013. 226 S., kt.
ISBN 978-3-515-10436-4

139. Tetsu Sakurai / Makoto Usami (Hg.)
Human Rights and Global Justice
The 10th Kobe Lectures, July 2011
2014. 167 S., kt.
ISBN 978-3-515-10489-0

140. Bernhard Jakl / Beatrice Brunhöber / Ariane Grieser / Juliane Ottmann / Tim Wihl (Hg.)
Recht und Frieden – Wozu Recht?
Tagungen des Jungen Forums Rechtsphilosophie (JFR) in der Internationalen Vereinigung für Rechts- und Sozialphilosophie (IVR) im September 2012 in Münster und im April 2013 in Berlin
2014. 206 S. mit 3 Abb., kt.
ISBN 978-3-515-10806-5

141. *in Vorbereitung*

142. Daniela Demko / Kurt Seelmann / Paolo Becchi (Hg.)
Würde und Autonomie
Fachtagung der Schweizerischen Vereinigung für Rechts- und Sozialphilosophie, 24.–25. April 2013, Landgut Castelen, Augst
2015. 216 S., kt.
ISBN 978-3-515-10949-9

143. *in Vorbereitung*